8th Tang - Running glazed - earthenware

Liao Dyn. 947-1125 - incised design -
w/ Floral pattern

late
Tang   10-11th
        smooth green w/ incised floral shapes
        smooth white

THE CHINESE POTTER

)) black

Song -

Northern Celadon - green stoneware -
        11-12th   sophisticated -
                        designs

Ru - Blue

Southern Celadon - greenish but w/o the decoration

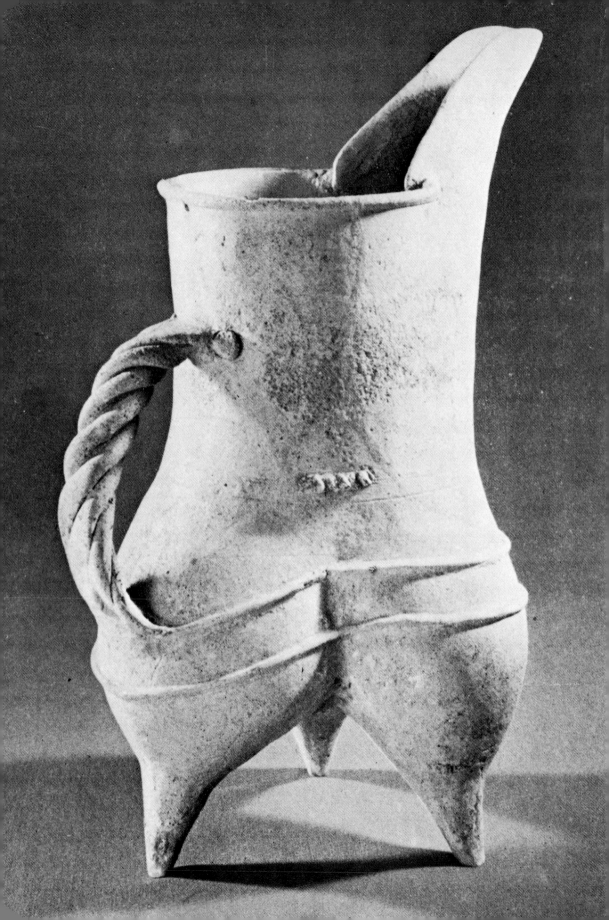

Margaret Medley

THE CHINESE POTTER

A Practical History of Chinese Ceramics

PHAIDON

OXFORD

Phaidon Press Limited
Littlegate House, St Ebbe's Street,
Oxford OX1 1SQ

First published 1976
Second edition (paperback) 1980
Second impression 1982
Third impression 1986

© Phaidon Press Limited 1976

ISBN 0 7148 1675 2

Filmset and printed in Great Britain by
BAS Printers Limited, Over Wallop, Hampshire

Facing title-page: Fig. 1. White earthenware jug, *k'uei*, hand built. Lung-shan culture, Wei-fang,
Shantung. Height 33.5 cm. 3rd–2nd millennium B.C. Chinese Government.

Contents

To

Sir Harry M. Garner

Preface

The aim of the following study is to present an up-to-date history of Chinese ceramics in terms of their technical development. Such development is an essential part of the history of any craft, and in Chinese ceramics the evolution of techniques of manufacture and decoration is of fundamental importance to the appearance of particular wares. An attempt is also made to set the ceramics against the social and economic background, and to relate the whole subject to the wider, world picture. The three parts into which the work has been divided would each make a full-length book, and perhaps at some later date it may be possible to expand each one, and do this as more material becomes available following scientific analysis of the materials.

The advantage of this approach is that there is a story to tell of the logical development from one stage to another. The limitation imposed by such a treatment is the need to disregard some of the ceramics. For instance, Hsin-tien and Li-fan pottery of the later period of neolithic culture is omitted, as is the so-called Donkhe ware in the Ming period, in each case simply because they contributed nothing to the main line of technical evolution. It will also be thought by some that the Ming and Ch'ing periods have been rather scurvily treated. This is deliberate, for from the technical point of view they added very little. The potters by then were more concerned with variations on established techniques, which, once these had been thoroughly understood and the practicalities mastered, is exactly what one would expect.

It also has to be remembered that there is ample literature on the last two periods, as indeed there now is on some of the others. I have therefore preferred a selected bibliography to a comprehensive one, which is apt to defeat its own ends. I have placed some emphasis in the bibliography on works which contain valuable references to related fields of study, as well as to the deeper levels of the main subject, and additional references will be found in the notes.

I would like, in closing, to pay tribute to friends and colleagues, too numerous to mention by name, who have patiently borne with me and given so much time to the discussion of many aspects. I owe a special debt of gratitude to Professor Henry Hodges for his encouragement and help, and particularly for the kiln reconstructions which he has so generously contributed. I am grateful, too, to Mr G. Davenport of Birkbeck College, and his staff, for redrawing my untidy maps, thereby considerably improving the usefulness of this book. In the matter of illustration I have to thank Miss Vanessa Stamford of the Percival David Foundation for her patience and care in carrying out a great deal of exacting work, and for the admirable new photographs, some of them in colour, which had to be made of objects in the collection of the Foundation.

Margaret Medley, London, 1975

Note to the Second Edition

In the four years that have elapsed since 1976 a number of important new books have been published. This means that while the main text in the following chapters remains unchanged, the bibliography has been revised and considerably enlarged. One exhibition catalogue that has been included is not at all easy to obtain, but is so remarkable that it could not be omitted. This is the catalogue of the 'Special Exhibition of Cultural Relics found off Sinan Coast', the spectacular ship find off the Korean coast which caused such a sensation in 1976, with its thousands of Chinese stonewares and porcelains still in their original packing, in pristine condition, and almost all datable to the early fourteenth century.

Margaret Medley, February 1980

Chronology of Chinese Dynasties and Periods

NEOLITHIC . . . . 8th or 7th millennium B.C.–18th/16th century B.C.
SHANG . . . . 18th/16th century B.C.–1028 B.C.
WESTERN CHOU 1027–771
SPRING AND AUTUMN ANNALS 722–481
WARRING STATES 481–221
CH'IN 221–206
WESTERN HAN 206–12
HSIN . . . . 12–23 A.D.
EASTERN HAN . . . . A.D. 25–221
THREE KINGDOMS AND WESTERN CHIN 219–316
EASTERN CHIN AND FIVE PRINCIPALITIES 317–419
NAN-PEI-CH'AO I 420–500
NAN-PEI-CH'AO II 501–580
SUI 581–618
T'ANG 618–906
FIVE DYNASTIES 907–960
LIAO 907–1125
SUNG 960–1279

Northern Sung	960–1127
Southern Sung	1128–1279

CHIN (Ju-chên or Golden Tartars) 115–1234
YÜAN (Mongols) 1260–1368
MING 1368–1644

Hung-wu	1368–1398	Hung-chih	1488–1505
Chien wên	1399–1402	Chêng-tê	1506–1521
Yung-lo	1403–1424	Chia-ching	1522–1566
Hsüan-tê	1426–1435	Lung-ch'ing	1567–1572
Chêng-t'ung	1436–1449	Wan-li	1573–1619
Ching-t'ai	1450–1457	T'ai-ch'ang	1620
T'ien-shun	1457–1464	T'ien-ch'i	1621–1627
Ch'êng-hua	1465–1487	Ch'ung-chêng	1628–1643

CH'ING 1644–1912

Shun-chih	1644–1661	Tao-kuang	1821–1850
K'ang-hsi	1662–1722	Hsien-fêng	1851–1861
Yung-chêng	1723–1735	T'ung-chih	1862–1874
Ch'ien-lung	1736–1795	Kuang-hsü	1875–1908
Chia-ch'ing	1796–1820	Hsüan-t'ung	1909–1912

REPUBLIC 1912

The Potter and his Materials

From the earliest ages of the civilization of China the potter has held an unique position in the social structure. From the very beginning he has been at the service of the community in which he has found himself, and he has served this community with a faithful devotion unparalleled by any other member apart from the tiller of the soil. While the farmer has cultivated what was immediately available for the survival of the group of which he was a member, the potter has had a creative task, to make vessels for storage, for cooking, and drinking, each essential parts in the chain of activities required for survival. His work in early ages was confined to the production of vessels of a purely functional character to suit the specific needs of the community, and if in later times the forms he created were esteemed on aesthetic grounds, this was because his mastery of the clay medium was sufficiently secure for him to be able to use his products as a vehicle for both invention and personal expression, the latter to some extent always reflecting the artistic climate of the age in which he worked. Indeed, without the potter's own appreciation of the material and its possibilities, as well as its limitations, and his ability to handle these with both imagination and skill, much that we now have would scarcely have survived down the centuries.

While the potter learned how to use his local materials to build vessels that satisfied everyone's needs and tastes, he also learned, and perhaps initiated, the technique of using fire for creative purposes. It is little wonder that in the Bible and other early religious and philosophical texts the potter plays such an important role. He creates for a specific purpose, and if what he creates fails to satisfy his own instinctive understanding of the basic material under his hands, whether he uses the wheel or not, he will destroy what he has made and start again, generally using the same material, for until it has been fired in the kiln the clay can be reused by damping it down; a fact all too often forgotten, especially by collectors unaware of what goes to making a pot.

It is perhaps fair to say that collectors in the past have displayed a strong tendency to envelop Chinese ceramics in a mystique and expend upon them an adulation wholly inappropriate both to the material and to the attitude of the craftsman. Nowadays we are perhaps able to approach Chinese ceramic history in a more realistic manner, with an eye to the practical problems and the purpose for which the finished works were originally conceived. For they were intended for household and ritual use and not just to grace the shelves of glass-fronted cabinets. Thus we have to view Chinese ceramics, like those of any other culture, in terms of social and economic structure, as well as of technology, in order to discover how they developed.

It was possibly the almost unequalled resources of suitable raw materials in nearly all parts of China that made the use of ceramic materials so natural, and contributed to the long and virtually unbroken tradition down to the present day. It may, indeed, account for the pre-eminence of pottery over precious metals, pewter, and wood, the very reverse of the situation in Europe, and it certainly stimulated the potter's search for high quality in his work. The early achievement of sustained and controlled high temperatures, and the use of high-fired glazes, before the appearance of low-fired lead glazes in the third century B.C., again the reverse of what happened in Europe, is of peculiar interest. So also is the fact that the lead glazed ware was always intended for furnishing tombs and not for general household use. Higher fired glazes on hard earthenwares were already current alongside the sophisticated painted lacquers in aristocratic households as early as the fourth century B.C.[1]

It may be worth repeating that the potter's primary purpose is to satisfy the needs of the community and himself, and to bear in mind that when a particular method of construction was mastered, and often indeed before this, decorative techniques were also being developed. Construction and decoration therefore evolved alongside each other. Sometimes they seem to keep pace with each other, and sometimes decoration appears to be abandoned and left behind. This may be due to the artistic climate of the age, as it is in some of the Sung period material, or it may be due to the character of the materials actually being used at the time, as in the T'ang stoneware, where the material imposes its own limitations. There is also the fact that the decorative techniques used on earthenware are not necessarily those most appropriate to stoneware, which may be made more aesthetically satisfying by some other means of decoration; then later it may be found that what was already being used on earthenware might under certain conditions also be used on stoneware, so an old technique is revived and appears a novelty in the different context.

Thus decorative techniques tend to vary not only on different wares, but in different periods and even regions. In fact the basic techniques in the decoration of earthenware can also be applied to stoneware and porcelain, but social and aesthetic factors are constantly seen in the evolution of ceramics in China, where with few exceptions all the techniques of construction and decoration with which we are familiar today had been developed by the end of the fourteenth century. How the potters achieved this, and what they actually accomplished with them is discussed in the following chapters.

Before turning to the proper consideration of our main subject and the background against which the developments took place, it is appropriate to describe the different types of pottery and clarify what is meant by some of the terms used; other terms encountered in the text will be found in the glossary. There is unfortunately much misunderstanding of what is meant, and confusions have arisen over the use of terms in many of the older books on ceramics, especially in those concerned with Chinese ceramics.

It is essential in the first place to understand that pottery is a generic term. It is the name for the product of the potter, whatever its form or distinctive material. Thus it applies without exception to all ceramic wares and comprehends earthenware, stoneware, porcelain and fritware, although we are not concerned with this last type in East Asian pottery. In writing of Chinese ceramics the tendency to introduce such terms as 'proto-porcelain', porcellanous stoneware, and porcellanous ware has confused the issue, and the first two should perhaps be altogether abandoned. The Chinese have two basic terms: *t'ao*, meaning pottery in general, is used in specific cases to indicate low-fired ware, or what we would call earthenware, and *tz'ŭ*, meaning high-fired ware, comprehending both stoneware and porcelain. The European distinction between these two is not made, although from our point of view it is a convenient one.

In studies of pottery in which the technology is a central theme it is the practice to speak of ceramic bodies. The term *body* is used of the clay material and any added temper in either the unfired or fired state and is applied specifically here to the interior part of the pot as distinct from the glaze. Earthenware bodies show wide variations in colour and texture, and are usually made from clays with a high degree of plasticity. The bodies fire well at temperatures between 800°C and 1,100°C, with an absolute maximum of about 1,150°C. If fired above this temperature they will slump, or collapse and melt. In the fired state they may be all shades from very dark grey, almost black, through all the greys to nearly white, and from dark reddish brown to pale buff or yellowish, and may in some cases be pinkish in colour. While it is not altogether uncommon to find clays which can be fired satisfactorily without modification beyond the necessary washing, potters generally add what is called temper, normally either crushed quartz or flint, which serves to improve the plasticity of excessively sticky clays, improve the silica content, and reduce the tendency to excessive contraction and even warping in drying. How much temper is added, and in precisely what form, the potter has to discover for himself, as naturally clays vary from one locality to another. As the grain size varies from the very coarse to the extremely fine and dense, so also the material in the fired state varies in its porosity, a matter which is also dependent on the firing temperature. If the body is coarse, which may be brought about by temper, it tends to be porous, but this is not an invariable rule. It is worth noting that an additional advantage of temper is that it opens the structure, or pores, and this helps the gases to escape during the firing, as well as helping in the initial drying process. Generally earthenware has to be glazed to make it impermeable, and the glazes need to be of the low-fired type. These may be lead glazes or leadless glazes; this is a subject which will be taken up at a later stage.

Stoneware is harder than earthenware, but similarly variable in colour and texture. It fires at temperatures in the range from 1,200°C to about 1,300°C.[2] As for earthenware bodies it may be necessary to make additions of temper. In firing, however, the material sinters and fuses completely to form an impermeable body. Stoneware is rarely left unglazed, though the glaze may not wholly cover the object; the reason for glazing appears to be aesthetic. The Chinese use glazes of an alkaline type on stoneware, and these may be high in feldspars, hence they are often called felspathic glazes.

Porcelain differs from the former two in being constituted of two distinct materials, and invariably being pure white or very pale grey. In the fired state it is vitrified and translucent. The two ingredients are kaolin, a white firing relatively non-plastic clay of which there are massive deposits in China, and white China stone, petuntse (*pai-tun-tzŭ*, 'little white bricks'), a refined non-plastic felspathic material derived from decayed granite, which when washed and prepared for use is dried in small white blocks. These two materials properly combined produce a vitrified body when fired at temperatures of about 1,280°C upwards; later temperatures in the region of 1,400°C were achieved by the Chinese.

When fired, of course, the body is impermeable since it is vitrified, but because it is not very attractive in this state, it is usually the practice to glaze it. This can be done using a felspathic glaze, which will fuse at a temperature similar to that required for the body, or the body may be fired first to the appropriate temperature to secure fusion, a process giving rise to the term 'biscuit', and it can then be covered with a low temperature glaze and fired a second time. In descriptions of objects fired in this way, first to the porcelain temperature and then with a low temperature glaze, the glazes, which in China are generally lead glazes, are often said to be enamel on biscuit, or 'decorated in lead silicate enamels'. This is really a rather elaborate way of saying that the piece is lead glazed, and it may be confusing since the word enamel is often associated with metalwork.[3]

The question of glazes is complex, but those used by the Chinese fall basically into two categories; those which mature at low temperatures, and those which mature at high temperatures, the boundary between them being roughly in the area between 1,150°C and about 1,250°C; it is impossible on the basis of our present knowledge to be more specific than this. The low-fired glazes are generally fluxed with lead, but some are leadless and thus alkaline. The high-fired glazes are alkaline and *may* be felspathic. It has been the practice for many years to refer to Chinese high-fired glazes as being felspathic, but this is not necessarily the case, and without expensive and highly sophisticated techniques of analysis the real facts cannot be determined. Many of the higher fired glazes probably are felspathic in as much as feldspars form a major part of the mix, as they certainly do in the case of porcelain. It therefore seems best in the present context to avoid the use of the term felspathic, except in the case of the pure white porcelain, and confine ourselves to the simpler and less controversial term 'high-fired' glaze.[4]

The colouring of glazes is rather simpler than the question of their constitution. Lead glazes are excellent as media for bright colours. Greens derive from copper oxides, brown and amber tones from iron oxides, and aubergine purples from manganese oxides. Good blues are achieved using cobalt, but they are less brilliant except in rare cases. The especially brilliant turquoise colours are obtained by using copper oxide in lead-free glaze.

High-fired glazes, with two exceptions, give more sombre colours. A variety of iron oxides in different concentrations and under different firing conditions are those most commonly used to colour the glazes, and these will produce all the soft greys, greens, lavender blues, browns, rusty colours, yellowish browns and blacks. The most brilliant black is actually produced using a combination of iron and manganese. The two exceptions, which produce really bright glowing colours, are cobalt blue, and copper for red used with limited inclusions of iron. The latter is fired under very carefully controlled reducing conditions, a technique which will produce a very wide range of variations, of which the deepest and strongest is that sumptuously described as *sang de boeuf*.

Kiln atmospheres are of two kinds, oxidizing and reducing. Oxidizing atmospheres are achieved by ensuring a good through draught during the firing and plenty of clear flame. Reducing atmospheres are created by damping down the firing at some stage, often by closing the kiln doors so that the amount of oxygen drawn into the firing chamber is drastically reduced. This process is very commonly used by the Chinese and accounts for a great diversity of effect.[5]

It is with these varied resources that the Chinese potter worked, only gradually achieving mastery and combining it with the decorative techniques, many of them complex. That the richness of the effects is so great is not surprising, but even so they are a tribute to his creative ability and his technical mastery of the materials that came to his hand. In the development of decorative techniques the Chinese potter showed himself imaginative and a master of selecting what was most appropriate to the material, and if sometimes he produced wholly repellent pieces in both shape and decoration, we can only say that he was no different from any other craftsman in any other society. That he so rarely falls down in this way may be partly accounted for by what appears to be an instinctive appreciation and understanding of proportion in relation to function, and of line in relation to form.

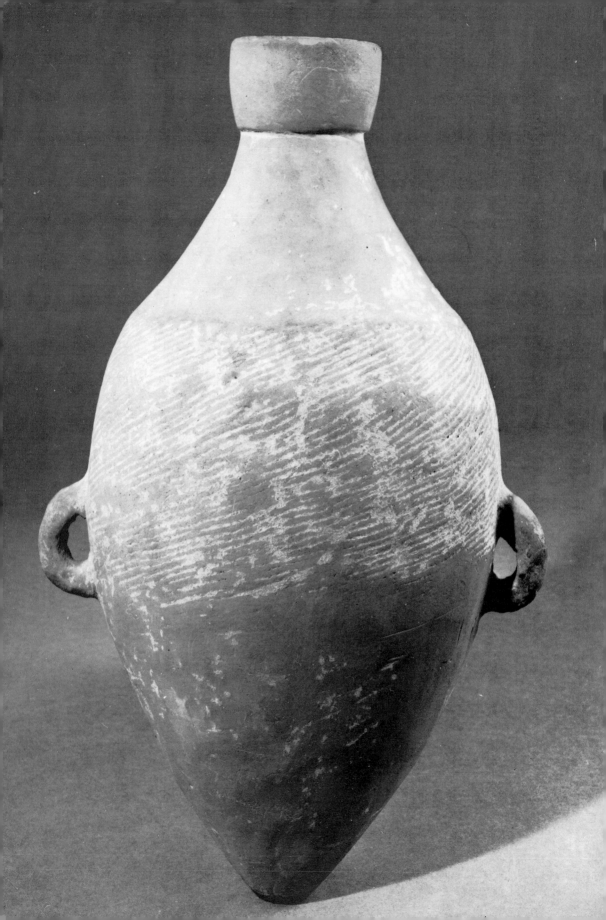

PART ONE

THE BASIC TECHNOLOGY

CHAPTER ONE

Pre-Han Unglazed Earthenware

The earliest pottery of China is the unglazed earthenware of the neolithic cultures of north China from the fourth to the early part of the second millennium B.C., and even at this stage it is possible to discern certain fundamental qualities which were later to become characteristic during the evolution of ceramics in historic times. There were two neolithic cultures in the north and it is necessary to distinguish them as clearly as possible.

The Neolithic Cultures of North China

One neolithic culture was centred on Honan, southern Shansi and through central Shensi, reaching out to an extension in the west in Kansu. The culture, called Yang-shao after the village of that name in Honan, where J. G. Andersson first identified it in 1922,[1] is confined to the loess region, the sites of which are generally found along the middle course of the Yellow river, although in Honan they may be found as far south as the Huai river and north into the flat plain of southern Hopei. The Kansu extension is now usually termed Kansu Yang-shao.

The second culture, called Lung-shan, lay to the north-east and east in a broad coastal strip reaching from southern Manchuria through Hopei, eastern Honan and Shantung, and as far south as northern Chekiang. The type site, Ch'êng-tzǔ-yai, lies in northern Shantung and was discovered in 1931,[2] the culture taking its name from the hill, Lung-shan, adjoining the settlement.

The two cultures overlap in central Honan and in the more common type of

Opposite: Fig. 2. Red earthenware amphora, hand built with corded paddle. Yang-shao. Height 30.5 cm. 5th–4th millennium B.C. London, British Museum.

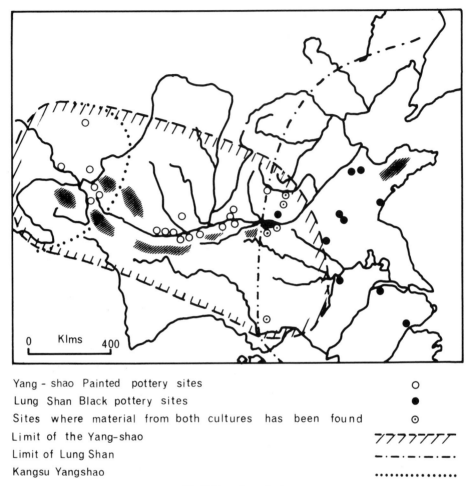

Yang - shao Painted pottery sites   ○
Lung Shan Black pottery sites   ●
Sites where material from both cultures has been found   ◉
Limit of the Yang-shao
Limit of Lung Shan
Kangsu Yangshao

Neolithic culture limits

pottery the distinctions between them are so blurred that positive identification as to proper cultural origin is virtually impossible, and on some sites, indeed, wholly impossible. Each culture, however, in its most distinctive form, is distinguished by totally different fine quality pottery, that of Yang-shao in the central and western areas being red and usually painted in slip colours, while that of Lung-shan in the east is black, burnished and often incised.

The question of chronology is particularly difficult and has not so far been satisfactorily solved, although there are relative chronologies within each of the two cultures. The Chinese view, put forward by An Chih-min, is that the Lung-shan succeeded Yang-shao and was an eastern diffusion from it, but this has not been finally confirmed and crucial questions still remain.[3] The only clearly established point is that at An-yang, the last Shang dynasty capital in Honan, a

Bronze Age site, the Lung-shan material overlies that of Yang-shao and is almost immediately succeeded by Shang remains. This only proves that in the western extension of Lung-shan this culture is later than that of Yang-shao, and not that the whole Lung-shan culture is later, or that it is in any fundamental way dependent upon Yang-shao.

It is customary to discuss the Yang-shao culture first and to follow it with Lung-shan. This is the order in which the type sites were found and is adopted here.

Yang-shao Pottery

The pottery of Yang-shao is basically of two kinds. First there is a coarse grey earthenware built up by hand using a pad and beater,[4] which if bound with cord leaves the impressions of cording on the outside; or the pots can be built up using coils of clay, and then either using a corded beater or simply smoothing the outside with a suitable tool to conceal the joins between one coil and the next on the outside. A smooth surface may often be pricked, pecked or otherwise patterned. Both techniques are widely used in other cultures and are in fact still practised. The grey earthenware made by these two methods was intended for ordinary household purposes, for cooking, storage and for carrying water. There are bag-shaped pots with everted rim (Fig. 3), deep jars with neatly finished rim, and tall amphora shapes (Fig. 2) for the collection and carting of water.

The clay for these often rather crude pots came from the sticky deposits at the base of the loess and was usually tempered to make it more easily workable, but relatively little care was taken in its preparation. The firing was carried out in a simple kiln chamber cut into the ground with the fire itself a little to one side and

Fig. 3. Earthenware jar, hand built with pricked surface. Yang-shao, Pan-p'o site. Height 11 cm. 5th–4th millennium B.C. Chinese Government.

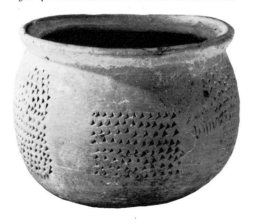

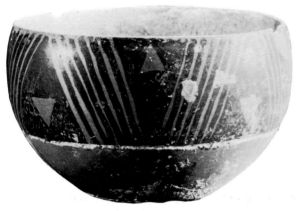
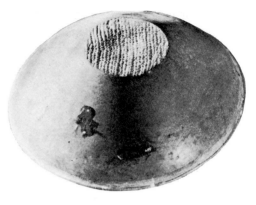

Fig. 4. Red earthenware bowl painted in black. Yang-shao, Pan-p'o site. Diameter 15.5 cm. 5th–4th millennium B.C. Chinese Government.

Fig. 5. Red earthenware bowl with textile impressed base. Yang-shao, Pan-p'o site. Diameter 13 cm. 5th–4th millennium B.C. Chinese Government.

at a lower level than the shelf or platform on which the wares were placed. There were a few holes in the platform for the passage of the flame and over the top was a lightly constructed dome, probably rebuilt for each firing, with a central flue to allow the escape of gases, flame and smoke. Thus already the pots were partly separated from direct contact with the fire. The temperatures for the firing of the grey ware were not very high; it seems that about 900°C was sufficient, although higher temperatures could be achieved with kilns of this construction. The grey ware is found throughout the region with only minor variations, unlike the wide variation to be found in more sophisticated wares.

The superior earthenware of Yang-shao is a light red, fine grained ware with a lightly burnished surface decorated with painted designs in black and red, maroon, brown and on some sites, especially in the east, with white slip. The most common vessels are wide bowls narrow at the base and turning in towards the rim, which is sometimes flattened; simple round bottomed bowls (Fig. 4); large swelling urns narrowing to the base, with narrow necks, and with two lugs set vertically at the maximum diameter; vases of more elongated shape, and jugs with straight necks and simple strap handles. There are also bag-shaped jars with handles or lugs at the slightly constricted necks. On the eastern borders of the Yang-shao area there is a slightly greater variety of shapes with some handsome vases with narrow or relatively long expanding necks.

All these vessels are made from carefully chosen and fairly well prepared clay of comparatively fine particle size with little if any added temper. The reddish colour is due to the iron content in the body which was fired in an oxidizing atmosphere at temperatures said to vary a great deal and believed in some cases to have been as high as 1,020°C.[5]

The pots were hand built by the coiling method, and in order to rotate them, especially in the final stages when the lip was finished, they were often set on a piece of matting which could easily be turned on a flat surface of earth or on a large flat stone, an early example of the turn-table. There is evidence of this on the base of some of the bowls from the important site of Pan-p'o in southern Shensi (Fig. 5). When the vessels were completed they were allowed to dry for a time, and then the surface was lightly burnished. In some cases, particularly the large urns from Kansu, the lower parts show signs of having been trimmed and shaved thinner with some kind of blade before burnishing, which does not always reach the base. The burnished clay, of course, provided an excellent surface for the subsequent decoration in slip colours.

The painting was executed with a primitive form of brush, the marks of which can frequently be seen. The bright red is due to iron, while the black and maroon are due to varying quantities of iron and manganese. White slip painting, which is largely confined to the eastern extensions of Yang-shao, is heavier and usually reserved for simple bands and geometric designs. The other colours are used with great boldness and fluency either for schematic designs of fish, animals, toads and human faces, or for rhythmically drawn curvilinear designs with additions of hatching and cross-hatching.[6]

The decorative styles varied from one region to another, but broadly there are three that are easily distinguishable. In the central area, of which Pan-p'o in Shensi is representative, the simple geometric patterns and schematic designs with animals, fish and human faces were relatively common, the painting being either on the inside or outside, rarely on both, and carried out in black sometimes with touches of red, and occasionally on a very thin red slip ground.

In the west, in the Kansu region, the so-called Kansu Yang-shao, where the culture is generally admitted to be later than that of the central area and which continues until some time in the second millennium, black is again the predominant colour (Plate I, opposite page 96). Some sites yield pieces painted only in black, but others have examples painted in black and maroon or black and brown. From this western area come the large urns with bold curvilinear decorations which constitute a unique feature of the culture of the region (Figs. 6, 7). It is noticeable that only the upper parts of the large urns, jugs and jars are painted and that the patterns are often bordered with a broad scalloping band round the lower extremity.

At the eastern end of the Yang-shao culture, in Honan and north-western Kiangsu, where there is an overlap with the Lung-shan culture, the red pottery, when painted, includes white slip used either as a ground for the other colours, especially black, or for simple rather static geometric patterns (Fig. 8). The other colours are the black already mentioned and a rather bright red. When curvilinear designs are used they may be poorly organized, tending to disintegrate into a series of interrupted rhythms, unlike the inventions of the far western tradition.

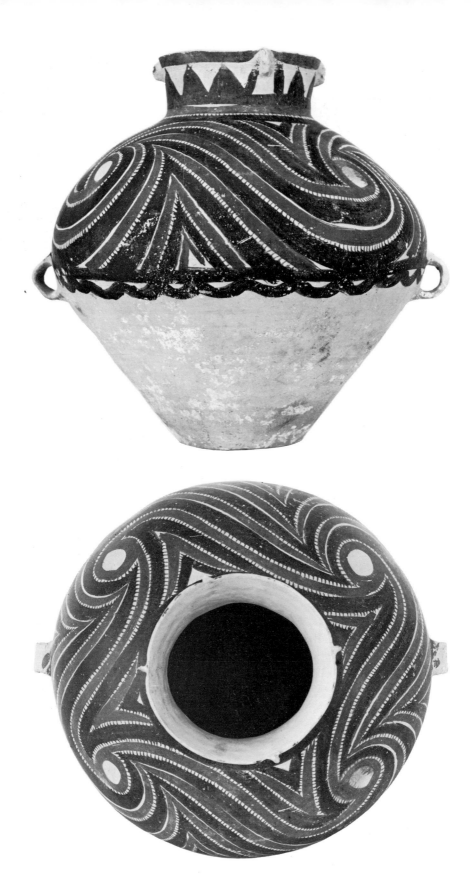

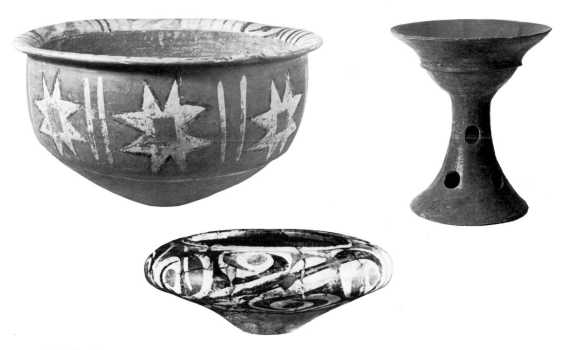

Left: Fig. 8. Red earthenware bowl painted in black and white. P'ei-hsien, Kiangsu. Diameter 33.8 cm. 4th–3rd millennium B.C. Chinese Government.

Centre: Fig. 9. Red earthenware bowl painted in red, white and black. P'ei-hsien, Kiangsu. Diameter 18 cm. 4th–3rd millennium B.C. Chinese Government.

Right: Fig. 10. Brown earthenware *tou*, tazza. Yang-shao ts'un, Honan. Height 22 cm. 3rd millennium B.C. Stockholm, Museum of Far Eastern Antiquities.

The shapes on which they appear are also to some extent different from those of the central tradition. The bowls, still hand-made, are often much smaller at the base and some, like the example from P'ei-hsien in Kiangsu, have an exceptionally deep inversion at the rim (Fig. 9).

In Honan there are numerous sites where the shapes and styles are found to be transitional between those of Yang-shao and Lung-shan. Among these are the solid legged *ting* tripod cauldron, the udder-shaped leg forms represented by the *li* and *chia,* and the open bowl supported on a tall spreading stem, called *tou,* all ultimate antecedents of early Bronze Age types of the Shang dynasty. These shapes are hand-made and the decoration on them is minimal; the use of cording, applied strips of clay pinched to stand in relief, simple scoring and grooving being most common. The hollow stem of the *tou,* however, may be pierced through ornamentally with circles or triangles (Fig. 10). Such vessels are found in both grey and fine grained reddish ware. If there is only coarse grey ware with corded

Opposite: Figs. 6, 7. Red earthenware urn painted in black and maroon. Yang-shao culture, Kansu. Height 42.5 cm. 3rd millennium B.C. Stockholm, Museum of Far Eastern Antiquities.

texturing on the surface to be found on these central Honan sites, it is usually impossible to determine whether the material should be attributed to Yang-shao or Lung-shan, unless stone tools of certain specific forms are also present.[7] Farther north into Hopei and east into Shantung the distinctions become clearer, while towards the south in Kiangsu and Anhui, the grey pottery to some extent gives way to a browner type.

Lung-shan Pottery

The Lung-shan culture, at its most characteristic in Shantung, differs in a number of important respects from that of Yang-shao in the Yellow river basin and westwards. In the first place there is a greater diversity of material in terms of the clays used. Not only is there a rough sandy pottery of grey colour common to both cultures, but there is a reddish brown type, some of it fine grained and some of it coarse and sandy. There is also a fine grained very dark grey ware and an unique black pottery with exceptionally fine particle size and thin structure when fired, and a rather rare pale yellowish or white ware, this last being confined to Shantung.[8]

The second important difference is that there is a much greater diversity of shapes. The variety is so great and the regional variations so numerous within the cultural area that attempts to create a serviceable classification of the material have not so far proved altogether satisfactory. In addition to this, although the surfaces of the black, dark grey and reddish ware may be burnished, there is no painting. Designs are normally impressed or incised, the latter being especially common on the black and dark grey ware. The patterns are usually simple geometric ones, lines horizontally grooving the body in what the Chinese call 'bow-string design', the fine scoring of limited areas on burnished surfaces. Occasionally bands are raised in relief and small bosses may be applied to the surface; this last treatment occurs on the pale yellow and white ware, but is sometimes found on the dark grey as well (Fig. 11).

The third and quite fundamental difference between Yang-shao and Lung-shan is that it is in Lung-shan that the fast turning potter's wheel appears for the first time. It was perhaps this that made an entirely new approach to clay essential, and must have been one of the factors responsible for the more diversified forms which are found, especially in the dark grey and black wares. The dark grey and the uniquely thin black earthenware, the latter averaging between one and three millimetres in thickness, are both thrown on the wheel and are indeed the only wares so made. Simple jars of various sizes and good proportion are natural shapes on the wheel, and there are many of these, but there is also a wide range of cup and jug shapes, while the *tou* with long stem also occurs, together with high footed basins and a series of long stemmed goblets of

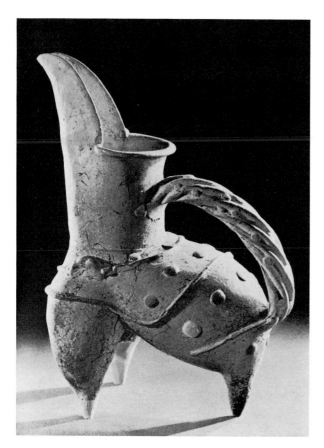

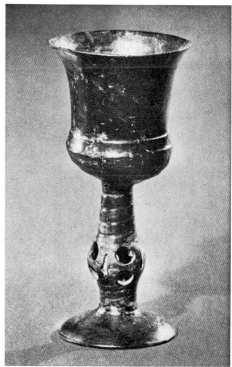

Fig. 11. White earthenware jug, *k'uei*. Lung-shan culture, Wei-fang, Shantung. Height 29.7 cm. 3rd–2nd millennium B.C. Chinese Government.

Fig. 12. Black earthenware goblet with burnished surface; wheel made. Lung-shan culture, Wei-fang, Shantung. Height 19 cm. 3rd–2nd millennium B.C. Chinese Government.

surprisingly angular contour (Fig. 12). This angularity in the black ware has often been remarked on as it is unusual in ceramics except when there is an immediate dependence on metalwork for the derivation of form. But no metal has ever been found on the Lung-shan sites, so the explanation must be sought somewhere else.

The answer almost certainly lies in the very mastering of a new technique and a delight in being able to handle the material in this novel way. With a well levigated fine grained clay of even particle size, the potter had a plastic material admirably suited to use on the wheel, and as a turn-table of a primitive kind was already in use for finishing, the wheel must very soon have been used for shaving the black wares, in particular, to the thinness possible and compatible with practical use. The combination of a fine clay, the wheel, and the ability to shave the walls of vessels successfully, is likely to have led to the enthusiastic exploration of form. It did lead to the introduction of new shapes as well as to a new handling of those

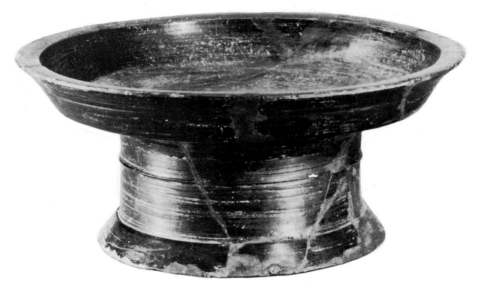

Fig. 13. Black earthenware *p'an*, basin; wheel made. Lung-shan culture, Wei-fang, Shantung. Diameter 43.8 cm. 3rd–2nd millennium B.C. Chinese Government.

already long familiar. But the wheel, while it makes construction faster and in some ways easier, also imposes limitations. Large shapes are ruled out if the potter is throwing off the top, that is, throwing a series of bowls or cups off a single cone of clay without pausing except to remove each in succession. Eccentric shapes are also impossible in a single operation. The need therefore arose to make several thrown parts in order to complete a single vessel, and this in itself must have stimulated the elaboration of structured vessels like the *tou*, the *p'an* basin on a high foot (Fig. 13), and a remarkably elegant long stemmed goblet, which are characteristic forms of the Lung-shan tradition.

The use of the wheel also extended to truing up hand-made earthenware, whose rims often show signs of finishing on the wheel. Many such wheel finished rims are simple, but they can be elaborated by grooving and carination, thus imparting a sophistication of contour to the rim such as would have required very laborious effort in hand building. It is perhaps significant that the use of the wheel for throwing was confined to the production of the dark grey and black ware. This is because it was not possible to throw satisfactory shapes with clays that had a variable or very coarse particle size; a relatively fine and even particle size is a prerequisite for this method of construction.

One of the consequences of this technical innovation was that it inevitably led to a greater degree of specialization in social terms, since those good at making pottery by the older coiling method, or by using the pad and beater, might not be sufficiently skilled in the use of well prepared clay to throw well on the wheel, while the skilled thrower might not have the patience to engage in coiling and using the pad and beater.

In any case the two methods continued side by side for centuries and one of the most remarkable of the hand-made pots of Lung-shan, found nowhere else, was the *kuei* jug on its udder-shaped tripod, with a cylindrical neck and elegant upward angled spout. It is a strange vessel known in two variant forms in pale yellowish or white clay. One form tends to stand somewhat vertically with the vertical handle rather to the rear, well away from the spout (Fig. 1), and the other, which is more horizontal, with the handle often composed of rolls of clay twisted in the semblance of a rope or of twisted thongs of leather, has it arching roughly horizontally across from the base of the spout over the dome-like body to the back leg (Fig. 11). The *kuei* and the use of the whitish clay seems to have been

Neolithic kilns: I. Lung-shan; II. Shang, Chêng-chou.

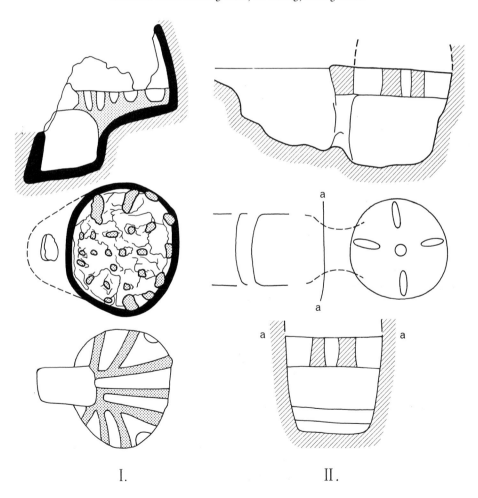

I.   II.

confined to Shantung, unlike the black ware which spread into Honan, though found with diminishing frequency as one moves westward (see map on page 30).

In Lung-shan there was not only the technical advance in the introduction of the potter's wheel, but also an improvement in kiln design. This was now slightly refined by an increase in the number of heat vents into the kiln chamber through the baked earthen floor (see drawing on page 27). Earlier kilns had a few rather large vents, which often meant that blasts of particles from the furnace were forced through on the draught into the kiln chamber, with the accompanying risk to the surfaces of the pots. By increasing the number of vents and reducing them in size, the risk of defacing the wares was much diminished, an important consideration where the fine quality black ware was concerned. Because the heat was now more evenly distributed, it was probably also more easily controlled. The firing temperatures, which could be high, were also easier to maintain, and reduction, which was essential for the black ware, was better controlled. It is in fact clear that the black ware and the dark grey were both reduction fired, whether by covering the top of the main flue at the appropriate time, or by using the imbibing method, or both, it is not at present possible to determine.[9]

The picture that emerges of the northern neolithic period is that there are two distinct traditions in terms of technique, form and decoration. The western tradition is characterized by hand built forms conceived as simple unities and composed in a continuous process, with only simple supplementary parts such as handles being added to suit a particular purpose, and by boldly painted decorations that support the unity of the form.[10] The eastern tradition, by contrast, is striking not only for the use of the wheel, but also for complex constructions, in which the vessels are conceived as a unity composed of a multiplicity of small parts, often of great diversity and each made singly to be assembled to form the whole, the proportions being carefully adjusted to each other and to the whole.[11] The complexity of the processes and the understanding of the raw materials imply an imaginative and creative intelligence of a very different order from that which in the west is best shown in the strength of the brush and the fluency of the curvilinear rhythms in painted decoration. The major traits of both these cultures were to be deeply embedded in Chinese ceramic development from this time on.

Southern Neolithic Pottery

The southern regions of China, too, had a neolithic culture. It differed in some respects from both those of the north, but because it was generally later and continued longer, it betrays influences of both Yang-shao and Lung-shan. At present the pottery is not very well understood, although sites have been found well up the Yangtse river in both Kiangsi and Hunan, as well as in the east in Chekiang, Fukien, and in Kuangtung as far south as Hong Kong.

The clay bodies tend to be more brown than grey, and there were some vessels produced in the eastern region that were thinner in the wall and harder in the body than was usual in the northern cultures. While most of the pieces were hand-made with pad and beater, the wheel was also used. The decoration of the surface was mainly corded, stamped or impressed, even shells being used for decorative texturing. Some of the stamps were of baked clay with patterns of spirals, both round and squared, herring-bone patterns, and matting designs. The decorations varied somewhat from one region to another, but were of the same general type. The shapes include the familiar bag-shaped pots, and with them some *ting* tripod shapes, the *tou*, and rather slack looking variants of the *li* and *chia*, which all indicate the impact of the more northerly cultures with which there is an overlap in the north on sites in the lower Yangtse basin.

The coarse products of the neolithic cultures continued over a long period and follow on even into the Shang period in the early Bronze Age, for the greater part of the population went on living in near neolithic conditions despite the sophistications accompanying a flourishing bronze culture.

Shang and Chou

It was in the northern provinces, an area in which cultural developments were in advance of those farther south that the next important steps forward were taken. It was in Honan, on the edge of the Yellow river basin where Yang-shao and Lung-shan overlapped, that the neolithic cultures in due time gave way to the first historic period, the Shang, generally believed to extend from the sixteenth century to the last quarter of the eleventh century B.C.[12] Dominated by the production of bronze, the period is regarded by many as fairly sterile as far as ceramics are concerned, probably because of the obvious and natural emphasis on bronze founding with which the first dynastic period is pre-eminently associated. While in certain respects this is true, there are aspects in which the Shang has to be viewed as an important period of innovation.

Progress was made in three ways. The first and fundamentally the most important was in kiln design. The second was in the use of high-firing materials such as are seen in stonewares, with which we shall be more concerned in the next chapter, and the third was in the use of white kaolinic clays for white bodied vessels.

If the less revolutionary aspects are dealt with first, it is found that all through Shang, and indeed right down to the end of the Bronze Age and at the beginning of the Han dynasty, unglazed earthenware underwent very few changes. The common, coarse, sandy grey ware continued to be made in the same rather crude

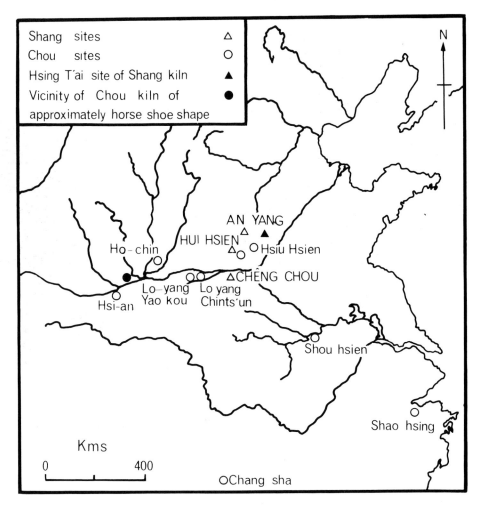

Shan and Chou kiln sites.

shapes for domestic purposes as it had been in neolithic times, but there was a notable increase in the use of the wheel for finishing the rims and for simple decorative horizontal grooving and banding, even when the vessel was constructed by hand using a pad and corded beater or a patterned wooden paddle. Strips of clay were still applied for decoration, often being pinched or serrated in the same way as before. The purely utilitarian function of the grey pottery ensured the continuance of this rather pedestrian line over a long period.

Alongside this coarse ware there was something a little more sophisticated. It was a fine dark grey, almost black ware, which was a survivor from the neolithic tradition. The shapes are closely allied to those of bronze, but rarely imitate them very closely either in detail or in decoration (Fig. 14). In most cases the handsome

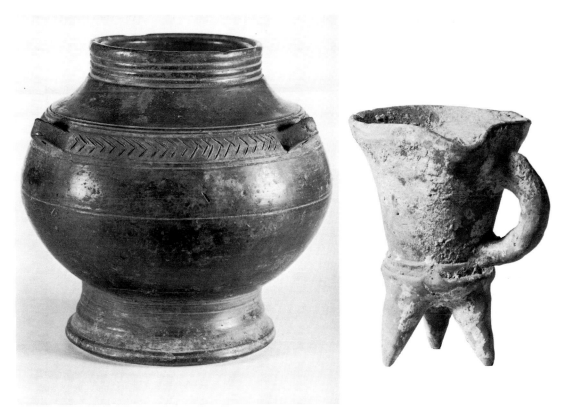

Fig. 14. Dark grey earthenware jar. Shang. Height 15.9 cm. Boston, Museum of Fine Arts.

Fig. 15. Grey earthenware *chüeh*, jug. Shang. Height 12.1 cm. Asian Art Museum of San Francisco, Brundage Collection.

bowls on a thick ring foot, large vases with a flat base, and tall beakers were made by using both hand building methods and the wheel. The surfaces were usually burnished while the vessel was still on the wheel by using a suitable implement such as a well worn stone. They were then grooved horizontally in bands to assign the surface into areas to be incised with simple geometric patterns including a range of chevron (Fig. 16) and lozenge designs, sometimes with impressed corded areas supplying a textural variation which gave emphasis to the main elements.[13] In many instances stamps bearing double and treble scrolling motifs, or diamond and lozenge patterns were used to form repeating bands well below the rim of a basin, or for a shoulder band on a large vase. Handles and lugs might be added, and these were moulded into shape before being luted on to the main body. All are thick, heavy pieces, and, while well enough made, will not stand comparison with the fine Lung-shan black ware to which they are technically related.

A few examples are more explicit copies of existing bronze forms, and of these

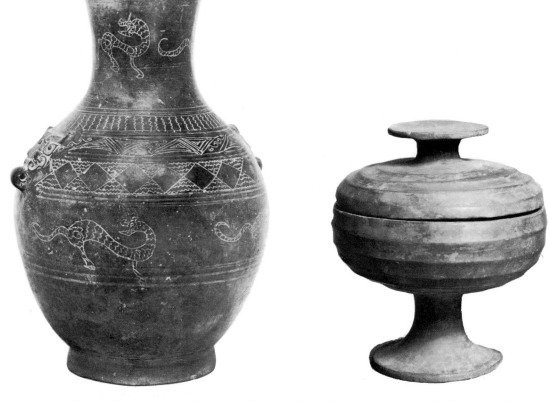

Fig. 16. Grey earthenware *hu*, vase, with incised decoration on a lightly burnished ground, with moulded relief mask escutcheons on the shoulder. Eastern Chou. Height 35.6 cm. Seattle, Art Museum.

Fig. 17. Grey earthenware *tou* with reversible lid. Height 24 cm. Late Eastern Chou. 4th–3rd century B.C. New York, Metropolitan Museum of Art.

the *chüeh* is the best known (Fig. 15). It is a crude, rather top-heavy vessel in pottery with three stubby legs supporting a slightly bellied lower section with a spreading open-spouted upper section, the handle at right angles to the spout being affixed to the belly below and to the upper section just below the lip. The dependence on the metal form is made obvious by the rib defining the connection between lower and upper sections and by the occasional addition of two protuberances of clay on the lip to right and left of the spout in imitation of the capped columns of the bronze prototype. Such ungainly vessels seem to have been discontinued after the end of Shang and are not encountered again until the later periods of antiquarianism from about the fifteenth century A.D. onward.

Despite the change of dynasty in 1027 B.C., and changing society, the fine grained rather compact dark grey ware continued during the following Chou with very little variation. Perhaps the wheel was more widely used, but definitive evidence is lacking. The shapes, too, remain largely unchanged, with the taller jars only gaining slightly longer necks and narrower bases, bringing them more into line with what the Chinese term *hu* (Fig. 16), which is more ovoid than the bronze *lei* and less rotund than the *p'ou*. One form reappears in a more elegant variation, the *tou*, the bowl section now rounder and the stem thinner with a wide spreading foot; it is usually made with a reversible lid (Fig. 17). With the reappearance of the *tou*, two other vessels in close imitation of the contemporary bronzes are seen for the first time. These are the covered *ting* and the *tui*,[14] a spherical vessel made in two halves with three projections on each half serving as feet. Both vessels are purely imitative and add nothing to the evolution of pottery. They merely reflect the current preoccupation with bronze, for which from about the sixth century B.C. they are frequently substituted in the tomb. Some finds, notably in the Lo-yang region, reveal a slavish imitation of gold and silver inlaid bronze forms such as would date from the fourth century B.C. onwards, and these are elaborately painted in unfired red, blue, and white designs approximating very nearly to those found in the bronze prototypes. This was a practice which continued well into the Han period, remaining current, until its ultimate extinction in the immediate post-Han period, as a cheap substitute for the costly bronzes.

In the east, in Kiangsu, Anhui, and Chekiang during the later centuries of Chou, in the Warring States period, there was a series of brown rather than grey ware, some of which was hand-made with pad and beater, the beater being covered with finely textured woven textile in simple tabby weave. These vessels are not as a rule large, and are surprisingly thin. In the smaller pieces the impression is given that the beater was covered with silk, so unusually fine is the woven texture. The vessels are mostly rounded with a contracted lip, and often have S-shaped reliefs applied near the lip. Another group also from this region, and probably made in Chekiang, consists of large, fairly thick jars well made on the wheel, and with wide shoulders, the body narrowing towards the flat base. There are often impressed patterns of matting, or carefully cut vertical grooves ordered in bands (Fig. 18). These pieces are rather harder than most of those produced at about the same time in the fourth or third century B.C.

Thus in the post Shang period nothing significant is added in unglazed wares in terms of shape. Much the same may be said of decoration, apart from the appearance of incised animals, especially rampant tigers, on the dark grey ware. Burnishing continued as a ground for incised decoration, but there was one new variant in the use of curvilinear patterns on a semi-burnished surface; there may also be geometric designs executed in a similar manner.

At this point it is possible to return to the real innovations of the Shang period, taking the white wares first. Although, as in later neolithic ware especially in the eastern extension of the Yang-shao, white clays had been used, they had hitherto been exploited only for slip coatings and simple surface decoration, or in the

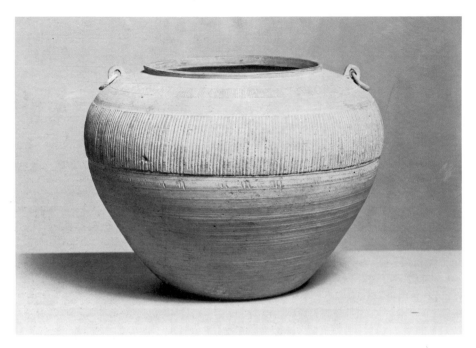

Fig. 18. Brownish grey earthenware jar from Kiangsu. Diameter 19 cm. 3rd century B.C. New York, Metropolitan Museum of Art.

Lung-shan culture for the peculiar vessel *kuei*, confined to Shantung. In Shang times, however, many large vessels were made using a white kaolinic clay, exceptionally free of those impurities, especially iron, which impart colour to the body in the fired state. These kaolinic clays lack much of the plasticity associated with earthenware and stoneware clays and consequently, in Shang times at least, the clays were used for rather thick hand-made vessels with only very limited use of the wheel.

Both in shape and decoration the white earthenware approximates closely to current ritual bronzes, although identity of design is hard to find (Fig. 19). The decoration is carved into the thick body while still leather hard and the blade marks are easily seen on many pieces. Of individual motifs the *t'ao-t'ieh* is the only one that can be clearly distinguished, together with a modified squared spiral or meander. The potters employed on the production of these vessels, which were related to the bronzes in form and design, were exposed to a similar artistic climate, but they evidently worked apart from those immediately concerned with the bronze founding industry, whose ceramic specialists only engaged in the construction of moulds for casting and not in the more generalized production of ceramics. This is once more an indication of the specialization within the society in which the craftsman lived, at a time when bronze was the aristocratic material, and its possession a mark of the owner's wealth.

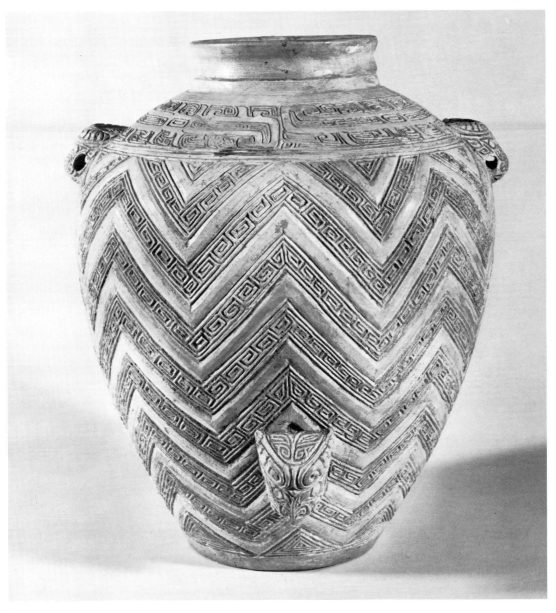

Fig. 19. Carved white earthenware *lei,* jar. Shang. Height 32.6 cm. 13th–11th century B.C. Washington, Freer Gallery of Art.

The firing temperature of the white ware seems to have been within the same range as that of the superior earthenware, fluctuating, according to tests carried out some years ago,[15] between 1,050 and 1,150°C. There have been claims that Shang white ware would have been porcelain had it been fired to a higher temperature, but this is not so as the body lacks the essential ingredient, china stone, necessary to produce porcelain at the correct temperature of 1,280°C. The kaolinic clays could only have vitrified at temperatures approximating to 1,750°C, a level impossible to achieve with any ease, and certainly not possible at that time. The result is that Shang white ware, although thick, apparently strong, and relatively hard, is in fact rather brittle. This may be the reason for its disappearance at the end of the Shang in the late eleventh century B.C.

The greatest innovation of the Shang dynasty, and the one to have the most lasting and important effect, was in kiln design. This was partly a spin-off from the need for high temperatures and reducing conditions for smelting metal, although the seeds of the development had already been sown in the neolithic period, when the desire for high quality ceramics, especially in Lung-shan, had resulted in the fine black pottery. The first step had been the separation of the pottery from the danger of ash falls and contamination of burnished surfaces by placing it in a chamber heated through vents cut in the floor, with the fire box well to one side and outside the walls of the kiln. This was a good kiln, so far as it went, with a good draught, but reduction was necessarily difficult to control because it was still fundamentally an up-draught kiln. Reducing conditions could only be imposed by applying a chimney-top damper in the form of a piece of broken pot or tile over the top of the smoke vent, or by using the imbibing method, which involves shovelling earth, straw, and vegetable matter on to the top of the kiln and then dribbling water over it as soon as the maturing temperature has been reached. This is a technique which produces a great deal of steam and a rapid drop of temperature within the kiln.

It was the Shang change in design which was ultimately to lead to the reduction firing techniques becoming predominant for Chinese stonewares up to and even after the great development of porcelain in the eighth and ninth centuries A.D. The change in design may have been one of the benefits of the bronze technology of the age and been dependent on the type of furnace necessary for smelting the ore ready for the foundry. The first step was taken in the new development towards an efficient down-draught kiln of a kind different from the later 'horseshoe' kiln common throughout north China.[16]

The design is ingenious, but operation was difficult, and it produced something more in the nature of a carbon soaked firing than true reduction, yet the principle of the down-draught kiln was nevertheless present. The placing of the smoke vents or flues at the side of the kiln wall and immediately in contact with some of the heat vents in the floor, combined with the introduction of dampers near the top of the heat vents, indicates clearly that the kiln was intended for reduction (see drawing opposite).[17]

No kiln door was found, since the upper parts of the kilns are almost invariably missing, so it is not possible to know whether the kiln was top loaded or packed from one side. The arrangement of the smoke vents round the side might have precluded an ordinary door.

After the setting of the kiln, the fire is lit and allowed to burn up normally; that

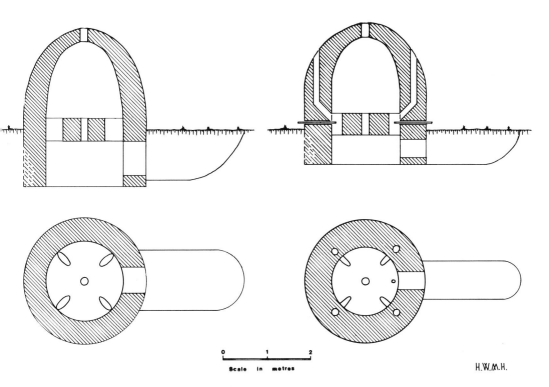

Shang kiln; ideal reconstruction. Hsing-t'ai, Hopei.

is, slowly with all the dampers open; this is essential for the first stage of drying the ware and warming up the whole kiln atmosphere evenly. When this has gone on long enough the fire is stoked more quickly, and when a really good roaring fire has been created and the temperature has begun to rise rather steeply, the dampers are slammed shut across the vents in the kiln. A great blast of heat then rises straight through the central vent, which has to be quickly closed with a tile. The interior wall of the dome deflects the heat back towards the floor of the kiln, the smoke and flame ultimately being forced through the chimneys which connect with the now closed heat vents. Because the heat is raised so rapidly the carbon content in the clay bodies is not dispersed in the normal way, but burned black in the clay before it can be dissipated by the combination of chemical and thermal reaction. The fact that grey pottery fragments were found in the kiln of this design at Hsing-t'ai in northern Honan in 1956 is evidence strongly supporting the design as ideally reconstructed. But there was still a long way to go before the horseshoe kiln emerged and the intermediate steps, which one would expect to find in Honan, southern Shensi or slightly to the east and south, have yet to be discovered on new archaeological sites.[18]

The unglazed pottery up to and including the Han period bears witness to the potter's fairly exhaustive exploration of the basic materials of his craft, and also to

37

his interest in form. The character of the Chinese potter in these early centuries is perhaps most clearly seen in the forms he created, whichever of the two principal techniques he employed. Each had its own limitations and its own potentialities, and he learned thoroughly to understand these. There are two ways of using clay, whichever technique is adopted. Either one can use the material to the limits of its natural potential in creating organic unities of great simplicity, as may be seen in much of the neolithic pottery of the Yang-shao culture, or one can go to the opposite extreme and construct vessels of complex form bound into a unity by the balancing of the proportions of the parts to each other and to the whole, a tendency most apparent in some of the early experiments with the wheel in the Lung-shan culture. By Han times these two streams, the single dynamic unity and the complex construction, had begun to merge into a characteristically Chinese tradition, which has remained unaltered to the present day.

At the same time the techniques of decoration of unglazed earthenware had been almost completely explored by Han times, but in the handling of design, both in the use of individual motifs and in the organization of patterns on the surfaces, there was much to be learned, indeed, the beginning had only just been made; the real development of ornament was still to come, and maturity lay far in the future.

CHAPTER TWO

Glazed Wares from Shang to Han

Even from neolithic times the north China plain was, as we have seen, an important area in which cultural developments overlapped and evolved. In the Shang period, from about the sixteenth century B.C., the region remained central to the cultural evolution, and it was here under the military autocracy of the Shang kings that the bronze founders, jade carvers, stone sculptors, and potters worked. The earlier of the two capital cities, which we know from archaeology, was Chêng-chou, south of the Yellow river in the modern province of Honan. Extensive areas of occupation, as well as massive royal tombs, and ordinary cemeteries have yielded a vast quantity of artefacts including pottery.[1] The area continued to be inhabited after 1300 B.C., when the Shang kings moved their capital about a hundred miles north of the Yellow river to An-yang, where excavations of an extensive kind have continued intermittently since 1928.[2] It was here that the cultural succession of Yang-shao, Lung-shan, and finally Shang was seen for the first time, and it was from here that the first glazed pots were excavated.

Shang was overrun and the dynasty obliterated in 1028 B.C. by the Chou ruler and his people from the west, where in the Wei river valley the capital city of Hao-ching in Shensi remained until 771 B.C. In that year the Chou king moved the capital to Lo-yang in western Honan, where he built a new one. The Chou state, unlike the Shang, was rather feudal in its organization, with most of the evils associated with that system, and after about 700 B.C. the king's power to control his lords waned until he was no more than a figurehead, a ruler in name only, yet at the same time the only person able to offer the sacrifices to heaven. The states, in what amounted to a loose confederation, steadily increased in both military and political power, and began to jockey for supremacy in the age known as the Period of the Spring and Autumn Annals. Some states disappeared altogether by peaceful absorption into greater states, or were split into a series of smaller ones, no one state being able to claim more than temporary power over a large area. It was also the period when statesmen began to take over from the hereditary rulers and diplomacy of a kind first developed. After about 475 B.C., however, came the period of the Warring States, which, as the name indicates, meant all-out war between the strongest states, and the ordinary people suffering accordingly when no holds were barred.

The Chou were finally wiped out, in fact as well as in name, in 256 B.C. by the first emperor, Ch'in Shih Huang-ti, the First Universal Emperor of the Ch'in dynasty. His conquests brought about the unification of China for the first time. It was in his reign that the Chinese script was unified and weights and measures were standardized, two measures of fundamental importance in the history of China. The second emperor, who was a cruel profligate, did not last long, and the realm to which he succeeded was taken over after his death in 206 B.C. by Liu Pang, the first emperor of the Western or Former Han, with whose reign the first great period of empire began. During this great age the Chinese, made restless in the preceding centuries of strife, first looked outwards from their own land and travelled the Central Asian trade routes to India, Persia, and other strange and exciting countries to the west, and to Korea in the east.[3]

The Han dynasty is divided into two parts, the Western or Former Han, which came to an end in A.D. 9 with the brief usurpation of Wang Mang, and the Eastern or Later Han which began in A.D. 23, when the dynastic family recovered the throne. In Western Han times Ch'ang-an was the capital city in Shensi, but the Eastern Han established a new capital at Lo-yang in Honan. During the late years of the second century A.D. the Han declined, losing the last remnants of empire and fading away completely in A.D. 221 to be succeeded by the short, and to the Chinese of later ages, romantic period of the Three Kingdoms.

The first great age of empire was over, but the dynamic qualities associated with it lived on in some degree for at least the next two centuries, as did the appeal of popular Taoism and the mythical stories associated with Taoist beliefs, some of which found visual expression in the decoration of ceramics in the following centuries.

Glazed Wares of Shang

The introduction of glazing into the technical repertory marks an important step forward, because it means that even the humblest pot can be made impermeable. It makes possible new uses for ceramic wares, new methods of decoration, and also, of great aesthetic interest, the exploitation of glaze transmutations of both colour and texture.

While there is a recurrent possibility of an unglazed pot emerging from the kiln with an entirely fortuitous glaze covering on the upper surfaces, what is known as kiln glost, through an accidental fall of ash, this is not the same as a deliberate application of certain raw materials in the expectation of achieving a glassy covering. Ash falls result in a fortuitous glaze because of the presence of silica and other minerals that fuse with similar ingredients in the clay bodies. Such a kiln effect is uneven and generally only apparent on the upper surfaces facing the top of the kiln, but in Korean wares, for instance, the effect was deliberately encouraged if not exaggerated by stirring the fire so that the glost covered a greater area, often including the underside of a vase lip and not just the shoulder. In colour kiln glost varies from greenish yellow to brown and occasionally, if there has been a heavy fall, it may be streaked in thicker parts with blue grey, the colour being partly due to the iron content, but also partly dependent upon the firing temperature, the speed at which the temperature has been raised and the atmosphere of the kiln, whether it is one of reduction or oxidation.

The surprisingly early appearance of relatively high-fired glazes in China, during the Shang dynasty, as an intentional effect cannot easily be explained, except as a deliberate attempt to establish the character of kiln glost as regular practice. Just how the potters set about the task can only be guessed at as there are so many variables needing investigation. At the moment it is sufficient to say that the glazes are of the leadless variety, fusing at temperatures between about 1,100°C and 1,200°C. Chemical analysis of the body material, which is paler than that of the unglazed grey wares, shows a high silica and low alumina and iron content, which is wholly consistent with the light colour and high firing temperature. Analyses of the glaze have not so far proved possible owing to the unusual thinness of the glaze layer, which has prevented separation of the one from the other.

The likelihood of finding the answers to these problems is at present fairly remote because there is little material available for study. In the west there is one surviving example in the William Rockhill Nelson Gallery in Kansas City in America, one in the Royal Ontario Museum in Toronto and one formerly in the collection of Professor W. Perceval Yetts. In China the number of pieces is about the same, with only one whole piece so far published. The material comes from the latest levels of Shang culture at Chêng-chou and from An-yang, so that it is possible to date it to the period between about 1300 B.C. and the end of the Shang dynasty in 1028 B.C., when the Chou took over the Shang dynasty territory from the west.

The surviving pieces can be divided into two types. One type, represented by the Kansas City piece and the one published by the Chinese and exhibited in Europe in 1973 and 1974, is hand-made with a round bottom (Fig. 20). The pots are about 28 cm high with a rounded bottom and sides, a fairly wide almost straight, sloping shoulder, and a wide expanding neck with a flared and slightly everted lip. The surface of the lower part is patterned with cord or textile from a paddle, or beater, and the shoulder with something resembling a twill woven textile or with a lozenge pattern. The neck, which is finished on the wheel, is left undecorated, the rilling lines alone bearing witness to the use of the wheel in finishing. The glaze, thin, yellowish and transparent, covers the whole of the upper part and right up the neck both inside and outside in a thin, evenly applied coating over a light grey body, which has burned a light brown where exposed on the lower part.

The second type, represented by the Toronto example and the one formerly in

Fig. 20. Glazed earthenware jar, hand built, from Cheng-chou. Shang. Height 28.2 cm. 16th–15th century B.C. Chinese Government.

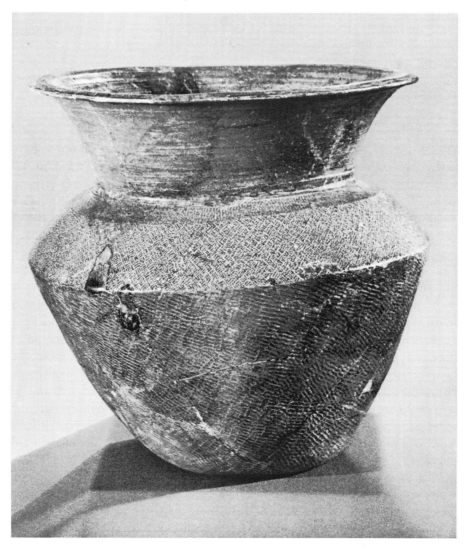

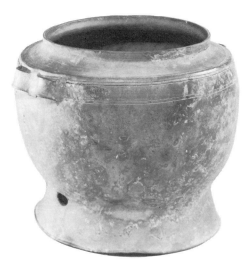

Fig. 21. Glazed earthenware jar from An-yang. Shang. Height *c*. 16.4 cm. 13th–11th century
B.C. Toronto, Royal Ontario Museum.

the Yetts collection, is quite different in shape and in the character of the glaze
(Fig. 21). The jars have a wide, straight rimmed mouth, a narrow, straight, and
nearly horizontal shoulder, from which the almost barrel-shaped body descends to
a deep, spreading foot-ring, which has been luted on to the rounded bottom like a
skirt. Just below the shoulder line are two pairs of lugs, luted on horizontally and
perhaps intended for tying down a lid. The body is perfectly smooth and of a fine
grained fairly hard grey fabric which burns a pinkish brown where exposed. The
glaze, of a thin greenish yellow colour, covers the whole of the outside except for
the base and the inner wall of the spreading foot-ring.

On both these types there may be greener patches, but reduction, or the
thickness of the glaze which may produce a greener tone, is not in this case
deliberately contrived, but is rather the simple chance of the kiln. It may be due to
the position of the piece in relation to the heat vents, the rapidity with which the
temperature has been raised or an accident in the firing cycle. It has to be
remembered that although a primitive form of reduction was known and used on
unglazed wares, it was probably too soon to anticipate this kind of sophisticated
experiment with an entirely new material on a different type of body, and one
which was fired at a higher temperature than the grey and black ware, but was still
not fired fully into the stoneware range. The important point to notice is that both
the bodies and the glazes could be fired to much higher temperatures, and that
with careful kiln control they were able to react to reducing conditions of the kind
which could be achieved with the type of kiln already used for the unglazed black
wares.

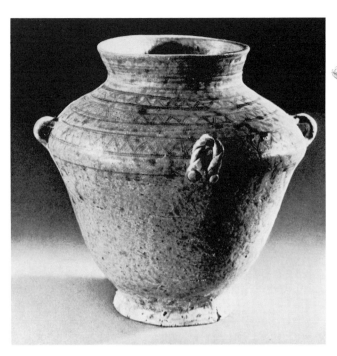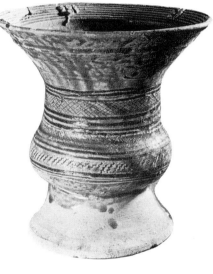

Fig. 22. Green glazed stoneware jar. Lo-yang. Western Chou. Height 21.5 cm. 10th century B.C. Chinese Government.

Fig. 23. Brown glazed earthenware vase. T'un-hsi, Anhui. Western Chou. Height 18.5 cm. 9th–8th century B.C. Chinese Government.

Chou Glazed Ware

On present evidence the evolution of glazed pottery was not an uninterrupted development, and the intermittent occurrence, without apparent connection in various parts of China over the succeeding seven or eight centuries, makes the plotting of any steady growth in glazing skill exceptionally difficult. The earliest find after the end of Shang, dating from early Western Chou in the tenth to ninth century B.C., from Lo-yang in western Honan, suggests, in at least one piece, a logical step forward from the Shang type.

In a group of tombs lying about a mile north of old Lo-yang a number of high-fired wares were found in 1964.[4] The Chinese report described these pieces as being made from a kaolinic clay of greyish white colour covered with a grey green glaze (Fig. 22). The fired body had a very low, if not non-existent, water absorption and a good resonance. The body material was also fine grained and the walls relatively thin. The firing temperature was calculated to be high on account of the low absorption and the good resonance, the report stating that the firing temperature was approximately 1,200°C. This means that here we have the first Chinese material known to have been fired properly into the stoneware range. The best piece to be illustrated is the vase similar in form to the contemporary bronze

44

lei. The body is well covered by the glaze, which is thicker than that on the Shang pieces. It seems to be a well-made piece and from the description and comment in the archaeological report it would appear that improvements must have been made, but whether these were in the realm of kiln design and control, or in the matter of the constitution of the glaze, it is not possible to determine.

A century or so elapsed before the next group of glazed ware occurred. This was found in Anhui far to the south-east, in two tombs at T'un-hsi. At first sight it seems to show little if any progress in technique. The pots are hand-made with the use of the wheel or turn-table restricted to finishing the base and mouth rim, the latter often with a rather elaborate contour.[5] The wheel was also used for simple decorative grooving and ribbing of the surface, the rest of the decoration consisting of incised hatching, chevrons and simple geometric patterns. There is also some impressing and a limited use of applied reliefs. In addition, on most pieces, there are small horizontally applied lugs, usually two or three, on the shoulder. On the base of some pieces are potters' marks roughly scratched into the still damp surface. Two types can be distinguished and in one an apparently retrograde step has been taken in the character of the glaze. The pieces in this series are very unevenly coated outside and on the inner side of the lip with a brown glaze, containing about two per cent iron oxide. It has a rather poor fit, that is it peels and flakes off, a fault usually due to a wrongly composed glaze mixture, in which the coefficient of contraction is unsuitable for the type of body to which it is applied. The uneven application results from the glaze having been brushed on (Fig. 23).

The second type, however, reveals no unevenness or bad fit. The glaze is similar in chemical constitution, but contains only about one per cent iron oxide (Fig. 24). It covers the whole vessel inside as well as outside, except for the foot and base, in a thin even layer achieved by using the dipping process.[6] The surface is smooth, glassy, and hard. It is an unusually consistent pale greyish green over the whole piece. Evidently a good deal of care was lavished on this type, and the indications are that the kiln atmosphere was one of deliberate and relatively well controlled reduction.

Examples of both these types have been found fairly widely distributed, and it is not known precisely where they were made. The unusually large find at T'un-hsi down in the south of Anhui strongly suggests that they were produced in the south-eastern region. The wide distribution further suggests that the wares were popular and regarded as valuable articles of trade. If and when a kiln is eventually found it may well prove to be an advance on the Shang type, in which the initial step was taken towards the construction of the true down-draught kiln.

After the eighth century B.C. there seems, at present, to be a long gap in the production of glazed pottery, and it does not reappear until the period of the Warring States in the late fourth or third century B.C. Again the wares are southern and mainly from Chekiang, Kuangtung, and possibly Hunan. Most

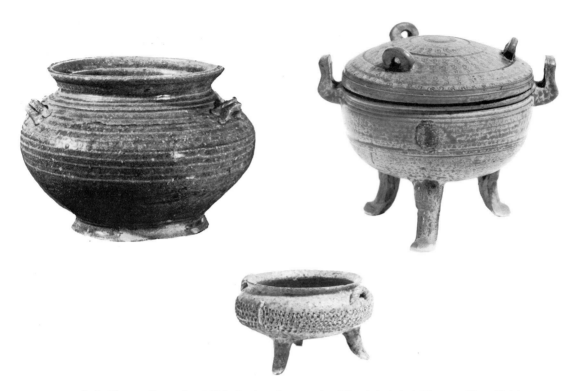

Left: Fig. 24. Green glazed high-fired earthenware jar. T'un-hsi, Anhui. Western Chou. Height 11 cm. 9th–8th century B.C. Chinese Government.

Right: Fig. 25. Grey bodied, yellowish glazed high-fired earthenware tripod. Eastern type. Height 13 cm. 4th–3rd century B.C. Oxford, Ashmolean Museum.

Centre: Fig. 26. Grey bodied, yellowish green glazed tripod. Eastern type. Height 6.3 cm. 4th–3rd century B.C. Oxford, Ashmolean Museum.

vessels are well made by throwing on the wheel, and have a fine grained grey body that may burn reddish or purplish brown where exposed.

The pottery from the more northerly of the three provinces, Chekiang, and probably from the vicinity of Shao-hsing towards the north of the province, follows very closely the contemporary bronze forms with impressed ornament and raised ribs in imitation of the main decorative schemes of the metal prototypes. Many of the vessels are ungainly, but some of the large jars, which owe less to metalwork form, are well balanced, the only reflection of the bronze founder's tradition occurring in the animal mask handles which are often applied to the shoulder. The glaze, thin and greenish, is only applied to the upper half, stopping abruptly at a well-defined raised rib or cordon running round the widest point. All the pieces are thick, stoutly constructed, and consequently heavy.

Closely related to these large jars and vases, but smaller and more refined, as well as very much paler in body and yellower in glaze, is a group of wares that imitate more faithfully the contemporary bronzes (Fig. 25). The pieces making up the group are in the direct succession from the T'un-hsi wares of late Western Chou. The body is pale grey and quite hard, the surface being decorated either with bands of impressed curls and thin relief cordons, or rather deeply pecked. Most specimens are well made on the wheel, and additions like legs and handles are carefully made and attached (Fig. 26). The glaze is thinly applied by dipping and is a light yellowish grey. The type appears to come from a kiln in the northernmost extremity of Chekiang, where a high-fired earthenware tradition must have been long established, and which from now on, in the late fourth or early third century B.C., began to show marked improvements in almost every respect.[7]

Much farther south in Kuangtung a hard, thin bodied ware was produced. Again it was well made on the wheel, but had fewer affiliations with the contemporary bronzes of the north. Some of the later pieces, however, which continue into the Western Han period, simulate a local southern style in bronze (Fig. 27). The shapes in other respects are sometimes unusual and include a jar on a spreading foot-ring, with an upstanding collar with slit perforations on the shoulder and a neatly made lid with a central knob (Fig. 28). The glaze on these

Fig. 27. High-fired earthenware vase with greenish brown glaze. Southern type. Height 20 cm. 4th–3rd century B.C. New York, Metropolitan Museum of Art.

Fig. 28. High-fired earthenware with greenish brown glaze. Southern type. Height 16.5 cm. 4th–3rd century B.C. Honolulu, Academy of Arts.

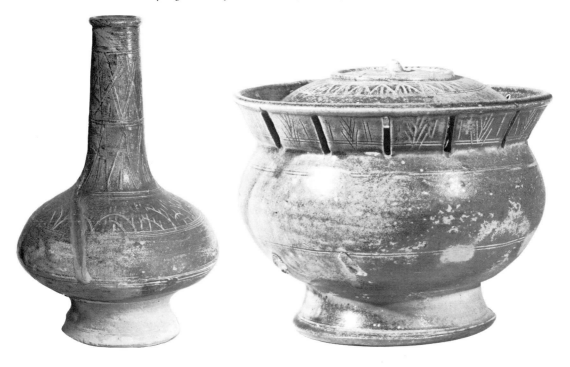

pieces tends to be rather uneven, and where it is thin is usually brown, but in thicker parts it is a pronounced greenish tone. This variation in the thickness of the glaze and in the colour suggests that the ware was subject to local reduction where the glaze was thick, but oxidation where the glaze was thin enough to permit the easy escape of gases from the body. The effects do not really justify the assumption that the ware was deliberately fired in a reducing atmosphere. Examples of this type have been found not only in Kuangtung in the vicinity of Canton, but also in Hunan near Ch'ang-sha. There has, as a result, been some uncertainty as to whether they were made in Kuangtung or Hunan, where many kilns of various dates have been thought to operate near Ch'ang-sha, and where some have been identified. On balance the evidence now suggests that Kuangtung is the more likely area, although no kiln has yet been found.

Han Period High-Fired Earthenware

In the Han period from 206 B.C. to A.D. 221, the hard glazed ware became firmly established, with northern Chekiang as the main region for its production, while Kuangtung continued for some time to make good pots of a similar type with increasing improvement in the control of firing. During the same period kilns in the vicinity of Ch'ang-sha opened up and over the next few centuries it became an important south central area for the output of a variety of wares.

From the eastern region came the vases which Laufer named 'proto-porcelain', under the mistaken impression that true porcelain developed from it. This could not have been so as it was to evolve into a hard grey stoneware, relatively rich in iron, which oxidized on the exposed surfaces to an almost purplish brown in many instances. Hochstadter, writing in 1952,[8] assigned these vases to the Han period, an attribution which has received confirmation in recent years, but his suggestion that these 'proto-porcelains' were made as far north and west as the province of Shensi has not stood the test of time, and the very wide distribution of the type would in any case make attribution to any particular centre, in the absence of strong evidence, a chancy business. Fairly recently the increase in the number of finds suggests more reasonably that northern Chekiang was the most likely source. The large vases and wine jars characteristic of these wheel-thrown pieces, with their ovoid bodies, are decorated with cordons in relief round the body, usually in groups of three, with the bands between them often incised with lozenge and triple lozenge designs which owe much to contemporary designs in textiles (Fig. 29).[9] Scrolling designs and birds, the latter depicted with varying degrees of realism, are also found. Handles are often luted on to the shoulders of vases and jars with an escutcheon in the form of an animal mask, echoing the contemporary practice on bronze vessels. Round the neck of a vase it is common to find combed wavy lines. The glaze is evenly applied; Hochstadter states that it

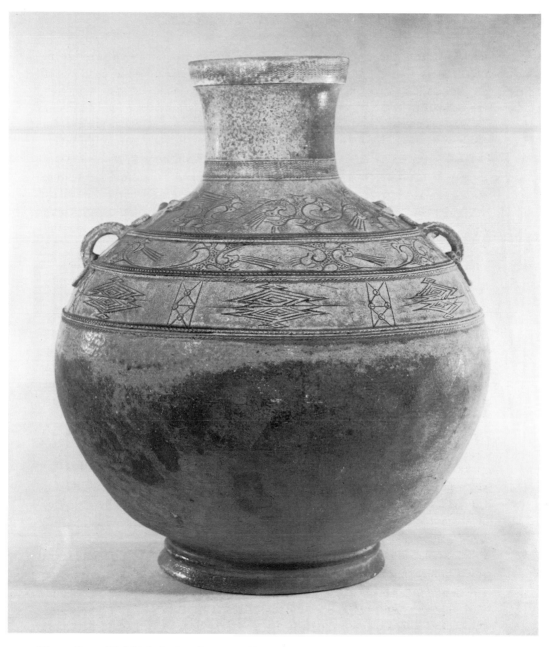

Fig. 29. Proto-Yüeh high-fired earthenware with greenish glaze. Eastern type. Height 45.7 cm. 1st century B.C. to 1st century A.D. Cleveland, Cleveland Museum of Art.

was sprayed on, but this is uncertain. It is brownish green, except where it is thick, when it appears more blue, or, where it is exceptionally thin, as sometimes happens on the neck, when it turns brown.

It seems therefore that, as in the case of the more southerly wares believed to come from Kuangtung, we cannot assume a controlled reducing atmosphere in the kiln. The lower part of the body is sometimes horizontally grooved where the glaze did not reach, and this gives the lower part a pleasing decorative impact as well as a contrast in texture. As time passed the mouth of the vase form ceased to be flared and gradually became dished, a change taken over from the somewhat similar bronze vases of the period, but given greater emphasis in the ceramic form.

Alongside these strong, large vases and jars, was a large number of small, rather characterless bowls, some of them like small tubs, flat on the bottom and without any kind of decoration. The glaze on these is generally less good than that on the vases and jars, which seem to have received the greatest attention.

The whole group marks the consolidation of certain aspects of earlier progress. The wheel was now well established, and the clays most suitable for throwing fairly large pieces were being carefully selected. It still remained to establish reduction firing as standard practice, and as a fully understood and controlled method of firing, although by now temperatures were reaching the stoneware range. Whether the glaze can be termed an ash one or a felspathic one cannot be determined as no analyses have been carried out in recent years. Until such work has been done and phosphorus, an element always present in vegetable ash but not in feldspar, has been identified, it is best to call these glazes high-fired in contrast to low-fired glazes which made their appearance in China early in the third century B.C.

Han Lead Glazed Earthenware

The origin of lead fluxed glazes in China is shrouded in mystery, and there is much speculation as to whether this type was introduced from the Near East or whether it was an independent development. In the Near East lead first appears in very small quantities in glazes well before 1000 B.C., but its early use was restricted to modifying the colours in glazes, which were still essentially of the alkaline type; the colourants affected were copper and antimony. Glazes in which lead was the principal flux, invariably coloured with copper, were a feature of the period of Roman domination, and hence contemporary with those of the Han dynasty. Nevertheless it has to be remembered that lead compounds are common in nature and were already known to the Chinese. They deliberately added lead to bronze to increase the sharpness of the casting, which was particularly important when fine delicate ornament was wanted on the backs of bronze mirrors. Lead in the form of red or yellow oxide, white lead, or as galena, is easy to powder on to a damp clay body, or the lead compound held in suspension in water could equally well be applied to the pot by brushing or dipping. Lead glazes have the advantage of being bright and smooth, and taking colouring metallic oxides very satisfactorily, and they are especially useful for earthenware bodies, particularly those rich in

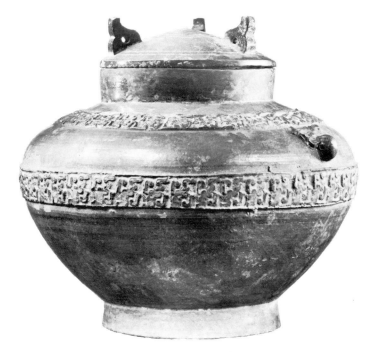

Fig. 30. Greenish lead glazed earthenware jar with moulded decoration. Diameter 22.2 cm. Early 3rd century B.C. Kansas, Nelson Gallery of Art.

iron, as the colourants conceal the nature of the body. The firing temperature is necessarily low as lead becomes volatile at about 1,150°C.[10] Since the glaze fit was normally good, lead was useful to make the soft, porous earthenware impermeable. If a lead glaze is to be used on a stoneware or porcelain body, it is necessary to fire the body to the biscuit, and only then apply the glaze and fire a second time to a suitably lower temperature. This particular process, however, still lay far in the future so far as the Chinese were concerned, and in the Han period, from which the earliest lead glazed ware is generally dated, only an earthenware body was used.

The earliest single example is a jar and cover dating from early in the third century B.C., just before the Han dynasty was established (Fig. 30). Based on a contemporary bronze form and with decoration strongly reminiscent of that used on the bronzes of the period, the body is a rather soft reddish earthenware and the glaze, which reaches right down to the base, is a glossy brownish green. The base of the jar is flat and unglazed. The decoration, standing slightly in relief is moulded, and indeed it seems likely that the whole piece was constructed using moulds.

The reddish body became standard in the following centuries, showing that the pottery was normally fired in oxidizing conditions. The glaze improved in colour, and was most frequently a good green from the addition of copper oxide. Less common is a warm amber brown, the result of using lead alone, the colour being

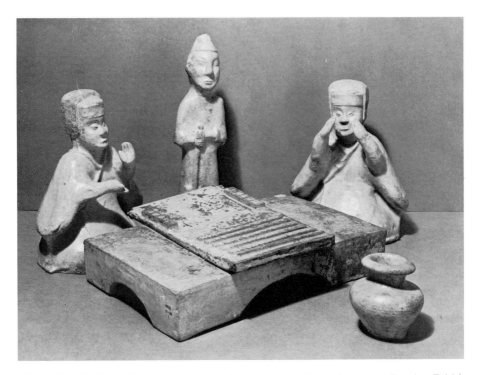

Fig. 31. Green lead glazed group of figures gambling. Han period. Height 20.3 cm. London, British Museum.

derived from the iron in the body. Even rarer is the evident addition of iron to the glaze material. A few pieces of the standard reddish earthenware are found covered with a very pronounced brown, which cannot wholly be accounted for by the glaze taking up the iron from the body. While it was obviously known that iron oxides coloured the glaze brown and copper oxides coloured it green, the Chinese rarely, if at all in the Han period, used the two together for polychrome effects;[11] this was to come much later. One characteristic of these lead glazes, which are rather soft, is that they are easily degraded in burial, and take on a silvery iridescence.

The use of lead glazes seems to have been confined to mortuary pottery. This was a wise decision since lead glazes are notoriously poisonous, and in fact probably contributed to a rise in the mortality rate among the potters themselves in the regions of both Ch'ang-an and Lo-yang, which are believed to have been the most important centres during the Western and Eastern Han periods.

During the whole period, the mortuary pottery was very rich in its variety of both unglazed, painted earthenware and lead glazed pieces. In the glazed ware practically every vessel current in bronze was copied, as well as most of those made in lacquer; indeed almost anything that could be modelled, either free-hand or using moulds, was reproduced in the ceramic medium. The great abundance of models of everything from a watch-tower or farmhouse to a simple pig-pen, and from cooking pots to men, women and animals provides a splendid reflection of the variety and vigour of the contemporary social scene. There are models of dancers, acrobats, musicians, and people gambling (Fig. 31), as well as some of labourers engaged in the serious business of food production, as represented by men milling corn.

Moulding added a new decorative element and in Han times it was extremely lively, with vases and hill jar censers encircled by bands in which there are scenes of animals, birds and human figures, often as hunters, 'fairy' figures with streamers flying from their shoulders, and figures of fantasy all dashing round the vessels with great animation in a primitively conceived landscape in which scale, either relative or real, has no place (Fig. 32). The upper sections of the hill jars are moulded in the shape of mountains piled up to a central peak, and in every part there may be small relief figures of men and animals, and even occasionally the figure of a man with a cart drawn by an ox.

Not only do the lead glazed models reflect the social scene, but also something of the beliefs that were current, as well as something of the artistic climate of the age. Most scenes which include 'fairy' figures can be linked to the beliefs of popular Taoism, while the hill jar form was connected with the concepts of both the Isles of the Blessed in the Eastern Sea, the home of the immortals, and with the Five Sacred Mountains of China. The artistic climate of the Han was dominated visually by a dynamic quality in which vigorous movement and bold rhythmic line are linked to a realism such as had not previously found expression in China.

Fig. 32. Amber glazed 'Po-shan-lu' jar and cover. Han period. Height 24.1 cm. London, Victoria and Albert Museum.

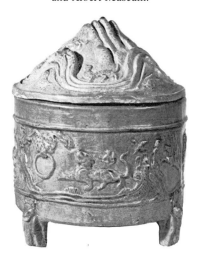

CHAPTER THREE

Technical Consolidation: The Period of the Northern and Southern Dynasties

The collapse of the Han dynasty, of which there were already indications by the middle of the second century A.D., marks the beginning of a period of disunity that was to persist until nearly the end of the sixth century. The four centuries between the fall of Han and the reunification of China by the Sui dynasty in A.D. 580, are characterized by a complex pattern of political, social and economic disintegration on one side and of relative stability and economic growth on the other, first in one region and then in another. The periods of economic growth were generally more extended and widespread in the territory south of the Yangtse, an aspect of the historical situation which goes some way to account for the ceramic developments in that area. The south was to lay the foundation for the most persistent and the richest tradition in China, that of the so-called celadon ware. For this reason the four hundred year period, so often known as the Six Dynasties, is better given its alternative name of the Period of the Northern and Southern Dynasties in the present context. The name clearly makes good sense because the major centres of activity lay in Chekiang and from there south into Fukien and Kuangtung, and west into Hunan, all of which are provinces south of the Yangtse.

The Northern Dynasties Unglazed Earthenware

It was only from about the middle of the sixth century, right at the end of the period of disruption, that northern kilns once more became significantly active. Few kilns have been located and our knowledge of their production has until now been meagre. Production of some kind must have continued over a long period, but what they made apart from tomb furniture is very uncertain. There is considerable wealth of this type of material together with some rather indifferent pots made for burial.

The tombs datable to these four centuries of turmoil, during which China was infiltrated from the north and north-west by tribes better acquainted with pastoralism than settled arable agriculture, are few and far between, and those that have been found have in most cases long since been plundered. That they were originally rich in tomb furniture is clear from contemporary literature, which tells of powerful men reduced to penury after ensuring their parents' interment with suitable pomp and ceremony. There is also the evidence of large numbers of tomb figures and models in collections all over the world. Even Ts'ui Shih, a statesman who himself condemned the extravagance and luxury of his age, fell victim to the need to conform to custom. He was left poverty-stricken following the death of his parents, for he was forced to sell the family estate in order to cover the expenses of the elaborate funeral. When he himself died, there was not even enough left in his house to cover the cost of decent burial.[1]

The practice of lavish expenditure on the burial of the dead was, of course, nothing new, and it was to continue for many centuries, but after the fall of Han until some time about the end of the sixth century, the tomb furniture was unglazed, even the familiar lead glazing of this type of material having been abandoned at the end of Han, although it probably continued for the glazing of roof tiles; but even of this there is no proof. Lead glazing was to be revived in the late sixth century and the hiatus remains unexplained.

The figures, models and vases that make up the tomb furniture are of heavy grey earthenware often covered with a white slip and painted in fairly bright colours after a rather low temperature firing, red, blue, white and green being the most usual colours. This in fact was to carry on the practice which had already been established in the Han period, but now the slavish copying of the shapes and decorative schemes of inlaid bronzes is abandoned in favour of more fluent decorations on simpler ceramic shapes (Fig. 33), while on the figures a decorative approach is seen in the robes and additional details.

The human figures include armed guards, many of them with western Asiatic faces and heavy beards, bearing witness to the incursion of western tribes from Central Asia and perhaps from as far west as Persia and Sogdia.[2] Some of these foreigners would have been bent on conquest, but others came for trade, which flourished especially in the later years of the period despite regional disturbances. The close links with Central Asian merchants are also illustrated by the appearance among the tomb figures, especially in the Northern Wei period, of the heavily loaded camels which carried most of the merchandise from the west into China. To remind us further of the troubled times, there are magnificently caparisoned horses of warring princes. These horses with small thin heads and long thin legs often seem weighed down by the weight of their saddle cloths. These have frequently been pressed out in elaborately decorated moulds and then laid

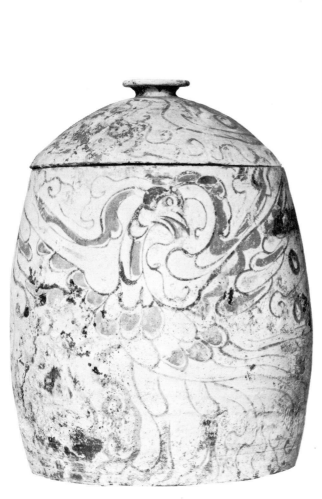
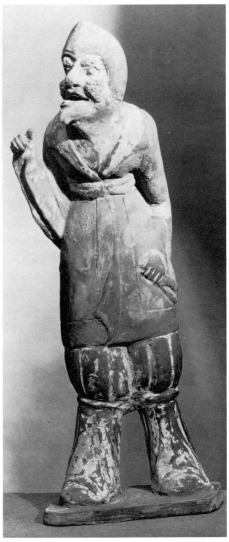

Fig. 33. Earthenware grain jar painted in unfired pigments. Height 25.1 cm. 3rd century A.D. Kansas, Nelson Gallery of Art.

Fig. 34. Unglazed earthenware figure of a foreigner. Height 31.1 cm. 4th–5th century A.D. London, British Museum, Seligman Collection.

over the backs of the horses before firing. The harness, too, is elaborate and often reflects the influence of the Sasanian Persian custom of hanging tassels on the harness straps and adding ornaments of various kinds to the bridle. The figures of most of the men and animals are pressed out in two-part moulds, which are then brought together until the clay has had time to dry for a time. The result is that many of the figures are almost identical, different only in small details of clothing, or in facial expression where the craftsman has done some hand tooling to please his own fancy.

There is surprisingly little variation over a long period in the style of the figures, and the fact that all are so much alike suggests that there were relatively few factories engaged on this production, and that they probably made nothing else. It was only at the end of Northern Wei, when Northern Ch'i took over in the west in A.D. 550, and Northern Chou similarly took over in the east in A.D. 557, that significant changes are seen. The only feature which seems to distinguish the early ones from those of obviously late date, is the stout, rather rotund construction of the early figures as compared with the late fifth or early sixth-century ones, which are usually tall and thin, occasionally with exaggerated elongation of the bodies and legs (Fig. 34). The faces of the later figures are often characterized by a sweet smile strongly reminiscent of that seen on the Buddha and Bodhisattva figures in contemporary stone and bronze sculpture.[3]

In addition to unglazed earthenware figures with painted decoration in unfired pigments, many tombs were lined with grey earthenware tiles and hollow bricks. These were ornamented with a wide variety of impressed or moulded decorations, many of which were frankly pictorial, but some were geometric repeating patterns, often with affiliations to contemporary textile designs.

The earlier material of the Eastern Han period included rectangular and triangular bricks with decorations of a few stamps used in a variety of combinations to create pleasing rural scenes such as hunts and leisurely strolls beneath trees. The figures, birds and animals were picked out in appropriate colours after the firing (Fig. 35). Other decorations were more formalized with simple geometric repeats in bands alternating with lively processions of dragons and men in chariots, and a large selection of figures drawn from mythology. Designs such as these were distant echoes of the splendid scenes found inside the funerary chapels cut in stone or painted on plastered tomb walls which survive as memorials of persons of greater wealth and prestige from the same period.[4]

During the period of the Northern and Southern dynasties the same practice

Fig. 35. Impressed tomb brick with details in colour. Toronto, Royal Ontario Museum.

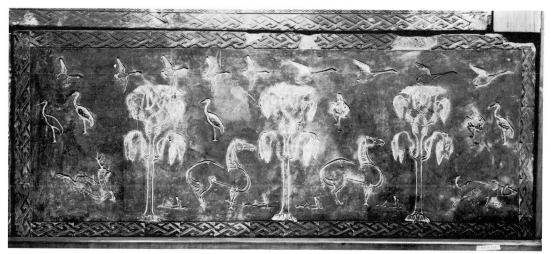

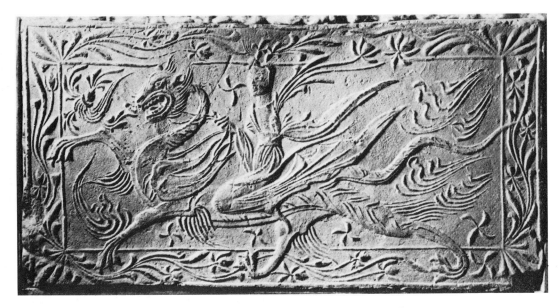

Fig. 36. Moulded brick from Têng-hsien. Length 38 cm. 5th century A.D.

continued, but became in some instances rather more sophisticated, as for
example in the series of bricks used to line the chambers of the tomb at Têng-
hsien in Honan.[5] Here the bricks are solid, measuring 38 cm long, 19 cm wide and
6 cm thick, each one decorated with a scene complete in itself, either with a
palmette scroll border framing the design, or with the design running freely over
the whole surface. In some instances the decoration intrudes into the border area
ignoring the firm constricting lines that retain the scrolling patterns (Fig. 36). The
extravagance of this treatment indicates a sophisticated taste tied to a spendthrift
attitude to the social customs of the period; ostentation even in death was not only
acceptable, it was meritorious. It is an ostentation particularly apparent here, as
every brick is different, each having been pressed out in its own mould. Even in
clay the designs in this series retain much of the dynamic quality which is such a
feature of the pictorial manner current in the fifth-century painting and in the
rock-cut shrines and temples of Yün-kang and Lung-mên.[6] In style, the
expression is quite different from that of the south where a less rugged manner
prevailed.

The southern equivalent of brick decoration in the tomb was softer and had a
warmer more dreamy quality. In place of dashing animals, swirling clouds and
boldly marching and dancing figures, we find the Seven Sages of the Bamboo
Grove seated on mats drinking and music making among trees, all of which are of
carefully differentiated species.[7] Technically there is no real connection between
the northern and southern method of execution. The bold heavy style of the north
is replaced by a sinuous, fluent linear style of great elegance, and instead of each
figure appearing on a single brick, each is in fact composed of a multiplicity of
bricks, each one bearing some part of the design and fitting together like a jigsaw

58

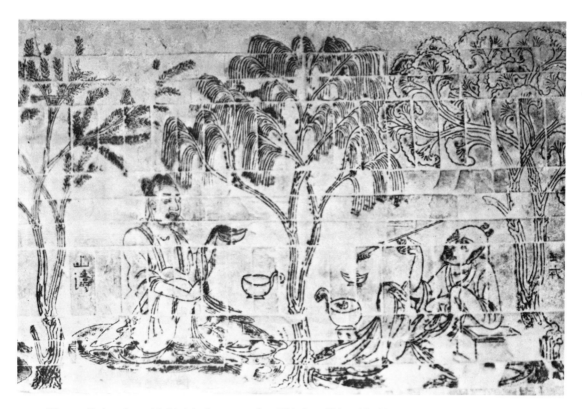

Fig. 37. Series of moulded bricks from a tomb at Hsi-shan Chiao, Nankin. Late 4th or early 5th century A.D.

to make a wall facing (Fig. 37). The bricks are numbered on one end to facilitate the setting into the two wall panels, each 240 cm long by 80 cm high. The whole design was probably executed from a painting transferred to wooden blocks which were carved and laid out ready for the clay to be pressed down on them. If anything this is an even more complex and extravagant way of decorating the tomb than that at Têng-hsien, and, from the technical point of view, one that demanded greater accuracy to ensure that the clay shrank in the drying and firing to about the same extent. Unless there had been intelligent understanding of the nature of clay shrinkage, the designs would have fitted very badly and been visually disturbing, besides making a poor wall facing.

These bricks from Hsi-shan Chiao near Nanking are probably rather earlier than the Têng-hsien series, but they demonstrate a more advanced attitude in terms of pictorial treatment, an aspect much discussed by specialists in the field of painting. Such elaborate treatment of the tomb, while indicating a degree of mastery in one direction, was ultimately profitless and of no great advantage to the general technological development or to the production of a wide variety of pottery. For our purpose, however, it shows more clearly than anything hitherto that the Chinese potter was fully aware of the problems of clay shrinkage and that he was able to make reasonable allowance for it.

Southern Region Glazed Wares

The general development of ceramic skills in fact occurred mainly in the south-eastern provinces, especially in Chekiang, but the skills were in the rather different area of kiln control.

Immediately to the south of the Yangtse river and reaching in a wide belt from Tê-ch'ing through Hang-chou, Shao-hsing and Yü-yao towards Ning-p'o on the east coast, large groups of kilns were established from the Han period until some time in the T'ang dynasty, in the eighth or ninth century A.D. The earliest groups were situated in the vicinity of Tê-ch'ing in the extreme north of the province, at Chiu-yen to the south-east and at Yü-yao to the east, both the last being east of Hang-chou. It was in these groups of kilns that the fundamental skill in firing to stoneware temperatures was gradually brought to perfection in the pottery called in Japan, 'Old Yüeh', in China, 'green glazed ware', and now in Europe, proto-Yüeh.[8] It is as well to explain that the name Yüeh, which has long been common currency in the West for all the products of these kilns from late Han to the end of the tenth century, was not at any time applied by the Chinese until the T'ang period, when the Chinese connoisseurs themselves named it after the ancient kingdom in whose territory the kilns were situated. The indiscriminate use of the name Yüeh should therefore be avoided and the precursors to the T'ang type called more suitably, proto-Yüeh.

It is unfortunate that although a great many kiln sites have been discovered, their ruined state has not permitted us to be at all confident about the construction of the kilns themselves, or how they improved over the centuries from the earliest ones near Tê-ch'ing to the latest T'ang ones around the shores of Shang-lin lake. The indications are, however, that the down-draught kiln, whose beginnings were seen in the Shang period, continued to be developed, probably with local variations, and must by now have attained a fairly distinctive design and a reasonable standard of efficiency. Whether the pattern in use was a single, or already a multiple chamber type we do not yet know and must hope for enlightenment in the future.

Most of the early kilns produced wares that were very similar in both form and decoration, but Tê-ch'ing was peculiar for its manufacture of a black glazed type of which numerous examples are now known. At Tê-ch'ing activity must have begun in the last years of the Eastern Han dynasty, or at latest during the Three Kingdoms period, and a similar date is likely for Chiu-yen, for examples of proto-Yüeh are datable from about the middle of the third century A.D., and were already beginning to show superior qualities and a new decorative treatment.

The vessels are normally made on the wheel, unless too eccentric to permit this method, when moulding takes the place of the wheel. The body material is pale grey, sometimes almost white when fractured, and it generally burns a light

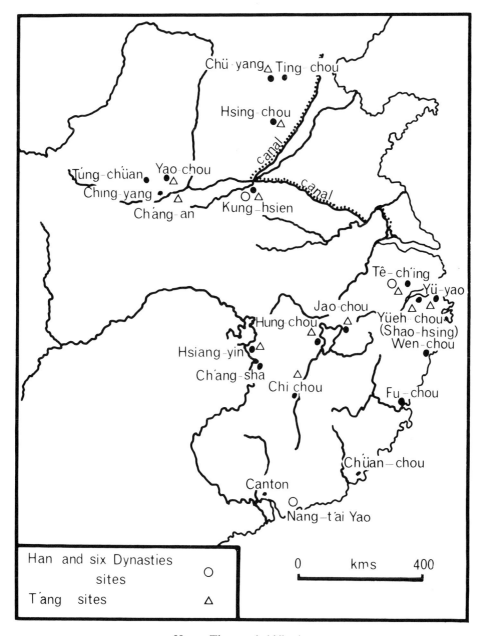

Han to T'ang period kiln sites.

reddish brown where exposed in the firing. The glaze on the early pieces is variable in thickness, colour, and surface gloss. The colourant is an iron oxide, so pieces tend to vary through shades of pale brownish yellow to grey green depending upon the success of the reduction firing cycle, which was now the one commonly adopted. The glaze in most cases is applied by the dipping method, proof of this being visible in the swag-like contour to its lower edge, which does

61

not always reach the base (Fig. 38). The vessels were fired on lumps of sandy fire-clay or heavily constructed spurred stands, whose marks are seen as pale patches haloed in reddish brown. The insides of vessels are generally glazed and the inside of the often surprisingly thin wall may display the concave encircling grooves which are characteristic evidence of the potter's hand in wheel-thrown forms. A foot-ring is fairly uncommon in the earliest pieces, most vessels being flat or slightly concave on the base. They are usually shaved, but not always very neatly, and the lower walls of jars and vases are frequently roughly trimmed with a knife without the use of either the wheel or the turn-table, thus betraying an unusual carelessness in finish.

Fig. 38. Proto-Yüeh jar. Late 3rd century A.D. Height 20.7 cm. Oxford, Ashmolean Museum.

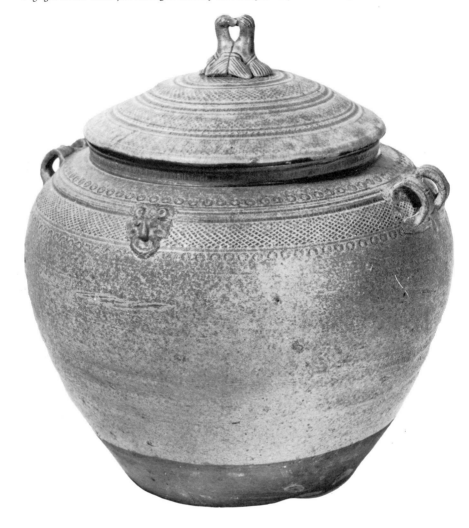

Among the most popular early shapes are large well-proportioned jars with wide shoulders, the body narrowing towards the slightly concave or flat base, while the mouth is either wide with a short straight lip (Fig. 39), or the shoulders contract into a narrow short neck with a fairly dished mouth. Also among the most popular early types are the bulbous ewers, similar in the neck to the second type of jar, but with a short spout rising from the shoulder ending in a cock's head (Fig. 40); sometimes there are two adjoining ones. Many of the spouts are false, so it would seem likely that examples with this feature were made primarily for the tomb. The handles of the ewers rise directly from the shoulder, curving outwards and round to the rim. As time passed the handles began to get taller until they rose well above the rim and had to be bent down to it. Later the handles were also elaborated and embellished with a dragon head at the junction with the rim. On the shoulders of both jars and ewers it was usual to add small lugs for the passage of a cord. In early examples these are simply strips of clay added either vertically or horizontally; sometimes the ones added vertically may be in pairs.

Before the lugs were added, and evidently intended as a guide to the craftsman as to how high to place the lugs, two wheel-cut grooves were run round the

Fig. 39. Proto-Yüeh jar with Buddhist figure. Diameter 17.2 cm. Late 3rd century A.D. London, Percival David Foundation.

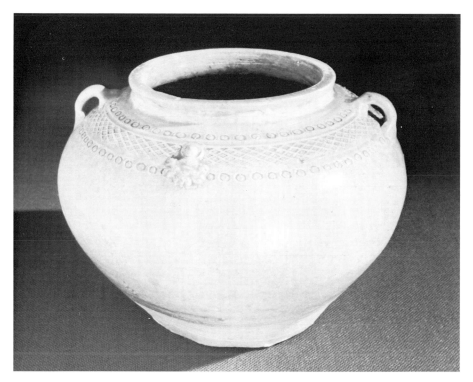

63

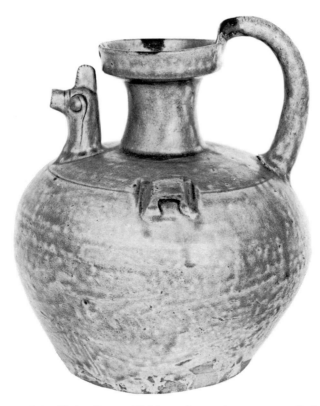

Fig. 40. Proto-Yüeh 'cock's head' ewer. Height 22.8 cm. 4th century A.D. Oxford, Ashmolean Museum.

shoulder, and after this a band of diamond diaper might be impressed all round between the lines. The diaper patterns are only narrowly varied and were applied with a roulette while the body was still quite soft.

The use of the roulette is at first surprising, but it probably evolved from the earlier moulding techniques of decoration when border designs of repeating lozenges occurred, as they did in borders to many of the tomb bricks in grey earthenware. It was a means of reducing the endless labour of carving the same design repeatedly on a long panel of wood, if this was the material used for the primary moulding. The roulette short-cut this by requiring only that the design should fit perfectly round a small cylindrical spool of wood slung on a spindle attached to a forked wooden element.[9] The craftsman using this new decorating tool seems to have been quite skilful. The pot would have been placed on a turn-table and the spool applied while it was being rotated on the table. Overlapping of the design is almost inevitable at some point, and evidence of this is to be seen on many pieces; in others where the overlap is not visible, it is because the lugs have been neatly applied at just this point, or in other examples there may be a sprig-moulded animal mask, a seated Buddha figure, a freely modelled animal or bird head spout, to conceal the join.

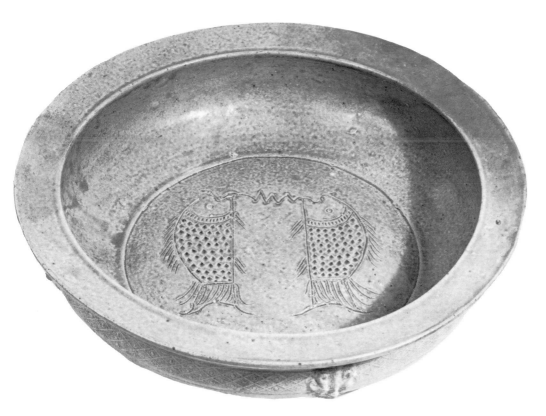

Fig. 41. Proto-Yüeh basin with incised and rouletted decoration. Diameter 33.5 cm. Late 3rd century A.D. London, Percival David Foundation.

Diaper bands are frequently bordered above and below, but still as a rule within the wheel-cut grooves, with impressed rings using a piece of neatly cut bamboo, sometimes decoratively trimmed to display a circular arrangement of tiny darts. The same kind of treatment is found on bowls and basins, the latter one of the few forms found at this time still not wholly divorced from the bronze repertory (Fig. 41). There are also a number of begging bowl shapes with rims sharply turned in; these usually have a coarser diaper band of larger scale and no moulded elements. Finally among the forms with this type of decoration is a series of small dumpy jars, with raised foot, a trumpet neck, and slightly dished mouth. The decoration is varied in that the design is applied in some instances using a triangular diaper-surfaced stamp instead of, or in addition to, a roulette, and the sprigged elements include dragons and men on galloping horses.

One peculiar vase form is a tall ovoid funerary urn surmounted by a group of neatly modelled buildings with press-moulded figures luted into the spaces under the eaves of the buildings and between the supporting pillars (Fig. 42). The scenes suggest the Taoist paradise with immortals, a subject popular in the literature and art of Eastern Han and later. The body of the vases may also have figures sprigged on, the outlines of the sprig moulds often showing as indentations in the body

65

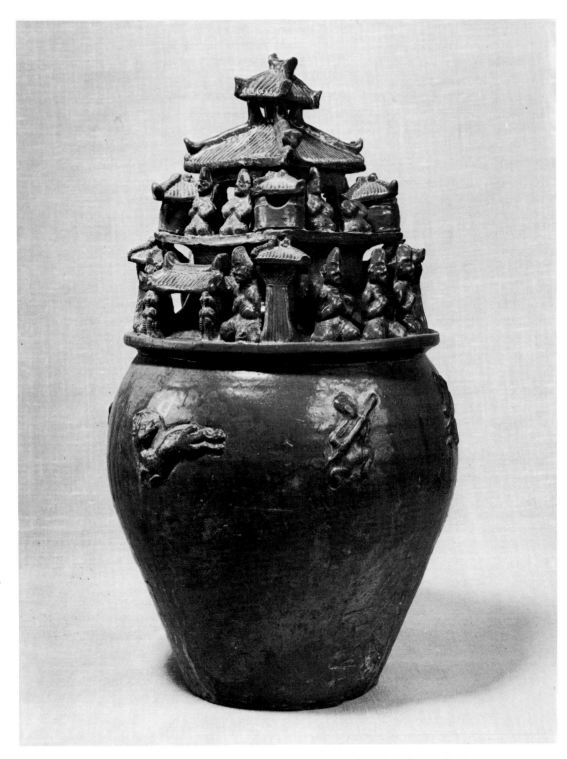

Fig. 42. Proto-Yüeh funerary urn with sprigged reliefs. Height 46.6 cm. Late 3rd–4th century A.D. Chinese Government.

where the craftsman has slapped the ornament on to the surface rather hard.

More appropriate to the scholar's desk than the tomb, in which so many of the proto-Yüeh pieces have been found, are the water droppers and candlesticks, the former commonly shaped like toads, sometimes with a small eared bowl at the mouth. The candlesticks were made as lions, in two-part moulds put together with the vertical join carefully smoothed and sometimes elaborately embellished with a curly mane and beard,[10] or as squatting bears with a tray on the head. There is usually additional incised detail such as light pecking of the surface to suggest fur (Fig. 43).

Also among the constructed pieces, either made as toys or tomb furnishings, probably both, is a wide variety of models of animals, hen coops with hens and roosters, and other simple models of the kind of equipment normally to be seen about the farm.

The glaze on these early pieces is very uneven in both thickness and colour, although it is clear that the potters were now deliberately trying to improve the glaze and aim at a greater consistency in both respects. There are instances where the glaze is very even but yellowish, and others where a good green is achieved over most of the surface, but it may have yellowish patches on one side due to local oxidation. Control of the glaze and firing were to be the points on which the potters concentrated during the following centuries, and improvements are slow but steady throughout the period. The black glazed types alone remain quite consistent, although the glaze sometimes fails to fit as well as it should. The much higher iron content made the firing of the black type easier, since it was of little importance whether the firing was one of reduction or oxidation. With the lower iron content of the green glazed type the control of the firing cycle in

Fig. 43. Proto-Yüeh lampstand. Diameter 15 cm. 4th century A.D. London, Percival David Foundation.

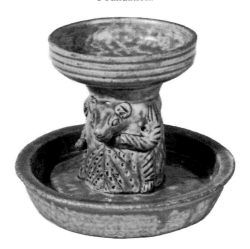

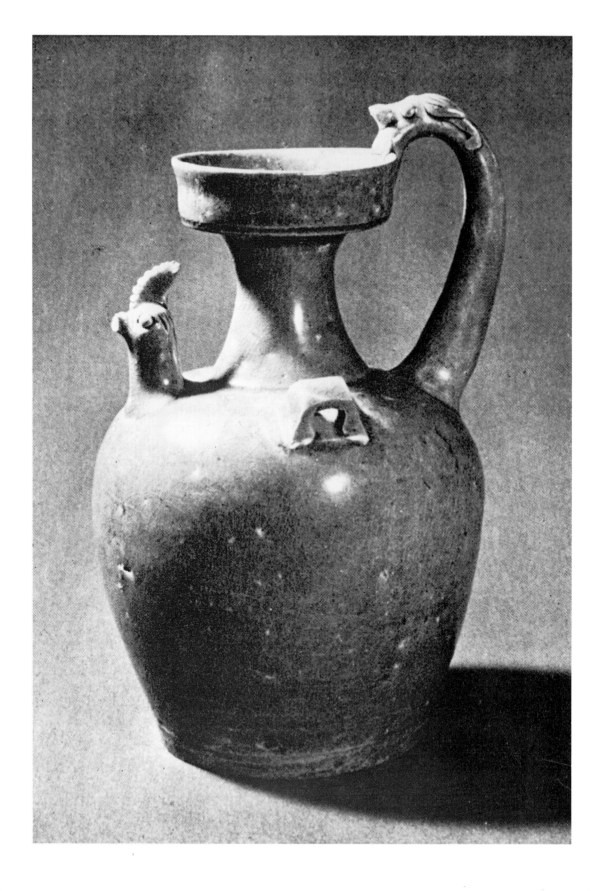

reduction was critical and could perhaps never be correctly achieved every time.

In the fourth century and later it is clear that improvements were having an effect, and the sensuous appeal of the better controlled clear green glaze exercised a fascination that gradually led to the elimination of much of the diaper decoration and less use of sprig-moulded elements. The contours of ewers and jars began to change, the shapes becoming taller and the necks longer, while the handles of the cock spouted ewers became more elaborate as though to compensate for the lack of decoration elsewhere (Fig. 44). There was an increase in the use of doubled spouts and handles, and for some reason the shoulder lugs began to be squared and luted on horizontally. One new decorative feature on the green glazed type was the introduction of black spots at predetermined intervals. These are usually found on covered bowls, boxes and jars, but sometimes also occur on ewers (Fig. 45); in the latter case the use of high iron oxide spots is more restrained than on other forms. The technique is the same as that found many centuries later in Lung-ch'üan wares, also from Chekiang, to which the Japanese give the name *tobi-seiji*, 'spotted celadon'.

During the late fourth and fifth centuries a restrained if slightly casual carving of petals on the upper parts of ewers and jars was introduced. At first these did not fit very comfortably and were often askew. They were always cut so that the tips pointed downwards. On the really large vessels they performed the useful function of relieving the plain surface and dividing the upper from the lower part of the vessel.

In the fifth and sixth centuries the improvements in both body and glaze are more obvious, the former becoming paler and finer in grain, while the glaze gets

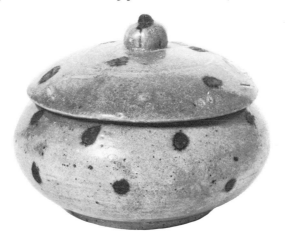

Above: Fig. 45. Proto-Yüeh jar with ferruginous spots. Diameter 10.2 cm. 5th–6th century A.D. Asian Art Museum of San Francisco, Brundage Collection.

Opposite: Fig. 44. Proto-Yüeh 'cock's head' ewer. Height 24.7 cm. 5th century A.D. Chinese Government.

slightly thicker and more consistently green. This certainly was partly the result of experience, but may perhaps also be accounted for by the stimulus from increased demands and competition as more kilns were opened, especially in north-eastern Chekiang. In any case the demand for the proto-Yüeh alone must long have been growing, for the material has been found widely distributed. Indeed the trade in this attractive ware was likely to have been a major factor in the appearance of new kilns in more distant parts of the country which attempted a similar pottery.

The kilns in the region of Ch'ang-sha for instance are among the best known for their imitations of proto-Yüeh, although the glaze is softer and the body at this time only a moderately high-fired earthenware. The glaze at its best is transparent green, but it tends to craze and decay quite easily, and, because the soil in which most pieces have been found is a bright gingery brown, the appearance of the less well preserved specimens is deceptive. In the shapes common to this region there is great similarity to much that was being made in northern Chekiang.

Northern Glazed Wares in the Sixth Century

Among the sixth-century pottery to which a northern origin may be attributed there are both high-fired stoneware and, once again, lead glazed earthenware. The stout jars found in both materials are fairly large and well constructed, sometimes with elaborate decoration, which owes much to the influence of the Sasanian Persians and the Central Asians. The sixth century in north China saw a lively trade growing up with the countries to the west, and many foreigners settled in the more important cities. Attention became focused on foreign manners and styles of decoration with the result that Chinese designs underwent a marked change. Evidence of this is seen particularly in a number of moulded earthenware flasks imitating leather bottles. They had either a green or an amber brown lead glaze over moulded reliefs of Central Asians or Persians playing musical instruments and dancing, all easily distinguishable by their dress, which was itself to become a familiar sight in the T'ang capital of Ch'ang-an in following centuries (Fig. 46).

Other lead glazed earthenwares and the stonewares were treated differently. There are a great many large jars with square lugs set horizontally on the shoulder, or with a doubled strip of clay looped into lugs and set vertically. The rest of the body is divided up into decorative bands reaching to just below the widest point. In the bands there may be sprigged reliefs of rosettes, imitations of cabochon jewels in beaded settings, or animal heads; or palmette scrolls may occur, the last being applied with a roulette. There are also instances in which the pendant lotus petal band, already used on the proto-Yüeh, receives more emphatic treatment, being heavily carved so that the tips of the petals stand out in harsh relief to break the smooth contour of the vessel (Plate II, opposite page 97).

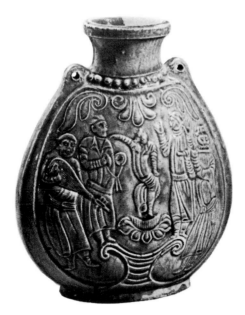

Fig. 46. Amber brown lead glazed earthenware pilgrim flask. An-yang, Honan. Found in a tomb dated A.D. 575. Height 20.3 cm. Chinese Government.

In one or two cases combinations of colourless glaze with streaks of green are found, foreshadowing the T'ang predilection for splashed polychrome effects.

More astonishing are a number of massive vases constructed from four or more thrown parts with somewhat grotesque sprig-moulded decorations of rosettes, heavy gadroon-like elements and trees, of a highly schematized nature, all applied in bands. The body material is a hard, light grey stoneware and the glaze an olive brown or green, or even yellowish (Fig. 47). These are totally alien to the Chinese tradition of form and would seem to be fantasies based on Near Eastern types of which we have no specific examples other than some unglazed and incompetently made earthenware from Central Asian sites. On these pieces the glaze reaches right down to the bottom, unlike that on the other wares of the north.

In the northern earthenwares and stonewares the glaze, with the exception just noted, rarely reaches more than two thirds of the way down the body, so that the danger of the piece sticking to the floor of the kiln or saggar was avoided. Significant is the fact that the body material is much whiter than hitherto and the firing now sufficiently well controlled, especially in the stonewares, for there to be little or no reddish oxidation of the unglazed areas. The indications are that kiln design and the technique of firing control had undergone radical improvements. Precisely what these were has still to be discovered, but it seems likely that the use of saggars had by now become part of the normal procedure, so the wares were well protected from accidents in the kiln.

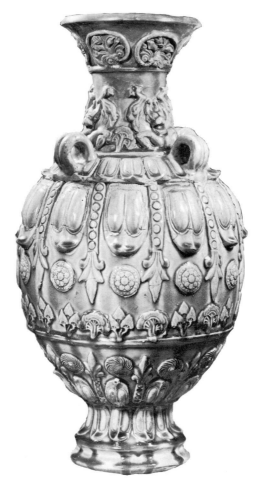

Fig. 47. Stoneware vase with sprigged reliefs and greenish glaze. Height 52.1 cm. Mid 6th century A.D. Kansas, Nelson Gallery of Art.

By the end of the sixth century the stages through which the Chinese potter had passed in the development of his craft were mainly of a practical nature. He learned the basic techniques of construction and firing, and the accumulated knowledge of these early centuries and the immediate practical experience gained were to make it possible in the future to exploit the clay and the glaze materials to their fullest extent. Hand building had been mastered in the earliest ages and then when the idea of rotating the pot on an easily turned wickerwork or basketry base had been put into practice, the first step towards a greater sophistication of form was taken. The fundamental advance in construction was made in the neolithic period, in east China, with the introduction of the fast-turning wheel, which required a thorough understanding not only of the balance of the wheel to ensure even rotation on the spindle, but also a sound acquaintance with the quality of clay materials. It was essential that both clay and any added temper should have a consistent small particle size so that the most suitable plasticity could be maintained. The need for consistency could only be learned gradually and the wheel would naturally not appear until the basic knowledge and experience had been gained.

A somewhat similar progression would be made in firing; the primitive bonfire with pots actually encased in fire would be abandoned only when some separation was found to have considerable advantages for even firing, consistent colour and relative freedom from surface blemishes. A further bonus from a separation of the fire from the chamber was the higher temperature that could be attained. Such a step in its own turn would force a renewed study of materials suitable for the higher temperatures, and would thus ensure an advance towards stonewares of a relatively impermeable character. The steps taken on both sides continued to react on each other in stimulating new experiments over a very long period of time.

With these combinations of reactions and developments the appearance of glaze was not far off. Either the effects of a rush of ash into the firing chamber, depositing a light glaze, was seen and imitated, or, perhaps more intriguing, a well-finished pot was carefully wiped or brushed over with a thin, clay charged liquid primarily to perfect the smooth surface, and it so happened that it included the right ingredients for the production of a glossy film which we call glaze; such a wholly unexpected effect would be tried again and imitated in its turn.

In decorative techniques cording, the simplest of all, was an inevitable concomitant of hand building with a pad and beater, and patterned paddles were a logical development, to which incising could quickly be added. The minor techniques like stamping, impressing, and ultimately rouletting, while sometimes practised extensively, were intermittently used, but were none the less valuable. Painting appears to have occurred quite spontaneously and nothing can be known as to how it came about. In the early stages it remained a decorative method for use on unglazed wares, and it was only after many other techniques had been mastered that it was satisfactorily employed on glazed pottery. Moulding was a different matter and, as already pointed out, it had affiliations with bronze founding techniques. What is surprising is that it took so long before it came to be used structurally on a large scale, but once turned to this use, it was to remain one of the most valuable techniques in the whole history of ceramic development.

With all these techniques, and the final addition, probably during the sixth century, of saggars to give better protection to the wares in the firing chamber and to ensure more consistently good results, the way was opened for more refined experiments in the use of both bodies and glazes with which the various decorative techniques could be combined. There is no hard and fast line to be drawn, however, for old practices lived on in one region, while new ones were being developed in another, or the old and the new were even practised side by side in the same kilns.

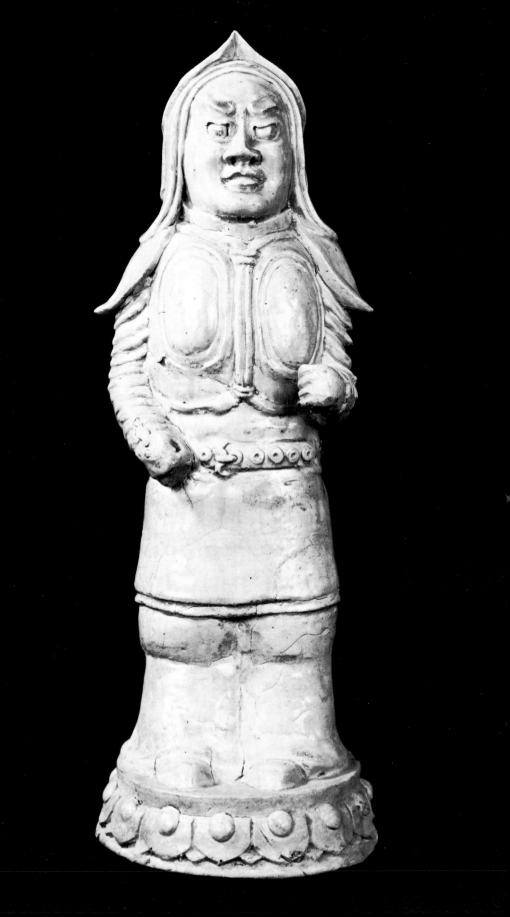

PART TWO

THE PERIOD OF DISCOVERY AND INNOVATION

CHAPTER FOUR

New Inspiration in T'ang

The T'ang dynasty is peculiarly significant in the history of ceramics because it was during this three hundred year period that earthenware was superseded by stoneware, and the foundations were laid for the supplanting in its turn of stoneware by porcelain, for whose discovery, or invention, the age was and is famous. The ultimate impact of the changes that took place under T'ang have been far-reaching and are still felt, even with our own advanced technology. It would, however, be misleading to tie the changes down chronologically to the T'ang dynasty alone.

A chronology based on dynastic successions is certainly a convenience, but it is singularly inappropriate to any account of art-historical, social or technological development, because changes in any one of these only exceptionally coincide with political upheavals. This is a fact which in recent years has been shown increasingly to be true in the history of Chinese ceramics. The new influences in north China, which had begun to become apparent in the sixth century, are themselves one aspect of the argument against the neat pigeon-holing involved in a politically oriented chronological scheme. The essence of ceramic development, as of all history of art, is a dynamism that makes nonsense of strictly defined stages between one recognizable type or style and another. Thus it is more helpful to outline the historical situation as it was from the latter part of the sixth century and early seventh century, irrespective of dynastic title, so as to provide a background against which the achievements of the whole period up to the tenth century can be seen in reasonable perspective.

During the latter part of the sixth century the slow process of reunifying China

Opposite: Fig. 48. Glazed whitish earthenware figure. Height 64 cm. Late 6th century A.D. Chinese Government.

was begun. This was not completed or consolidated until the second quarter of the seventh century. The whole process involved expansion, and the territorial expansion of the early seventh century under T'ai-tsung of T'ang was exceptionally rapid, taking in the whole of Central Asia as far as the borders of Persia, Sogdia, and Khorezm in the west. The policies pursued in the Sui period were to have far-reaching effects, since in aiming at the reunification of the empire it was necessary to fight off the Eastern and Western Turks in the north and north-west. To succeed in this the emperor used military force on the frontiers combined with diplomatic manoeuvring, in conjunction with the Persians, to create a split within the Turkish tribes aimed at reducing their power to threaten invasion.[1] This approach to the external defence of China, while internal problems were settled, was remarkably successful and went some way towards establishing conditions desirable for the territorial expansion in early T'ang.

At home unity and stability were seen partly as a matter of securing good communications. As a consequence improvements to the canal system and the roads were undertaken and carried forward with vigour, but at enormous expense. It was the cost of these, the massive repairs to the Great Wall, and the Sui military campaign against Korea, combined with the extravagance of Yang-ti, the second Sui emperor, that brought about the fall of the dynasty in A.D. 618, when Li Yüan forcefully established the T'ang after defeating other rebellious elements.

The achievements of Sui, however, were to bear rich fruit in early T'ang, when the emperor, followed by his son T'ai-tsung, continued the Sui diplomatic policy, but with a minimum of force. The latter pushed the frontiers of China out across the now relatively peaceful Central Asia, which already in Sui times had begun to look admiringly towards the east and the profits of trade with a China emerging once more as a political force in Asia.

The new stability of China was due to a number of factors, one of which was the improved internal system of communications of Sui, on which work continued in T'ang, but another of major importance was the efficient government administration. Economic security, which in the preceding centuries had barely existed, at least in the north, now became a reality, and the Chinese as well as the people of adjacent countries felt the advantages of the new situation. Trade across Central Asia grew rapidly and not only did merchants flood into China bearing luxuries of all kinds from Western Asia and India, but all kinds of people came too, Buddhist monks, Nestorian Christians, Zoroastrians, Manichaeans, and with them craftsmen and entertainers all anxious to enjoy the opportunities that the new and prosperous empire offered.

The merchant class, which had grown considerably during the previous centuries of unrest, when it was difficult for governments to keep private enterprise under strict control, now began to achieve a real identity, especially in the metropolitan areas of Ch'ang-an and Lo-yang, where the markets increased in number and size.[2] Luxury goods coming from abroad included Near Eastern textiles with complex weaves, and metalwork, as well as glass and precious stones, which all found a ready sale among the *nouveau riche* of the great capital cities, especially Ch'ang-an. The effect was startling on almost all aspects of Chinese art as the Near Eastern forms in metalwork and some of the decorative techniques made their impact. The foreign influences are easily discerned in almost every medium in use during the period of T'ang rule.

In ceramics many forms were wholly alien to the Chinese tradition, and although some were accepted, and adopted with suitable modification to suit Chinese taste, many were novelties of little lasting significance. The novelties, however, were snapped up by a public bent on keeping up with the latest fashions and delighting in extravagant, if not ostentatious display. The evidence is most clearly seen in the splendours of the lead glazed pottery intended for the customarily elaborate furnishing of the tomb, in which both figurines and vessels were included in great numbers for the use of the dead.

Lead Glazed Wares

The reappearance of lead glazing in the late sixth century differed from its original introduction just before the Han dynasty in that it was no longer applied to a strongly coloured pinkish or reddish body, but to a pale almost white body. Not only this, but at first it was nearly colourless; the only evidence of colour was a pale straw yellow tint due to the iron content, which in the pale clay was obviously much lower than in the earlier Han body. Occasionally a splash of copper green is found on the earliest pieces, but it was not until the end of the seventh century that coloured lead glazes were once more used, and then the first half of the eighth century saw the production of a great quantity of polychrome glazed wares of remarkable splendour.[3]

The lead glazed wares fall into two main groups, one consisting of figurines and the other of quasi practical objects, and it is significant that, as in the Han period, both groups seem to have been intended for the tomb. The glaze may at first have been applied raw, but by the beginning of the eighth century it seems to have been fritted; this is certainly the implication of the sudden appearance of cobalt blue among the colours. The pigment is known to have reached China in the eighth century, probably in the form of glass cabochons from the Near East, virtually ready for use, only needing to be ground down and fritted with the lead glazing material.[4] The other colours were amber and brown from iron, and greens from copper, in addition to the neutral glaze, which is occasionally made white and opaque,[5] but whether intentionally or not is unknown.

The earliest figurines of the late sixth and early seventh centuries are rather simple and generally less well executed than later ones (Fig. 48). Many are made

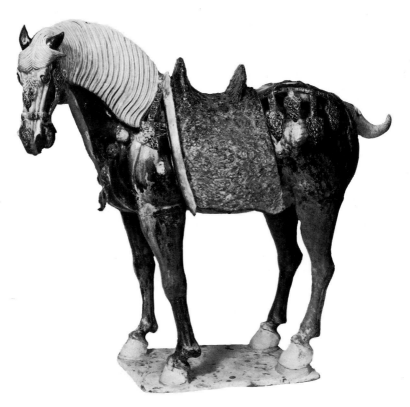

Fig. 49. Polychrome lead glazed horse with sprigged reliefs. Height 70.2 cm. 8th century A.D. London, Victoria and Albert Museum.

in a two-part mould, the vertical join up the legs and arms to the head often being only roughly cleaned up. The glaze is a pale straw colour, transparent and frequently crazed, and marred by a tendency to peel off. Later the bodies were roughly moulded, the head being made in a separate pair of moulds and luted into the body on a shanked neck. Details vary, especially the arrangement of the arms and hands, and what an individual figure may be holding. These parts were worked by hand after the main structure had been taken from the moulds. The heads, with their identical facial features endlessly repeated, were given individual expression and variation by the angle at which they were luted into the upper part of the body. The same general principles of construction were followed in making horses and camels, although of course the number of moulds used was necessarily greater. Both animals are known in a number of fairly set poses, but individual features and ornament are remarkably varied, particularly in the eighth century (Fig. 49).

A significant feature of the figurines is their realism, and this despite the mechanical methods by which they were made. Realism as such is rare in Chinese art in any medium, and is exceptional in the T'ang period for the immediacy with which it reflects the potter's lively interest in the world around, his keen observation and very real sympathy with his subjects. Figures are depicted with

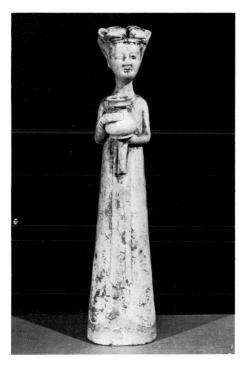 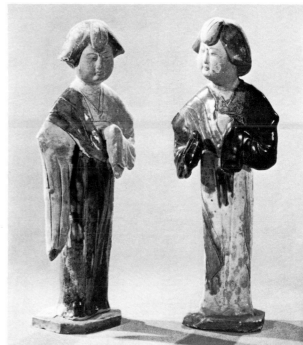

Fig. 50. Slim white glazed figure. Height 30.5 cm. Late 7th century A.D. Barlow Trust, Sussex University.

Fig. 51. A pair of matronly figures, polychrome glazed and with faces painted with unfired pigments. Height 42 and 45 cm. Mid 8th century A.D. Chinese Government.

astonishing power, in which there is an impressive sense of volume. The earlier realism of the Han dynasty was always in some degree subject to formal abstraction, but in the T'ang figures, the tactile sense, perhaps now more highly developed, demanded a perfectly articulated structure and a proper treatment of essential detail. Vitality and a sense of movement, dignity and a quality of individual character all have their place.

The contemporary ideal of feminine beauty is exemplified in an almost endless stream of figures, sitting, standing and variously occupied (Fig. 50). Up to the end of the seventh century the most acceptable concept of feminine beauty was evidently one of slenderness, great simplicity, and elegance. Early in the eighth century the figures became more matronly, until the middle of the century, just before the An Lu-shan rebellion in A.D. 756, when the polychrome figures come to an abrupt end, they had become heavier, stouter, and much rounder and fatter in the face. This was often left unglazed, and afterwards painted in colours using ordinary cold pigments (Fig. 51). The difference in palette and surface texture of these pigments on the bare body against the bright glaze colours of the rest of the figure gives a greater impact to the realism, although the expression of the face is usually one of vacuous complacency. In the figures of foreigners a different approach is seen; there is a delight in caricature, as in the splendid horseman

79

flexing his muscles (Fig. 52). Although this particular figure is unglazed, the same characteristics are seen among the glazed figures.

The greatest value of all these figurines, which, in their most characteristic form, seem only to have been produced in the metropolitan areas of Ch'ang-an and Lo-yang, with Kung-hsien near Lo-yang as an important centre of production, lies in their reflection of the society of the time.[6] As social documents they reveal a cosmopolitanism which has never been surpassed in any Chinese capital in any other age. They also mirror the pastimes and domestic occupations of the people in a noble household, as well as current fashions in dress, whether Chinese, foreign, or combinations of both.

To the figures of men, women, horses, and camels, which are the most common, are to be added the strange monsters which squat with bulging eyes, and the massive armed figures of guardians with exaggerated physical features. Both reflect the popular beliefs of the period: the former, the Ch'i-t'ou, a made-up animal intended to keep evil spirits penned down in one place, the latter, the Fang-hsiang, whose duty it was to frighten away sickness and evil spirits. In the course of the preceding centuries the Fang-hsiang had become assimilated into the pantheon of popular Buddhism, and by T'ang times was equated with the Dvarapala, or Four Heavenly Kings, who were guardians of the four quarters (Fig. 53). He is represented stamping on a dwarf or an evil-looking beast, and usually brandishes a sword or spear. In pottery figures the weapons may have been made of wood and been slotted through the upheld fist, but of course they have long since decayed. Figures of this kind were made to guard the entrance to the tomb, and one would be placed at each of the four corners of the tomb chamber.

It was not until the eighth century, when polychrome glazing came into its own and elaborate figures began to be made, that the potters started to apply a wide variety of moulded elements to the surface and to take great pains over the modelling. There was a lot of hand work done on these figures and the detail is often finely executed. All the figures were covered with a white slip before the glaze was applied; the use of slip helps to impart a clearer, brighter quality to the colour than would be the case if the glaze were applied directly to the body, whose iron content would tend to discolour it. The most intriguing feature of the polychrome glazed figures is the often careless, or even inconsequent, employment of the different colours. In some cases the colours have been applied to produce a harmonious and pleasingly patterned effect appropriate to the particular figure, but in others they have been splashed on without regard for design or contour, or they may be wholly inappropriate to the figure, like the unusual use of blue on a horse instead of the normal black or brown. When the

Opposite: Fig. 52. Unglazed horseman, from the tomb of Princess Tung-t'ai at T'ien-hsien. A.D. 706. Height 30.5 cm. Chinese Government.

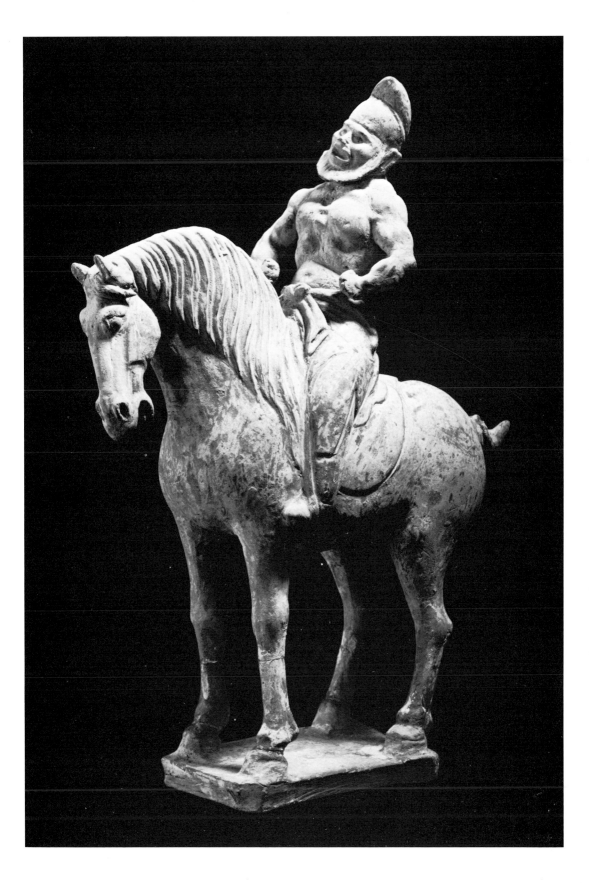

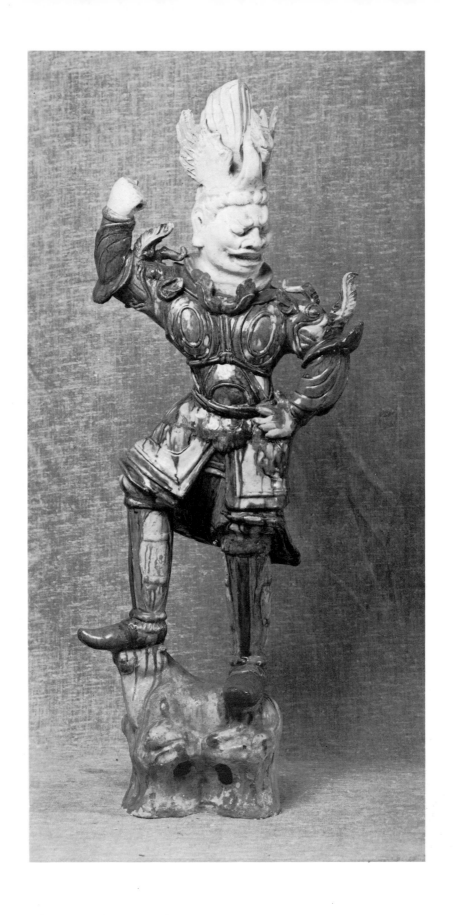

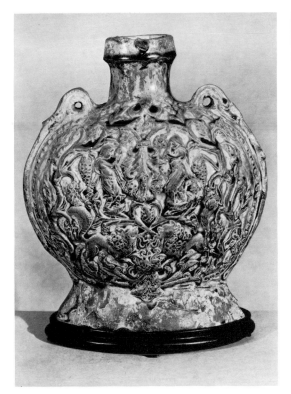
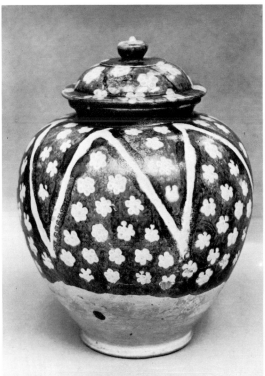

Fig. 54. Brown glazed moulded pilgrim flask with classical figures among vines. Height 23.9 cm. 7th–8th century A.D. Chicago, Art Institute.

Fig. 55. Polychrome glazed jar and cover. Height 25 cm. 8th century A.D. London, British Museum.

coloured glazes have been carefully and thoughtfully applied, they impart great splendour to the often massive figures.

The many vessels such as jars, jugs, ewers, bowls, cups, plates, and offering dishes with either monochrome or polychrome glazes are notable for their heavy dependence upon alien forms, especially in metal, as well as on foreign sources for their decoration.[7] Both foreign form and decoration may appear incongruous in the context of Chinese culture, as for instance in the leather bottle-shaped pilgrim's flask. Pressed out in a two-part mould, it may incorporate a design of late classical figures dancing among vines (Fig. 54). Like the figures, the vessels, too, are slipped to give greater brilliance to the colours, which are either splashed on carelessly or painted on in carefully organized designs. The latter treatment's success or failure depends to some extent on the viscosity of the glaze.

On the large jars and vases it is difficult to prevent the glazes running down in the firing and disrupting the design, but good examples show that the problem

Opposite: Fig. 53. Polychrome glazed tomb guardian, Fang-hsiang. Height 65.5 cm. 8th century A.D. London, Victoria and Albert Museum.

was at least partly solved by the careful use of a wax or grease resist, which to some extent isolated the colours from each other (Fig. 55). The resist was painted on as an outline to every part of the decoration, then the different colours were applied with a brush, failing only to adhere to the resist painted lines or areas. In the firing, which was to a rather low temperature, probably not much more than 900°C in many cases, the resist was dissipated, and although the colours may blur into each other slightly at the edges, especially on horizontal lines across a vertical plane, the basic pattern remains distinct.

The ewers with flattened ovoid body and phoenix-head lip area, based on a Near Eastern form made in metal, were habitually constructed using two moulds. The two pieces were luted together vertically, with the decoration of huntsmen, phoenixes, or lions, with flower and leaf elements forming a conceptual frame, all in low relief (Fig. 57). These ewers were more carelessly finished and glazed than the round-bodied type. This, also Near Eastern in origin, was similarly made in moulds, but this time with the parts stacked one on top of the other so that the joins lay in the horizontal plane (Fig. 56). The joins were then camouflaged by placing the piece on a wheel and shaving the surface, and sometimes also cutting simple grooved lines round the body and sprigging on relief elements of various kinds. Some examples of this type have a handle in the form of the head and neck of a dragon with its jaws clamped firmly to the rim of the ewer opposite the spout; other examples have a pinched type of spout and closely resemble the classical oenochoe, a form which was current in glass in the Near East at this time. Also ultimately Greek in origin was the amphora, and in most cases the handles were made in the same dragon form as on some of the ewers (Fig. 58). The glaze on the amphorae was rarely applied below the mid-body line because of its tendency to run down in the firing.

Plates, offering trays, and other vessels that would stand with the main glazed surface in the horizontal plane in the kiln, have a much more satisfactory appearance. The control of the glaze was naturally much easier and better, with comparatively little flooding of colours (Fig. 59). This was only partly owing to the impressed outlines for the patterns, where the gutters between the different colours tended to inhibit excessive running. Another reason was probably a slightly more viscous glaze, although this was not always the case. The viscosity of the glaze batch seems to have been a hit and miss affair. Careful arrangement of the colours could be combined with careless splashing, as on some of the offering

Opposite top left: Fig. 56. Polychrome glazed phoenix-headed ewer. Height 32.5 cm. 8th century A.D. Tokyo National Museum.

Opposite top right: Fig. 57. Polychrome glazed phoenix-headed ewer. Height 32.8 cm. 8th century A.D. Tokyo National Museum.

Opposite bottom: Fig. 58. Polychrome glazed amphora. Height 47.4 cm. 8th century A.D. Tokyo National Museum.

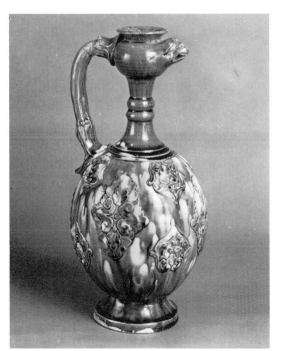
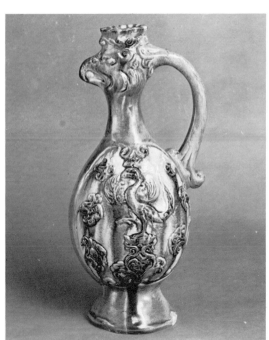
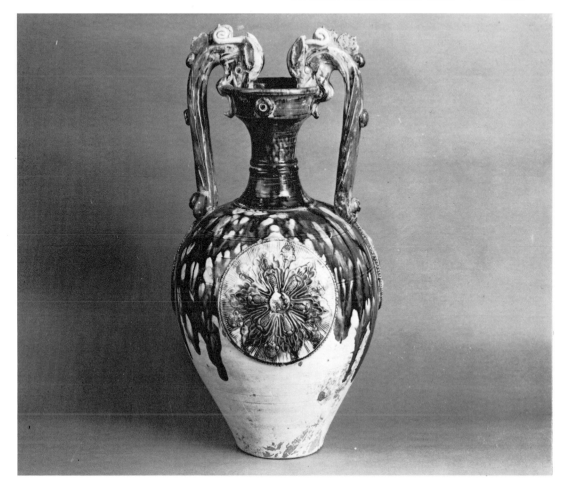

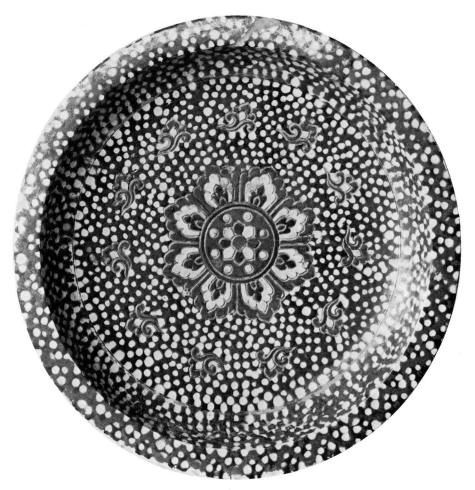

Fig. 59. Polychrome glazed offering dish with dye impressed design. Diameter 38.2 cm. 8th century A.D. London, Victoria and Albert Museum.

trays which have a well organized central pattern with splashed or stippled colours on the surround.

The offering trays are a particularly handsome type, with their central roundels made up of lotus leaves and ducks in flight, or formal palmette medallions. A number of very similar designs are constantly used, but they are visually saved from monotony by the varied alternations of the colours in the different parts. Like all other polychrome ware, the trays were slipped, but the slip does not cover the whole of the underside, which is supported on three cabriole feet. Nor does the glaze do more than cover the short sides down to the base on the outside. It seems to have been the practice to fire the offering trays in stacks, or at least with another vessel on top, as in almost every case there are three neat spur marks on the glaze of the decorated surface.

Among the much smaller lead glazed wares is a group of marbled cups and small bowls, and even one or two small vases, covered with amber or green glaze. In these two clays of different colours are combined either in a disordered fashion or in calculated patterns, the colours of the clays affecting the depth of glaze colour after firing (Fig. 60). Marbled ware has to be pressed out in moulds in order to ensure that patterns are not disrupted, as they would be if the combined clays were thrown on the wheel.[8] The pieces in this group are not very numerous, but their existence indicates that the potters were interested in experiment and invention of a kind for which they probably had little occasion or opportunity in earlier periods. Now, with well developed skills and a ready market for novelties, they had the opportunity to try out new ideas.

The rich effects and robust character of the metropolitan funerary potteries were in marked contrast to the more sombre hues of the only other polychrome wares of the period, which came from the southern province of Hunan and from one kiln in Ssech'üan in the west. The better known material is that from Wa-chia-p'ing and T'ung-yüan Hsien in Hunan, some distance north of Ch'ang-sha.[9] The earthenware from these kilns was grey bodied, and painted in copper green and iron brown fritted colours in an alkaline glaze, which is sometimes opaque white as the result of under-firing (Fig. 61). There is a variety of bowls, some of

Fig. 60. Marbled earthenware head-rest with transparent glaze. Width 24.8 cm. 8th–9th century A.D. London, Victoria and Albert Museum.

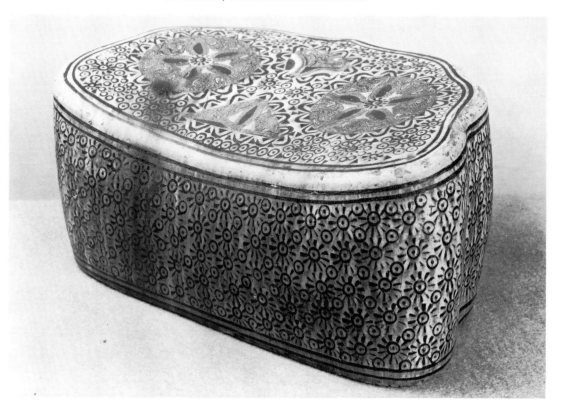

them rather shallow and wide open with a flared or everted lip, some are lobed. All are unglazed on the base, showing a fine grained grey body with a gingery discolouration of both body and glaze owing to burial in the reddish soil characteristic of the area. The decoration consists of simple florets, short thick lines and simple curvilinear patterns of an indefinable abstract kind. Sometimes the copper colour, which has to be fritted with a little lead to ensure the green in an alkaline glaze, seems to have been overloaded so that it appears almost blue; this has given rise to the mistaken idea that the potters of Hunan were using cobalt blue. Many fragments of this softly coloured ware have been found on archaeological sites in the Near East, notably at Siraf on the Iranian shore of the Persian Gulf, and so can be dated to the ninth and early tenth century.[10] This type is thus about a century later than the major production of the north and there appears little if any connection with the northern metropolitan pottery.

Fig. 61. Green painted alkaline glazed bowl. Diameter 14 cm. (Cup, 9.5 cm.) Late 8th or early 9th century A.D. T'ung-yüan Hsien type. London, Victoria and Albert Museum.

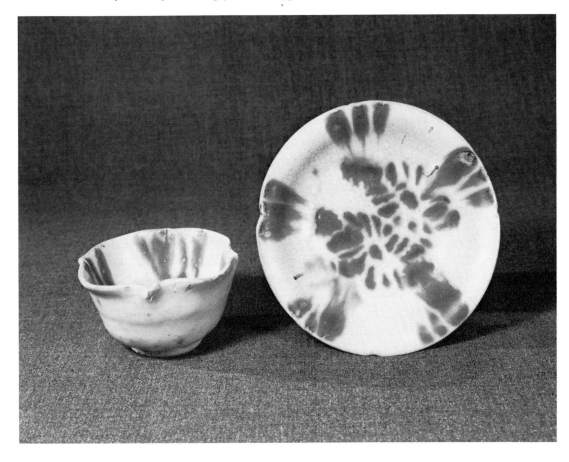

Stoneware with Coloured Glazes

Unlike the lead glazed pottery, the stoneware from the late sixth century onward was sombre in tone and such decorative effects as there were in terms of colour were subdued. This was because the high-fired glazes of China were at this time dependent upon iron oxides as colourants.

As a whole the high-fired material with a coloured stoneware body can be arranged conveniently in three regional groups, and is most easily studied in this way. First there is the pottery from the north central region, with southern Shensi and Honan as the main area of manufacture. Second there is the material from the eastern and south-eastern region with Chekiang as the most prolific area, but Fukien and Kuangtung farther south also contributed a considerable amount. Finally there is the south central region with Hunan and Kiangsi, which produced a much smaller quantity.

It is a remarkable fact that while there is considerable appreciation and some knowledge of the earthenware of the period, surprisingly little is known about the stoneware, particularly with regard to dating, and this applies even to the Yüeh from northern Chekiang, some of which has been attributed to the T'ang, but most of it to the tenth century and even slightly later. Recent work suggests that much of the Yüeh should be dated to the eighth and ninth centuries. Kilns found over the last few years are also beginning to suggest that the wealth of stoneware recovered should be similarly dated, and the excavations now proceeding in China should do much to better our understanding of the development of this ware from the late sixth century onward.

North Central Region

Kiln sites yielding material identified as T'ang have been found in both southern Shensi and in Honan, with a preponderance from Honan; there have also been finds in Hopei, the remains from these kilns being similar to those of Honan. The fabric of the northern stoneware is either very fine grained grey bodied or pale buff, sometimes speckled with brown from clay particles more heavily charged with iron. Some of the material from Hopei is a pale whitish grey, and may be coarser than the grey bodied ware of Honan and Shensi.

How early the northern kilns came into operation is still a matter for speculation, but most, in the opinion of the Chinese, date from the middle and later years of T'ang, that is, from the late eighth and ninth centuries. Clearly there are more sites to be located, because some pieces generally regarded as seventh-century cannot yet be assigned to any known kilns.

An early group is represented by a number of small stout ewers with short straight spouts set high on the shoulder, with rather small loop handles, and with

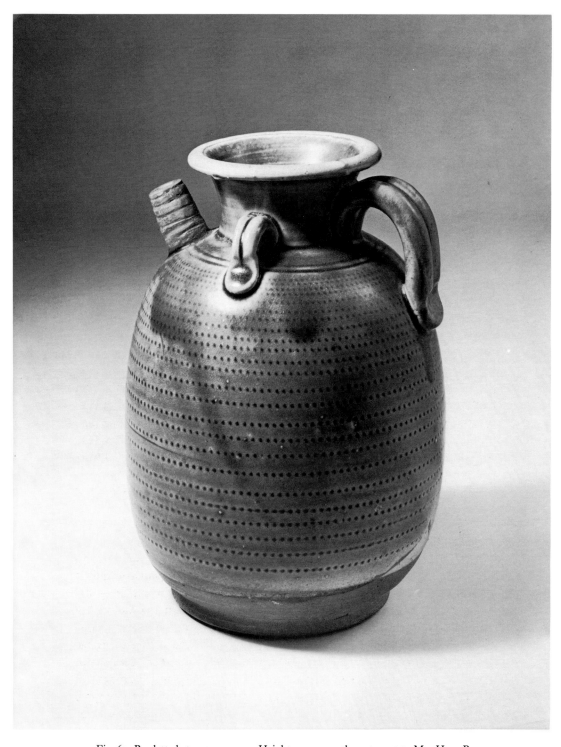

Fig. 62. Rouletted stoneware ewer. Height 20.3 cm. 7th century A.D. Mrs Hans Popper.

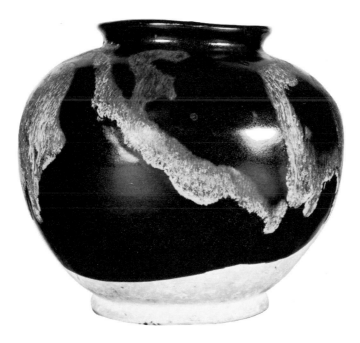

Fig. 63. Stoneware jar with bluish suffusions on a black glaze. Height 12.7 cm. 8th–9th century A.D. Bristol City Art Gallery.

lugs at either side. The body is pale buff and the usual practice was to cover it with a thin whitish slip, almost to the base, before rouletting the surface with either a dotted or a fine chevron pattern (Fig. 62). The glazes are those which are commonly seen on T'ang stoneware, being brown or a pale yellow of rather soft tone, thinly applied and not as a rule reaching below the lower limit of the slip. These are dated stylistically to the seventh or eighth century, the later examples of the type being taller in the neck.

More securely dated to the middle and late T'ang is the material from Hao-pi-chi in T'ang-yin Hsien and Chia-hsien both in Honan, the latter a district a little to the south of Yü-hsien, which was to become a major centre in the Sung and Yüan periods, but was already operating on a small scale in the late eighth century.[11] Recent excavations have yielded a variety of wares, including yellow, black, and white glazed types. Most important of all was the find, at the Huang-tao kiln in the Chia-hsien group, of a buff stoneware covered with a very dark brown or almost blue-black glaze with pale bluish grey mottling, and another type with a greyish glaze and dark mottling (Fig. 63). The pieces of this type include some handsome jars, deep bowls and some vases, some of them gourd-shaped with lugs at the waist between the upper and lower bulbs. All are now regarded as precursors of the famous Chün ware of the Sung and Yüan periods, some of which was made at the Yü-hsien kilns just mentioned. The quality is high, with good

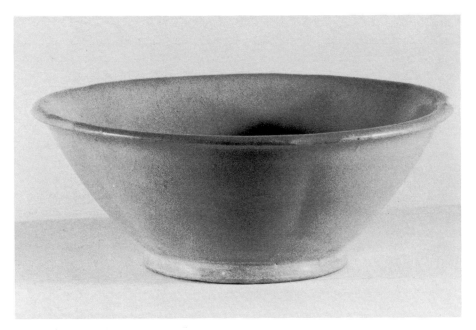

Fig. 64. Stoneware bowl with greenish grey glaze. Depth 16.5 cm. 9th century A.D. Dr P. Plesch.

proportions as a central feature. The glaze, which is high-fired, is usually thick and viscous, so that the suffusions do not run very much. The pieces are well finished, having a neatly cut edge to the smooth flat base.

Other glaze colours found on the Honan kiln sites are a pale yellowish brown, a deep brown with a tea-dust effect and a greyish green. The shapes are characteristically stout and strong; the bowls have thick walls and are sometimes thickened at the rim. Most are well finished and pleasing in appearance. Black glazed stoneware seems to have been common currency throughout the north and is particularly frequent among the products of southern Hopei.

From Shensi at T'ung-ch'üan, where a large number of kilns have been excavated in a group in Yao-chou, has come a grey bodied stoneware with a grey green glaze, the forerunner of the Yao-chou northern celadon of the Sung period. Bowls seem to have been the main output with this glaze covering, not only at Yao-chou, but at Lin-ju Hsien in Honan as well, a kiln centre which also became famous in Sung times (Fig. 64).

The Yao-chou kilns are reported to have come into production in 'late T'ang' as the Chinese report puts it, and this implies a date about A.D. 800 or soon after.[12] The kilns did not confine themselves to green glazed ware, indeed these were probably the least common, for they also made black, yellow and white glazed ware, some of the last being covered with a white slip and then painted in black before being covered with a transparent colourless glaze. A number of small boxes were found with black painted decoration, which marks a new departure in decorative technique, and is the first step towards the complex decorations of some of the stoneware of the following centuries included under the type name Tz'ŭ-chou.[13] The designs are simple linear abstractions based on an arithmetical division of surface. The colourless glaze over the very white slip and rather dense black painting produced a brilliance which must have been found extremely attractive as a contrast to the sombre tones of the rest of contemporary stoneware.

The glazes of the northern pottery, with the exception of that with a colourless, or neutral, glaze, all include iron oxides as colourants. The proportion of iron to the glaze mix increases in proportion to the depth of colour. The yellow glazes contain about one half per cent to one per cent, and the darker browns and black from about five per cent upwards. The grey green glazed pieces from Yao-chou were also coloured with iron oxide and were fired in a well controlled reducing atmosphere. It would seem that most of the stoneware of the north was fired in an oxidizing atmosphere at this time, and if so the reducing cycle necessary for the grey green glazes from Yao-chou and Lin-ju Hsien was an important exception. It

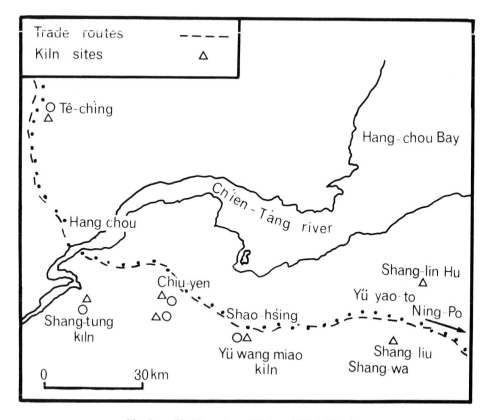

Northern Chekiang Proto-Yüeh and Yüeh kiln sites.

was most probably the result of the growing influence of the Yüeh tradition of Chekiang, from which province some pieces have been identified in the northern metropolitan area of Ch'ang-an, a notable example being an octagonal vase with a tall narrow neck from a tomb dated A.D. 871.[14]

East and South-East Region

In the course of the last few years there has been a very substantial increase in the number of known kiln sites in the region, the greatest number having been found in the northern and eastern part of Chekiang. The kiln sites are no longer numbered on the fingers of one hand as they were in 1939, but by hundreds, and a

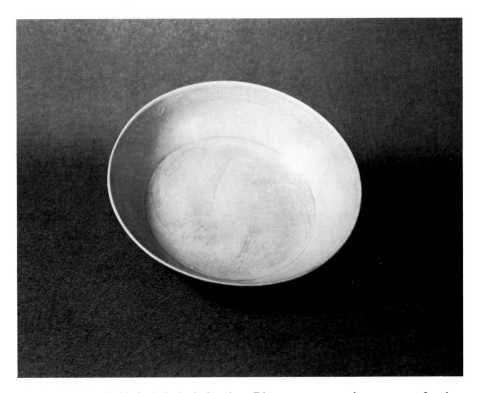

Fig. 65. Yüeh bowl with finely incised phoenixes. Diameter 17.4 cm. 9th century A.D. London, Percival David Foundation.

relatively large proportion of them produced Yüeh and Yüeh-type wares in the T'ang dynasty. It was during this period that the products of the region were properly named Yüeh for the first time, from their political and geographical association with the ancient kingdom of that name located in the area.

The most important kilns were those of Shang-lin Hu during the T'ang period,

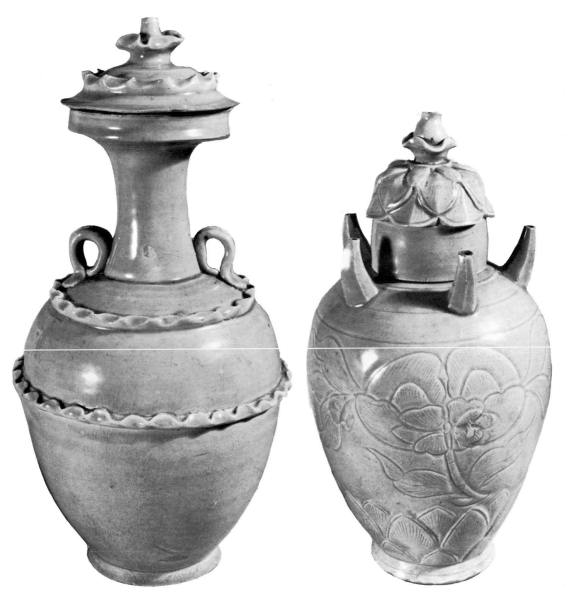

Fig. 66. Yüeh-type vase with dished mouth. Height 39.4 cm. 9th–10th century A.D. Captain Dugald Malcolm.

Fig. 67. Yüeh-type vase with five false spouts and carved decoration. Height 33 cm. 9th–10th century A.D. Captain Dugald Malcolm.

as Tê-ch'ing and Chiu-yen had been in the preceding four centuries. Further east was Hsin-hsien, nearer to the port of Ning-po, which came into production during T'ang, and has only recently been found and archaeologically reconnoitred.

The earlier proto-Yüeh was replaced in T'ang times, from these two sites at least, by a refined ware of great elegance. The body is light grey, very fine grained, hard, and extremely compact. The glaze at its best is thin and a pale, almost silvery olive green, applied over a plain undecorated surface, or sometimes over designs incised with a fine point in an almost pencilled style. There are a few moulded pieces with incising reduced to a minimum. When the glaze is greener and thicker there may be bold carving, especially of floral motifs, with finely incised detail. In some cases the glaze has become brownish yellow as the result of poorly controlled reduction.

There is a great diversity of shapes, with bowls, boxes, jars of lotus bud shape, and ewers among the most frequent. Many of the bowls are dependent on contemporary silver for their shape and decoration, the latter closely resembling the chased designs in metalwork, with birds (Fig. 65), flowers, butterflies, clouds and ribbon motifs among the most popular. There is one group of bowls which differs in being wholly free of decoration. These have a lobed rim, whose edge is turned outward and downward; the foot-ring is rather higher than that of the pieces based on silver prototypes, which generally tends to be low and splayed. The origin of this second group is to be found in lacquer, at first sight a surprising source of form, but in fact a natural one, since the other major product of northern Chekiang was lacquer ware of the highest quality.

The true Yüeh of northern Chekiang was widely distributed through the local markets, and many kilns further south, especially around Wên-chou on the coast, imitated it. One type, always called Yüeh, has a softer modelling to the carved decoration, and it includes a fine series of tall vases, ovoid in body, with a long neck expanding at the top to a cupped or dished mouth closed by a low-domed lid with a bud-shaped knob in the centre (Fig. 66). There are also vases of approximately the same shape, but with a shorter, straighter neck and a cover dropping down over the outside, while on the shoulder are five false spouts sticking up (Fig. 67). The purpose of these vases is not precisely known, but they are at least furnishing for the tomb. The carved decoration of these two types of vase is usually rather large in scale, consisting of handsome flower sprays and boldly carved lotus petals arranged in bands. The glaze is pale grey green, glassy, and remarkably consistent, indicating efficient kiln control. Where these handsome pieces were made is still not known.

All this Yüeh ware and many of the imitations continued well into the tenth century, when some of the finest was made, and all except the last group of vases was widely distributed inside China as well as being exported from mid-T'ang times to the Philippines,[15] Indonesia, and westward to India, the Persian Gulf, and the Red Sea, from where it travelled to Egypt. The popularity of Yüeh and

Opposite: Plate I. Kansu Yang-shao jar painted in black. Height 15 cm. Stockholm, Museum of Far Eastern Antiquities.

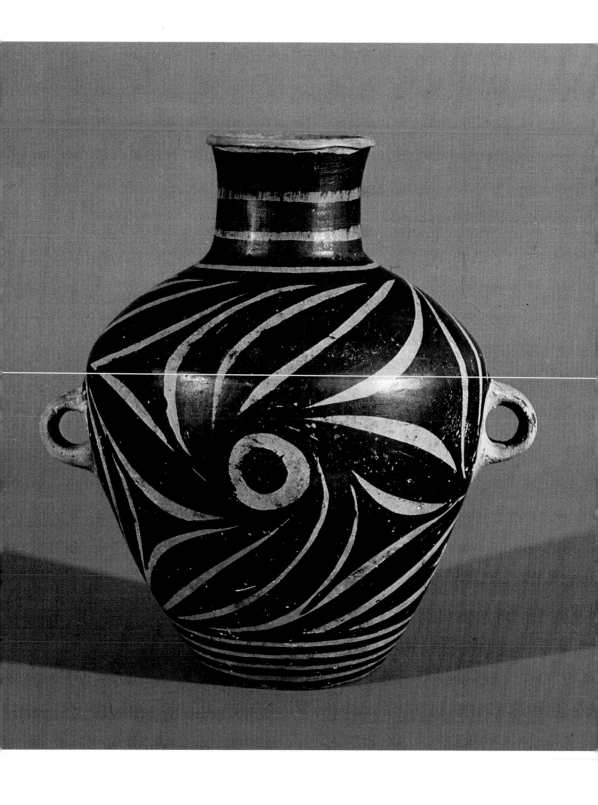

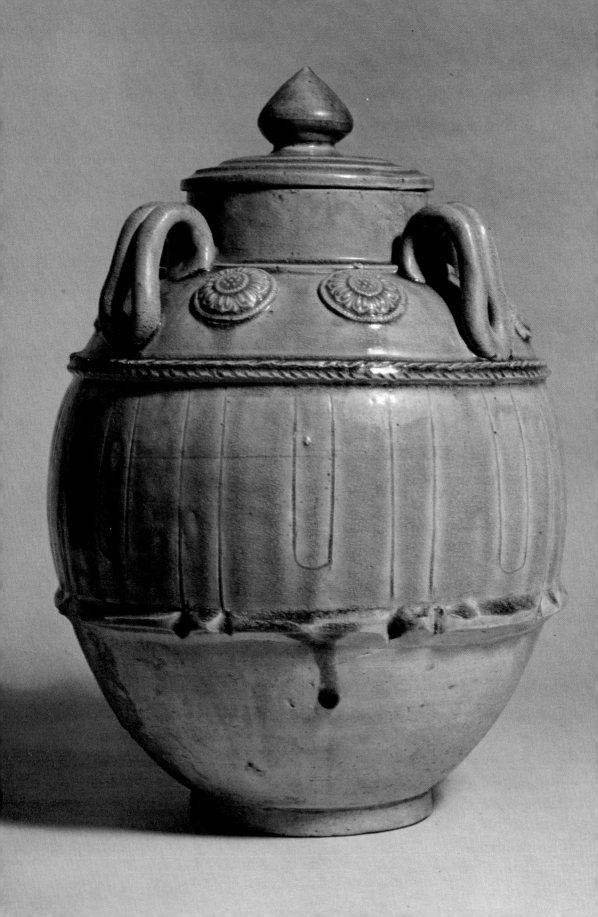

Yüeh-type ware was undoubtedly due to its hardness, which had no parallel in the potteries produced outside China at the time.

South Central Region

The main centre for this region was in Hunan, in the neighbourhood of Ch'ang-sha, where kilns have been located in recent years. Some like Wa-chia-p'ing and T'ung-yüan Hsien, referred to above, produced earthenware, but others seem to have made cruder imitations of Yüeh. There was, however, a distinctive stoneware with a greyish or brownish body. The type seems largely to have been confined to a standard type of ewer of stout proportions with a short straight spout set high on the shoulder, not unlike the northern type of the earlier seventh and eighth centuries, and like the earlier type it also had a simple strap handle (Fig. 68). The decoration is limited to sprig-moulded elements applied before glazing. The designs of the elements are varied and include lions, shrubby looking palm trees, and figures, often astride galloping horses. The glaze over the decoration is a transparent darkish brown, but over the rest is a neutral transparent one which shows up the buff body.

These ewers proved popular, for they have been found in many places, not only in China, but also overseas. Finds in a fragmentary state have occurred in Indonesia, at Siraf in Persia, at Nishapur in north-east Persia, and in the enormous accumulation of refuse at Fostat, old Cairo, in Egypt. The route by which they travelled from the kilns so far inland was south-east over the Mei-ling pass to Canton, where Muslim traders, who formed an important component in the mercantile population of the city, would ship them out with other wares from the southern kilns, together with silk, another valuable export commodity.

White Wares and Porcelain

It is necessary to separate the white ware from the stoneware of the T'ang period, because it was out of the gradual improvements in the white earthenware and whiter bodied stoneware that porcelain was finally born, in the sense defined in the introductory chapter, in the late eighth or early ninth century. Its discovery was due ultimately to the persistent search for a pure white body. The ordinary stoneware with its coloured body could not have developed in this direction at the northern kilns. The pale grey bodies of the south-eastern tradition of Chekiang, however, did eventually produce a comparable material, but not until after the end of the eleventh century. In the south central region it was to be in the hitherto

Opposite: Plate II. Stoneware jar and cover with greenish glaze. Height 34 cm. Late 6th century A.D. Formerly Mr Frederick Mayer.

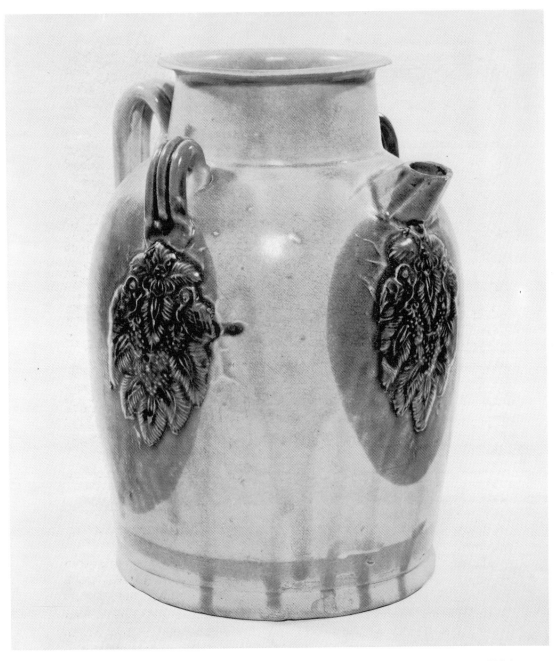

Fig. 68. Stoneware ewer with sprigged reliefs and brown glazed areas. Chang-sha type. Height 22.5 cm. 9th century A.D. Chinese Government.

more retarded region of development in the province of Kiangsi that the final breakthrough was made and porcelain in the European sense was to appear.

We are still ignorant of the exact development, and the problems with which we are faced are aggravated, as Ayers pointed out in his introduction to the Seligman

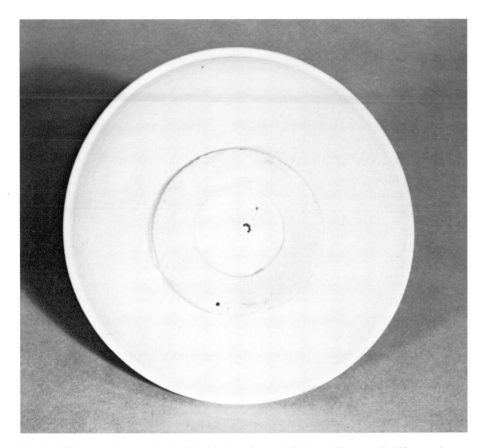

Fig. 69. White porcellanous bowl with wide foot-ring and thickened lip; so-called 'Samarra' type. Diameter 14.4 cm. 9th century A.D. London, Percival David Foundation.

collection catalogue, by the confusion of terms.[16] This is a particular obstacle in the description of the white potteries of the north, which are more varied in body material than those of the Kiangsi area.

The search for a pure white body had continued intermittently for centuries in the north, but from the middle of the sixth century work towards this end became more concentrated. The bodies became cleaner and whiter, more compact, and gradually much harder as the temperatures were raised and firing control improved. By the later years of the sixth century, fairly hard alkaline glazes were in use on white clay bodies. When the glaze lay thick and pooled in hollows it tended to be slightly greenish or pale straw yellow, but there was a tendency for the glaze to become crazed and even peel off, indicating that there was still some way to go. The clay bodies themselves were essentially kaolinic, being supplemented, whether intentionally or not, with other ingredients which helped towards a degree of vitrification. It is to this type of material in north China that the term porcellanous is applied.

In Kung-hsien in Honan, where the kilns produced a variety of wares, including a whitish bodied earthenware with polychrome glazes in the eighth century, the Chinese have also found some white sherds of a hard high-fired type, but the exact nature of the material and the shapes of the pieces to which the sherds belong are not known. Kung-hsien was only one of a large number of locations producing white wares, which seem to have been made at many of the Honan kilns. Some of the other white pottery was rather coarse in body and slipped inside and often outside as well to conceal the imperfections. It was the habit at most kilns to stack the wares, especially those of less fine quality, so many of the bowls, for instance, have five or six spur marks scarring the glaze on the inside. The most characteristic bowl shape was rather shallow and wide, with a thickened rim and a low, wide foot-ring, but there were also deeper types with narrower foot-ring (Fig. 69).

The old tradition, handed down in the literature, of the white ware of Hsing-chou in Hopei has been something of a stumbling block, since no kilns have been found there. The city, however, like Chü-lu Hsien, which was inundated by the disastrous change in the course of the Yellow river in 1108, may have been a market centre of sufficient importance to give its name to the best of the high-fired pottery of the period. If so, the source of the ware may have been Chü-yang, farther north in Ting-chou, which was to become so important in the Sung period. Preliminary studies on the Ting-chou sites have shown that bowls with a low wide foot-ring and thickened rim were made there, and were of fine quality, comparable to the type found at Samarra, the important early Islamic site on the Euphrates, some material from which dates to the latter part of the ninth century.[17]

The body seems to have been carefully constituted of a kaolinic clay of exceptional whiteness, and it is believed by Sundius to have had inclusions of dolomite in order to obtain a higher degree of translucency and vitrification.[18] The bowls were generally slipped both inside and outside, and then covered, usually by dipping or pouring, with a colourless glaze, which fired either a cold faintly blue tone like skimmed milk, or a pale ivory colour. The glaze fit is excellent and pieces are rarely crazed. How early activity at the Chü-yang group of kilns began remains an open question, but there is no reason why this high quality material should not have been in production by the beginning of the ninth century.

In the south, in the province of Kiangsi, both in the vicinity of Jao-chou and of Chi-chou further south up the Kan river, good quality white ware was being produced at this time, and it is in the south that porcelain as we know it seems first to have been made. It is here that the most abundant resources of the basic ingredients are found, the kaolinic clay being not only extremely plentiful, but also of exceptional purity in having a very low iron content. There was also an abundance of the felspathic China stone, petuntse (*pai-tun-tzǔ*), easily available for addition to the clay, to produce in the firing the vitrified translucent body associated with

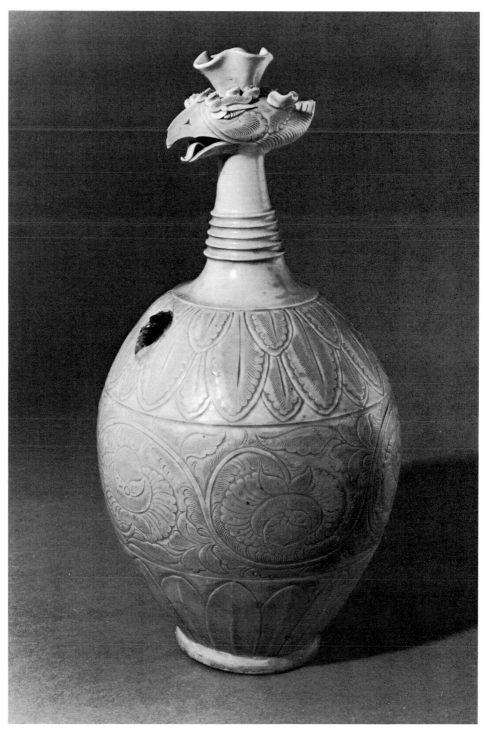

Fig. 70. Phoenix-head ewer from Chi-chou. Height 39.4 cm. 9th–10th century A.D. London, British Museum.

the name of porcelain. Unfortunately relatively little is known of the early developments in this region and there is a lack of dated material. A kiln at Yang-mei-t'ing near Ching-tê Chên was certainly making white ware in T'ang, and so were kilns at Yung-ho near Chi-chou. The nearest we have to datable material is the phoenix-head ewer in the British Museum and some companion pieces which have been identified in Indonesia and the Philippines in recent years and which date from the tenth century (Fig. 70). Some of the more recently found pieces may be earlier than the British Museum example, which seems rather elaborate. The body is often rather putty coloured, but the material is very hard and the glaze fit good.

The appearance in the last few years of some heavily constructed bowls, covered with a hard, transparent, faintly blue tinged glaze over a body coarsely carved with overlapping lotus petals round the outside, and having an unglazed base with reddish burn marks from the firing stand, set something of a problem. They would seem to be southern in origin and certainly are characterized by a more glassy fracture than is found in northern products; one indeed more consistent with the western conception of porcelain, and fairly near to the famous *ch'ing-pai* of the province of Kiangsi in the following centuries.

That a high-fired, vitrified, and translucent ware was discovered in the T'ang period is not really open to doubt, but its exact centre of origin and the precise constitution of body and glaze remain mysteries to be solved. The evidence we have for any one centre is still inconclusive, but the probabilities would seem to be heavily weighted in favour of the south.

The effects of the discovery of the new type of body and the shift to the well fitting felspathic glaze was to have far-reaching effects, not only on the ceramic wares of China, but on the whole approach to ceramic materials in the countries to the west, and also, perhaps less easily recognized, on the concepts of decoration.

The virtual abandonment of lead glazed earthenware, except for roof tiles and ornaments, and the concentration on stonewares resulted in rapid improvements in the latter and a notable expansion in production. The lead fluxed glazes were not wholly abandoned for domestic or funerary ware, but some centuries were to elapse before a new use could be found for them on the porcelain body, which in the first instance required firing to a temperature considerably higher than the old earthenware.

In the past the study of the stoneware of the period has been somewhat neglected in favour of the charms of polychrome tomb figures and vessels, a situation likely now to be remedied as Chinese excavations become more numerous. The avowed intention of the new excavation is to clarify artistic achievements and technological developments, which, in the T'ang period especially, had a profound impact on the art of Asia, and ultimately of Europe.

CHAPTER FIVE

North China from the Tenth
to the Fourteenth Century

It is during the centuries immediately following T'ang that the division between the northern and southern production can most easily be distinguished. The northern kilns made rapid advances in their technology that placed them ahead of the south-eastern kilns, which for so long had held the lead. The potters in the north were imaginative in their use of material and showed strong initiative in the development of decorative techniques. That the northern provinces were not able to take full advantage of their opportunities to build up overseas trade and work towards industrialization was due to two factors: the threat of invasion, to which the area was constantly subject, and the geographical and geological situation, which was unalterable. These factors, combined with the problems involved in political and economic changes from the end of the T'ang to the new period of unity under the Yüan Mongols, inevitably had an impact on the whole northern region and resulted in the shift of the major centres of production to the south, which already in T'ang times had begun to become the more important economic area of the empire.

During the Sung period the true focus of economic wealth became more obviously centred on the south, which was more easily accessible to foreign trade through the ports of the south-eastern coast. Shipping replaced the land routes and, so far as ceramics were concerned, was more profitable, as well as safer as an outlet to the world at large. But it does not alter the fact that wealthy patronage of the arts in the first two centuries following the fall of T'ang was mainly in the north, which, up to the twelfth century at least, remained predominant over the south in both invention and quality.

It is for this reason that the ceramics made at some of the northern kilns during the first part of this period of about three and a half centuries are regarded as 'classic' wares and have been esteemed especially highly by the Chinese, as indeed they still are by anyone familiar with them.

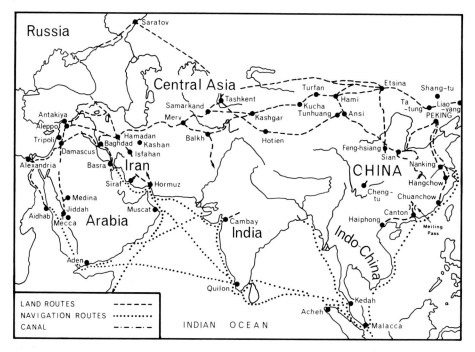

Trade routes of Asia: tenth to fourteenth centuries.

During the first part of the period the Sung dynasty ruled over a now much shrunken empire. The northern provinces were only held until 1127, when the Jurchen tartars invaded from Manchuria, after defeating the Khitans, who were known in history by the dynastic name of Liao. The Liao, at first holding southern Manchuria, Inner Mongolia and parts of the northern provinces of China, are important in Chinese ceramic history for their influence on the northern kilns, especially in the eleventh and early twelfth centuries. They inherited T'ang traditions in metalwork and lead glazing in the tenth century and brought to them elements of their own culture. For a short time the Liao actually held a large part of Hopei where the famous Ting kilns were situated, and even after their withdrawal, following a precarious and, for the Chinese, humiliating peace treaty, trade between the Chinese and the Liao was lively and cultural influences flowed into China from the north right up to 1127, when the Sung fled south.

For about a century after this date north China as far south as a line drawn from west to east along the line of the Chin-ling mountains to the Huai river and the sea, a traditional cultural frontier in China, was ruled by the Jurchen, who took the dynastic title Chin, 'Golden'. Barely a century later the Mongol invasion started; Peking was lost to the invaders in 1215 and the rest of north China down to the same west-east territorial limit in 1234. Then in 1250 the Mongols began the final assault on south China and finally united the empire in 1275 under Khublai

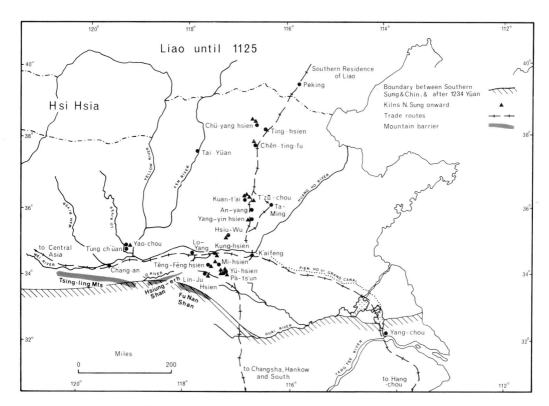

Kiln sites of north China: tenth to fourteenth centuries.

Khan, who took the dynastic title Yüan and established his capital, Cambalic, or the Chinese Yen-ching, the old name for Peking, in 1280.

From this brief outline it will be seen that one cannot employ the dynastic name of Sung in north China, except in a rather limited sense, because the whole situation changed after the defeat of the imperial forces in 1127. Not only was there political change, but also very serious economic change affecting the ceramic industry, and artistic influences combined with technological changes also had effects which have to be taken into account.

In the course of the whole period there were some very significant changes, whose beginnings can be traced back to the late eighth and ninth centuries of T'ang when an increased emphasis was placed on stoneware. The proliferation of kilns in the later years of the ninth and in the tenth centuries, despite local disturbances, was undoubtedly due to the easy availability of materials combined with a rapidly growing assurance in the handling of techniques. What was to emerge in the following centuries under Sung, Chin and Yüan was an industrialized system of production. This is particularly apparent at the small number of kilns which developed their own specialized output, to the virtual exclusion of the more diversified production of earlier times and of the greater number of the northern kilns. The economic distribution of labour and the concentration of specialization among the potters meant that great strides towards a systematically organized industry were not only possible but necessary. The question as to why all this should have happened when it did is partly answered by the technological changes involved in the evolution of the only white bodied porcellanous ware of north China, the Ting ware from the province of Hopei.

'Classic Wares'

Ting Wares

The kilns making this easily distinguished type were discovered in 1941 at Chientzǔ Ts'un and Yen-shan Ts'un, sixteen miles north-east of Chü-yang and about thirty-five miles north of modern Ting-hsien in Hopei.[1] The sites were visited by Chinese specialists in 1947 and in 1961–2, when some exploratory archaeological work was carried out.[2] From the work and the general survey of the area with its vast refuse heaps, it has been possible to distinguish the main groups of wares produced over the whole period from late T'ang to at least the end of the thirteenth century.[3]

The predominant output was the white ware with transparent ivory toned glaze which made the kilns famous. The other wares were a soft, dark brown or dense black glazed type, which is rare, a white ware painted in soft iron brown of rather light tone, again a rare type, and a group of uncertainly dated monochrome and polychrome lead glazed earthenwares about which there is at present relatively little information.

The kilns clearly specialized in the production of the porcellanous ware. It is characterized by the extreme whiteness and hardness of the body, which may be translucent, and the glassy, transparent, and warm ivory tone of the glaze. On some bowls this may show what the Chinese call 'tear stains', slight thickenings where the glaze has run down towards the foot after dipping. That the kilns confined themselves very largely to the production of bowls, basins, dishes and plates, is evident from the immense waster heaps in the vicinity of the kilns, and from the predominance of these shapes in collections all over the world. There is by contrast a very small number of vases. It was good economic sense to limit production to the most popular and practical forms; for it made the achievement of high quality and large output easier; moreover it may well have contributed to the long survival of the kilns in this somewhat remote area.

During the late tenth and early eleventh centuries production was more varied than it became later. There are, for instance, vases and jars dating from this fairly early stage with rather heavily carved decoration in which lotus petals played a large part (Fig. 71). By the second half of the eleventh century production was already concentrated, to the virtual exclusion of other shapes, on the manufacture of open and flat wares with carved and incised decoration of floral scrolls and

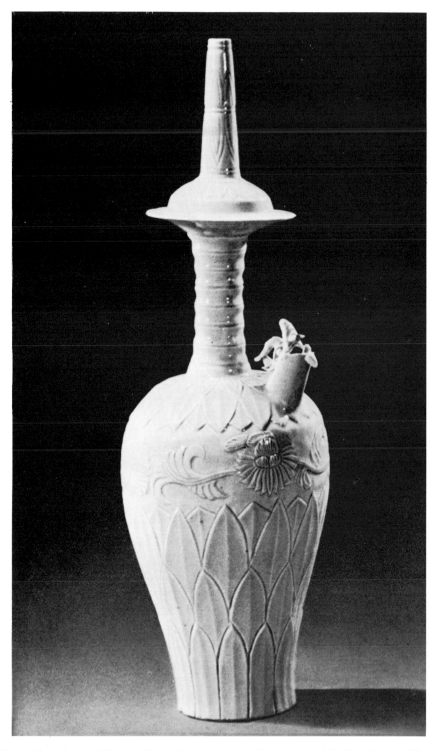

Fig. 71. Porcellanous Ting *kundika* with carved decoration. Excavated in Ting-hsien in Hopei. Height 60.5 cm. Late 10th or early 11th century A.D. Chinese Government.

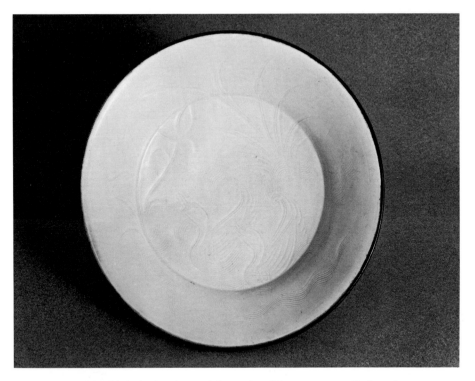

Fig. 72. Ting dish with incised and carved decoration. Diameter 22 cm. Early 12th century A.D.
London, Percival David Foundation.

sprays (especially lotus), of ducks and geese among reeds, dragons, and of fish.
The carving and incising was a highly developed skill and must have been carried
out by craftsmen specially trained in this work. Were this not the case it would be
almost impossible to account for the consistency in design, the fluency of line and
the almost unequalled high quality (Fig. 72).

The economic division of labour in the kilns and the consequent concentration
on particular skills are especially apparent in an unusual group of bowls in which
the contour of the wall changes direction completely between the foot and the lip.
The bowls were thrown on the wheel in the ordinary way with slightly rounded
wall, and were then, while still damp and plastic, carved at high speed by the artist
skilled in this work. When the carving was completed the bowl was passed to a
craftsman who placed it upside down on a blank undecorated mould, which was
made with a reversed contour half way between the base and the rim. By exerting
precisely the right amount of pressure the new shape could be imparted to the
bowl without impairing the decoration. The result was a bowl which suddenly
flared outwards from about half way up the sides.[4] After this the piece was shaved
and the foot-ring cut in the usual way. Each operation, the throwing, carving,

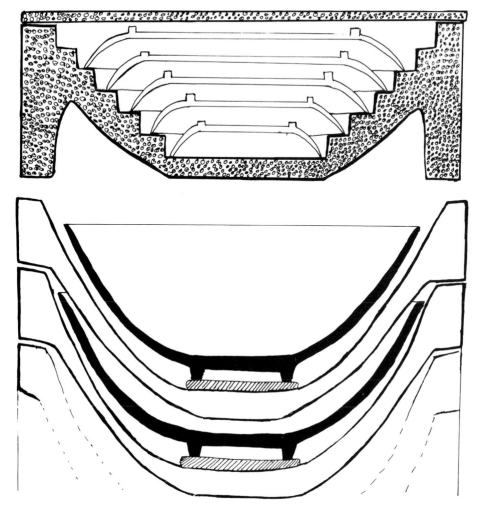

Saggars: I. Ting; II. Chün and other northern wares.

pressing over the mould, and finally the shaving and the cutting of the foot-ring demanded great skill and accuracy.

After sufficient drying time had elapsed the pots were glazed, stacked in saggars and fired to a temperature of about 1,260°C and probably not above 1,300°C.[5] The glazing of the open and flat wares was unusual in as much as they were completely covered except for the lip, on which they were fired. This is the reverse of normal practice, which is to fire on the base or foot-ring, so that these are the parts left free of glaze. There are two advantages to firing bowls, dishes and plates on the mouth rim. The first is that by distributing the weight of the vessel evenly over a wider area, the likelihood of warping during the initial drying out period in the kiln is slightly reduced, and the second is that a larger number of pieces can be fired in a single setting. The reason for this is that by designing a saggar with a series of steps round the inside a number of pieces from smaller to larger, working from the bottom upwards, can be put together in the one saggar. The practice involved a degree of standardization previously unknown. If vessels are fired on the foot it is necessary to place each piece separately in its own saggar, thus taking up a great deal more space in the kiln (see drawing on page 109). In some cases this is an inconvenience overcome by stacking several pieces in a saggar with stilts separating them so that they do not stick when the glaze melts; this has the serious disadvantage that the fired glaze is scarred by marks of the fireclay stilts. The disadvantage of firing the Ting pieces upside down was that the unglazed rim had to be concealed, so a very thin copper alloy band individually cut for the object, was applied to the unglazed rim after the firing.

At about the beginning of the twelfth century a new decorative technique was introduced in Ting. This was the use of moulds. The moulds were made of a slightly greyish, compact stoneware clay with a concave recess on the underside, the upper surface being richly ornamented with a design neatly carved *intaglio* (Fig. 73). The decorative vocabulary of the moulded vessels is much larger than that of the carved wares and included phoenixes, many more varieties of flowers, children and landscapes. The mould was placed on a turn-table with the decoration upwards, a thick disc or wedge of clay was laid on it, and it was then beaten over the mould with a wooden paddle with one hand while turned with the other. It was a task requiring much less skill than throwing and was guaranteed to produce a stream of identical patterns. When plates were made, the moulds for these were sometimes placed on a fast wheel, a disc of clay dropped on to it, and then while the wheel was spinning a profile was brought down on the clay, sufficient pressure being exerted to force the clay to accept both shape and decoration, and to shear off the excess clay as it spread towards the edge. The process is known today as jolleying and is the normal method of producing dinner plates in the modern industry, when of course it is done mechanically. In the use of these methods important steps were taken towards industrialization, whose economic benefits were to be very great in the future.

Even after the introduction of moulding, the carved pottery continued to be made, for it clearly had a good market. The astonishing fluency, sensitivity and elusive linear rhythms of the designs had an enormous appeal and were justifiably acclaimed at the court. In the eleventh and twelfth centuries the Sung court used to send buying commissions up to the kilns to cream off the best for imperial use, and even after the end of the Northern Sung period in A.D. 1127, the succeeding Chin patronized the kilns, so that during the twelfth century there was no deterioration in quality. It was only after the Mongol invasion at the beginning of the thirteenth century that the kilns began to decline and the quality became noticeably worse. Even the moulded pieces became much more careless. The kilns must finally have closed down about A.D. 1300 or soon after.

So far we have considered construction and the accompanying element of standardization, to which quantity production was concomitant. But decoration, its motifs and organization, is also important on account of its reflection of the artistic climate in which the potter lived and worked. Prior to Ting only Yüeh ware had to any extent mirrored the decorative taste, and in the best instances this depended upon metalwork for its inspiration. In the early stages in carved decoration Ting differs from Yüeh in being more obviously spontaneous in the treatment of natural elements. The designs only fell gradually under the influence of metalwork, and perhaps textiles, when the introduction of the moulding technique in the early twelfth century opened the way for a tighter, more repetitive approach to decoration.

Fig. 73. Stoneware mould with decoration carved intaglio; dated on the back to A.D. 1184. Diameter 22 cm. London, Percival David Foundation.

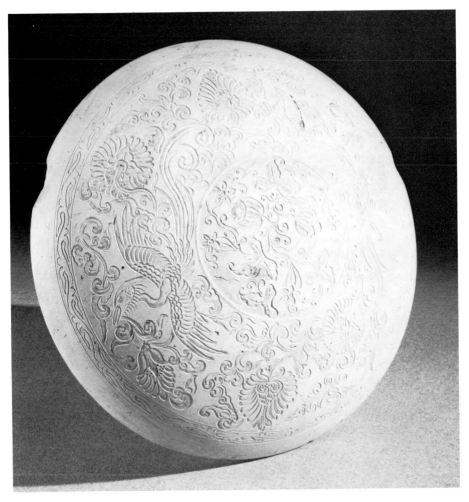

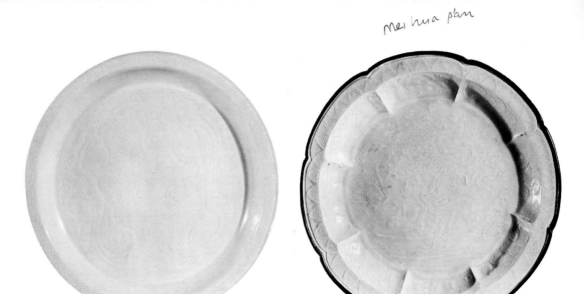

mei hua pan

Fig. 74. Ting plate with *ch'ih* dragons. Diameter 21 cm. 12–13th century A.D. London, Percival David Foundation.

Fig. 75. Ting plate with moulded decoration. Diameter 21.5 cm. 13th century A.D. London, Percival David Foundation.

The predominant motifs on the carved ware are the lotus, the peony, ducks and reeds, dragons, and, on a small number of pieces, fish swimming among waterweed. There are three ways of handling these motifs. If they are floral they are organized either as scrolls encircling the object round the inside, or sometimes the outside of a bowl or basin, or all round a vase such as the *mei-p'ing*. They can be oriented in one direction only, as on a small number of plates dating from the late twelfth century onward and on bowls. The peony particularly may be ordered as a series of sprays in panels, usually six, with the flower head towards the rim, again a twelfth-century treatment.

Dragons, which are relatively uncommon, especially in the earlier examples, are usually arranged almost heraldically round a conceptual centre point, so that like the floral scrolls they appear to rotate. On early pieces they are vigorous three-clawed creatures cleanly and fluently carved, but by the late twelfth century, this type had been replaced by that known as the *ch'ih* dragon. It is a curious newt-like beast with a snub nose, fleshy body and limbs, and sometimes a bifurcated tail (Fig. 74). The *ch'ih* dragons generally occur in pairs chasing each other round a central jewel. On these the rather clean carving is replaced by a softer grooving with less fluency than in the earlier examples.

The duck and reeds, and the fish and waterweed themes, are necessarily organized as a single pictorial scene. They are treated with great simplicity, every part having ample space in which to breathe and exist individually, yet composed in a perfect series of relationships to form a unity. Pieces with these two themes

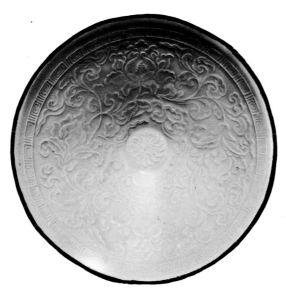

Fig. 76. Moulded Ting bowl with pomegranate decoration. Diameter 20.6 cm. 13th century A.D. London, Victoria and Albert Museum.

are to be dated mainly to the late eleventh century and the early years of the twelfth century, the period when the kilns achieved their apogee in both quality and quantity.

Moulded decoration is much more complex than carving and incising because the technique lends itself naturally to a more laborious treatment. More time could be spared to cut into the large thick pieces of clay, which dried out more slowly than the relatively thin walls of a thrown piece. Carefully prepared drawings could be transferred to the domed surface of a mould for a bowl or dish, or to the flat surface of one for a plate (Fig. 75). Much more time could be spent on precise and accurate carving, since the clay surface could be slightly damped down without fear of damage if the mould seemed to have dried out too much to allow the cutting tool to move smoothly. Once the mould was finished and properly dried it was fired almost to a stoneware temperature, and the decoration became indelible. The greater elaboration of the designs had two main sources of inspiration, one was metalwork with repoussé decoration, much admired in the north east at this time, and the other was probably the richly embroidered textiles, which one may see depicted in paintings attributed to the period (Fig. 76).[6]

The motifs include a large number of different flowers and fruits including the chrysanthemum, which is not found in the carved ware, both the flower and fruit of the pomegranate and melon gourds. To these are added somewhat abstract foliage scrolls and a debased form of key-fret, the only geometric motif in Ting decoration. Birds such as the phoenix, pheasant, a short-tailed bird resembling the hoopoe, ducks and geese, and even occasionally peacocks are used among the floral scrolls or in garden or landscape settings (Fig. 75). Animals include deer,

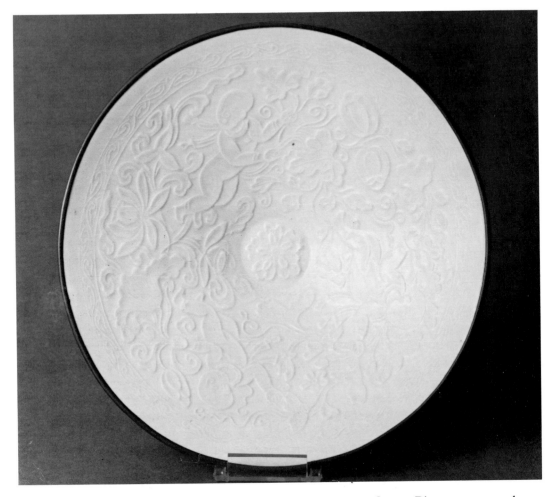

Fig. 77. Ting bowl with moulded decoration of infants among flowers. Diameter 22 cm. 13th century A.D. London, British Museum.

lions, kylin and some curious fish-like dragons as well as the newt-like *ch'ih* dragon. There are proper fish among aquatic plants and in lotus pools. Finally there are chubby infants, wholly or partially naked. It seems unlikely that they were incorporated into the decorative vocabulary much before the late twelfth century.

The organization of the surface is similar to that of the carved ware. The designs circle or rotate round a central point or sometimes a larger ornamented field. There are many examples with landscape and terraced gardens in which small naked or semi-naked infants appear; they may even hang precariously on floral scrolls (Fig. 77). What does not occur in the moulded series of Ting is the system of division of bowls into panels radiating from a central point.

Northern Celadon from Yao-chou and Lin-ju Hsien

Another ware made in the same way as Ting and decorated using similar techniques, though very different in style, was the stoneware broadly called Northern Celadon. It had a grey body and olive green or olive brown transparent glaze. It is now one of the best documented of the northern wares and the Chinese have rightly adopted the practice of naming it after the kiln at which it originated. The most important of the kilns were those at Yao-chou in Shensi, about 70 miles north-east of Ch'ang-an, the capital of the T'ang dynasty. A second group of kilns was found in Honan at Lin-ju Hsien in the mountains south of Lo-yang. The body material from both areas is very similar and the products are only distinguishable by very small technical differences in the carved wares and of style in the moulded ones.

The Yao-chou material is of particular importance because the report of the excavations there answers many questions that have arisen with regard to the ceramics of north China as a whole, as well as questions on the techniques and actual designs used in this type of green glazed ware.[7] The finds also provide a valuable framework for the chronology of a type, of which there are examples in many collections. Furthermore by identifying their particular designs such pieces can be allocated to their proper source, either in Yao-chou or Lin-ju Hsien.[8]

As in the case of the Ting ware, the roots of the tradition go back into the ninth century, and it is not until the late tenth century that, again like Ting, the potters began to concentrate on a particular ceramic type, this time on the so-called Northern Celadon with a reduction-fired glaze. The glaze, compounded with a small amount of iron oxide and reduced from ferric oxide to ferrous oxide, is rather variable in tone, but in the good pieces it is bright and glossy, very transparent and remarkably free from trapped gas bubbles. In later examples and less good pieces this may not be the case and the glaze is sometimes slightly or even completely opaque and crazed. The colour, too, is not always good; it often tends to yellowish or muddy brown tones, owing mainly to badly controlled reduction.

The early output included a wide variety of forms; cups, saucers, dishes, bowls, vases, ewers, and lampstands, but later bowls and dishes began to predominate. Nearly all the shapes are thrown, but naturally those with moulded decoration were made using a turn-table and paddle to beat the clay over the mould. The use of the fast wheel and template does not occur in either Yao-chou or Lin-ju ware, so far as it has been possible to discover.

The carved decorations were bold continuous floral scrolls and abstract foliage scroll patterns. They were sometimes rather carelessly executed, but they showed up well on the grey body under a transparent glaze which thickened in the hollows (Fig. 78). There is a remote dependence on Yüeh, but it is hardly apparent in the eleventh century, unless one is aware of the early history of the kilns in the T'ang

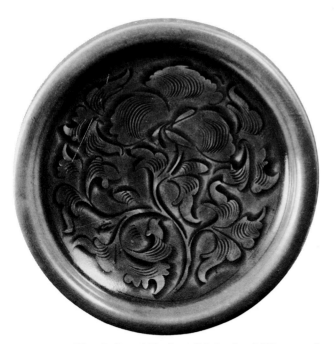
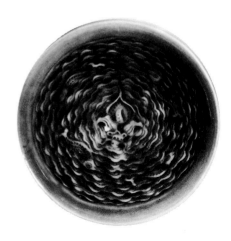

Fig. 78. Carved Northern Celadon bowl. Diameter 18 cm. 11th–12th century A.D. Baur collection.

Fig. 79. Moulded bowl with fish in a river from Yao-chou. Diameter 9.7 cm. 12th century A.D. London, Percival David Foundation.

period. Early in the twelfth century the technique of moulding was introduced, but it is of a very different character from that of Ting, in which the small scale and extreme delicacy of handling are striking features. The designs in Yao-chou ware are larger in scale and very deeply and sharply cut into the heavy grey stoneware moulds, so that the finished bowls and dishes nearly always look as though they have been carved. Indeed many examples cited in old books are described as being carved, and it is only because of the large number of discarded moulds found during the excavations, that it is now possible to identify most as having been moulded.

The peony and lotus are the most common decorative motifs and occur in both carved and moulded wares. In the early carved wares these are generally arranged in scrolling designs on the outside and perhaps on the inside as well. On the moulded wares they naturally only appear on the inside, the outside sometimes being carved rather roughly with overlapping lotus petals, or simply sliced. During the twelfth century fish and waves, lotus ponds and ducks, cranes, butterflies, and children playing among flowers make their appearance (Fig. 79). These designs at first rotate round a central point, but later they were sometimes organized into six panels with a different motif in the centre. In the very late carved bowls, most of which are rather thick and of which there are quite a number, the decoration may be oriented in one direction only.

The usual practice in firing was to place each piece in its own saggar, and to stack the saggars one on top of another in the kiln. All pieces were fired on the foot.

However, in the last years of activity at the Yao-chou kilns it became common to stack bowls and shallow dishes immediately on top of one another in a single saggar, which entailed leaving an unsightly unglazed ring inside each vessel so that the pieces did not stick together in the firing. Coal was obviously the fuel used in the kilns, as large quantities of coal ash and clinker have been found in the kiln stoking areas and among the refuse.

The most important find at Yao-chou was certainly the group of three kilns with an adjacent workshop. The middle one of the three kilns, which were built in a row, was sufficiently well preserved to permit an accurate reconstruction of the northern kiln type, which is known as the horseshoe shaped kiln. The name admirably describes the shape in plan (see drawing below). The fire box is on the perimeter of the roughly semicircular kiln chamber directly opposite the straight back wall. In this there is a series of vents set vertically from ground level, and behind it rises the double chimney. When the kiln had been stacked a light wall, known as a bag wall, was built to about two thirds of the height of the chamber to separate the wares from the fire outside; the fire was over a grating with a deep ash pit beneath. The side walls of the kiln, built of old saggars and firebrick, were surmounted by a domed roof. This deflected the heat and flame downward through the stacked wares as it came into the chamber over the bag wall. The heat and flame were then drawn out through the vents in the back wall and up the two flues which merged into a single massive chimney several feet above the floor. When reduction firing was needed the stone doors outside the stoking area could be closed. Shattered stone doors were in fact found in the stoking area. The

Yao-chou kiln: isometric reconstruction and elevation.

operation was simple and evidently quite efficient, for this type of kiln has been found at many other northern sites well-known for their reduction fired wares, though on most other sites they have been too ruined to permit reconstruction.

A variant of this type was actually discovered quite recently at Yü-hsien in Honan with two fire boxes side by side, each with its own flue into the firing chamber, which, as a consequence of this arrangement, is rectangular. Because of the low positioning of the fire boxes the need for a bag wall was eliminated, but an interesting addition to the construction is the small stoke-hole on the top of the left-hand flue into the kiln, for the insertion of additional small billets of wood. Further variants have been discovered in the far south of China, in Kuangtung, some of them dated on very flimsy evidence to the T'ang period; a Yüan or Ming date is to be preferred. Some of these are of the horseshoe shape but operate as cross-draught kilns in as much as the vents in the back wall are replaced by slits reaching up most of the height of the wall.

Chün Ware

A close relative of the so-called Northern Celadon is the type called Chün. The chief kiln centres were in Honan, in the neighbourhood of Lin-ju Hsien and further east around Yü-hsien, but it was produced at many other kilns scattered over a wide area. The wide distribution accounts for the great variations in body colour and texture. It is classified as a stoneware, but is not always fired into the stoneware temperature range. The less good quality pieces are usually of the lower fired kind with a rather porous body, and these seem to have been green fired. The best quality pieces have been twice fired, the first firing, without any glaze, to a relatively low temperature.[9] The glaze was then applied before the second firing at a slightly higher temperature.

The Chün glaze is one of the very few that can with certainty be termed an ash glaze; it has been possible to isolate the phytoliths in the fired glaze structure. Phytoliths are the minute silica particles that survive from plant ash in the form of opal bodies. In the plant itself phytoliths often have their own characteristic form according to the species of plant, and, provided the firing temperature is not high enough to destroy them completely, it is possible to detect them microscopically in a thin section. If in the firing the temperature has been raised so far that the phytoliths have been totally destroyed, it is necessary to undertake laborious laboratory analysis in order to establish the presence or absence of a significant amount of phosphorus, which is always present in plant ash, but not in purely felspathic materials. If there is a substantial amount of phosphorus, then the glaze is justifiably called an ash glaze. Such an analysis was carried out on Chün in the 1930s before microscopy had developed to the extent it now has.[10]

The bluish colour of the Chün glaze is due to the presence of small quantities of iron oxide in the glaze combined with the reduction firing to which the ware was

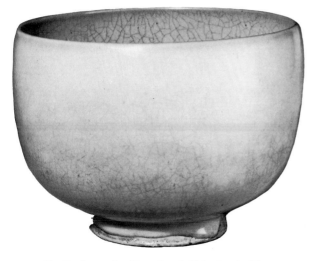
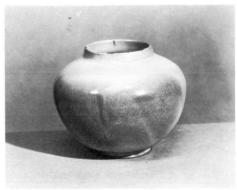

Fig. 80. Lavender blue glazed Chün bowl. Diameter 19.5 cm. 11th–12th century A.D. London, Percival David Foundation.

Fig. 81. Chün jar with crimson splashes. Height 8.9 cm. 12th century A.D. London, British Museum.

always subjected. Because of this there is a good deal of variation in colour from one piece to another. There is also variation in the surface texture and brilliance, depending on the firing temperature and the speed at which the temperature has been raised, and whether or not the ware has been soaked for any length of time, that is, whether the critical temperature has been maintained for a longish period in order to disperse the gases from the body and glaze (Fig. 80). In Chün ware such a practice as soaking does not appear to have been normal and the glaze structure is characterized by the vast quantity of trapped gas bubbles. However in the finest quality ware the surface may often be smooth, glossy and brilliant, despite the presence of these innumerable bubbles which help to impart the opacity inseparable from Chün. The reason for the high gloss probably lies in the fine grinding of the basic materials.

It was not until the early twelfth century that additions of copper were made. The first use of this oxide was apparently casual and limited to simple splashes (Fig. 81). After reduction firing the resultant colour was red or purple, making a startling contrast with the soft rather subdued tone of the glaze. It is not known what the potters were trying to achieve by using copper, and the result was certainly very different from that achieved by the Korean potters at about the same time; they used it quite simply to paint spots on the black and white inlaid celadon-type ware, which was their most important product. In the thirteenth century there are signs in Chün of attempts at definite patterns, and in at least one instance a Chinese character was used as decoration. It was painted boldly on the surface of a head-rest and read prosaically, 'pillow'. The final stage in the use of copper is seen in its lavish employment for colouring the outsides of flower pots, narcissus bowls, pot stands and the like (Fig. 82).

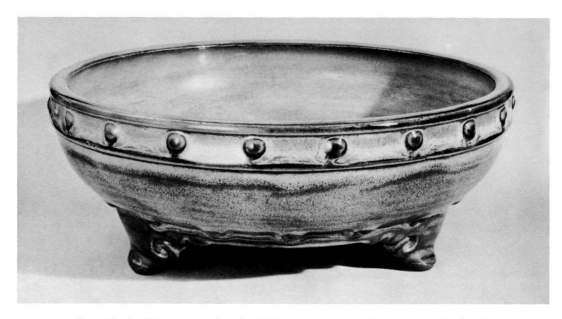

Above: Fig. 82. Chün ware narcissus bowl. Diameter 25.1 cm. 13th century A.D. London, Percival David Foundation.

Below: Fig. 83. 'Bubble bowl' of Chün ware. Diameter 8.9 cm. Late 13th century A.D. London, Percival David Foundation.

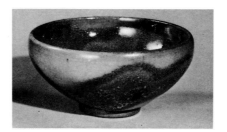

A characteristic feature of the use of copper, especially in the twelfth and earlier thirteenth centuries, was the tendency of an excess of it to oxidize a bright moss green in small patches on the surface. This peculiarity together with the unpredictability of its reaction in the firing adds much to the attraction of the Chün ware and to the intriguing problems regarding the technique of its production.

The shapes most common to Chün are bowls, rather flat small dishes and saucers, plates (Plate III, opposite page 128), stout jars and a few vases; in later times tripod incense burners in a wide range of sizes were popular. The bowls may be of the simple open kind with rounded sides, or they may be small with an incurving rim, a shape referred to by the Chinese as a bubble bowl (Fig. 83). It was not until the fourteenth century that the massive flower pots, narcissus bowls, incense burners and large basins were introduced. Some of these late, massive pieces, which continue into the Ming dynasty, are different in character from the early ware in being dark grey in the body, very fine grained and extremely heavy

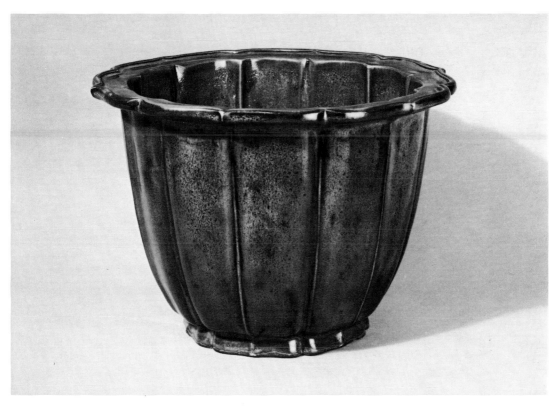

Fig. 84. Deep crimson Chün flower pot. Height 18.7 cm. 14th century A.D. or later. London, Percival David Foundation.

for their size. Moreover the eccentric shapes of the flower pots and narcissus bowls of various patterns were made using a complex system of moulds. In some instances a twin moulding process is possible, for instance, one for the inside of a flower pot and another for the outside, but for those pieces with the so-called 'cloud feet', either the feet had to be applied separately and be hand cut, or they could be included in a series of moulds keyed together to make an outer casing. The large wedge of clay was placed inside the outer mould and the inner mould was then pressed down until the excess clay was squeezed out round the edges and trimmed neatly off as the edges of the two moulds met. These mechanically produced pieces are perfectly consistent in size and in the thickness of the walls. Pieces made in this way were also numbered; each pattern was evidently available in ten sizes and the number of the size was impressed on the base (Fig. 84). This facilitated ordering since the authority placing the order could simply ask for so many flower pots of such and such a pattern in such and such a size, as the case might be. Such a development brought a degree of industrialization into ceramic production, and in the fourteenth century and later this was of great importance.

Whether these large mechanically produced pots with lavish amounts of copper in the glaze should be called Chün is something of a problem since the material does not appear to be quite the same as the earlier types from Lin-ju Hsien and

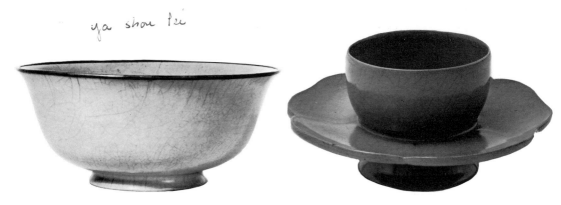

Fig. 85. Ju ware bowl, the metal band concealing damage. Diameter 16.7 cm. Early 12th century A.D. London, Percival David Foundation.

Fig. 86. Ju ware cup-stand. Diameter 16.2 cm. Early 12th century A.D. Sir Harry and Lady Garner.

Yü-hsien in Honan. It may be that they were a product of Chên-ting Fu in Hopei farther north, a centre which became very well-known from the fourteenth century onward and famous for its 'red' ware.

Ju-yao

Closely related to both Chün and the so-called Northern Celadon, and most probably deriving from the latter, is the very refined, rare ware called Ju-yao (Fig. 85). Like Chün it is classified as a stoneware, but again it appears to be an earthenware, although relatively high fired. There are only about thirty recorded specimens.[11] The body is a fine grained pale buff and the thick glaze is an opaque greyish blue from iron oxide and reduction firing. The glaze is in all but two cases crazed; the crackle is almost certainly not deliberately contrived at this stage. It is usual for the glaze to cover the object completely. This is then fired on a stand with three or five spurs, which leave small elliptical white fireclay marks on the base, spur marks which the Chinese refer to as sesamum seed marks.

In the form in which it has been recognized as an imperial ware and hence 'classic', we only know for certain that it came to an end abruptly in 1127 when the Northern Sung court fled south from K'ai-fêng in Honan, where the kiln is believed to have been set up. As to when it achieved the refined form that gained it its reputation, there is no clear evidence, earlier information on this subject having been found to be wholly unreliable. It seems unlikely that it can have been of the highest quality for more than about a quarter of a century, so it can scarcely have attained perfection much before the beginning of the twelfth century.

The few surviving specimens do not allow generalization as to the shapes most common to the ware, but they fall broadly into two groups. The first comprises bowls and dishes of great simplicity, with a low splayed foot-ring. The second is composed of objects dependent for their form on other materials such as bronze, silver or lacquer. The unusual cup-stand form is an excellent example of adaptation from either silver or lacquer, in which materials this was a common form from at least as early as the eighth century (Fig. 86).

Popular Wares

Tz'ŭ-chou Stoneware

The name Tz'ŭ-chou has always been associated with one of the most varied and popular types of stoneware, and is not now regarded, as it once was, as a kiln name. It is the name for a series of stonewares of great diversity manufactured in north China at a very large number of kilns, from late T'ang times to at least the end of the fourteenth century. In broad terms it is characterized by strong shapes and bold decoration on a slipped body; many of the pieces are also unusually large in size. As a type it takes its name from Tz'ŭ-chou, modern Tz'ŭ-hsien in the province of Hopei, where it has long been known to have been made. In many areas kilns which produced the type have been found alongside others whose production was more specialized and superior, such as fine quality Chün in Yü-hsien. It was in effect a popular line, such as would always have a market. The early history is not yet well known, although by the early eleventh century it was already well developed at a number of kilns. By the middle or end of the eleventh century the number of kilns producing it had increased sufficiently for it to be easy for us to say that the main centres were in Hopei, with the Tz'ŭ-hsien region in the former province being particularly prolific, and in Honan with Mi-hsien, Têng-fêng, Tang-yang and Yü-hsien of major importance, while other minor centres were to be found in Shansi in Sung, Chin and Yüan times.

The type can be defined as a stoneware, fired at 1,200°C and upwards, whose body varies widely in colour and texture, grey, dirty white and buff being most usual, but with dark brown and dark grey known, especially among the later ware. The dark bodies continue until at least the end of the fourteenth century and probably even longer into the Ming in the fifteenth century. The glaze is normally transparent and may be colourless, or green or turquoise, the last not being introduced before the thirteenth century. The glaze is always applied over a slipped body. A variant type often associated with the name Tz'ŭ-chou has a black or intense dark brown glaze, and this will be considered in a following subsection.

The shapes are all those common to the traditions of north China and include the usual diversity of bowls, basins, jars, vases, including the special form known as *mei-p'ing* (Fig. 87), ewers, boxes and head-rests, as well as small figures, many intended, it is believed, as toys. The later examples of these may be decorated with polychrome lead glazes.

The decoration is technically the most varied of any ceramic type ever

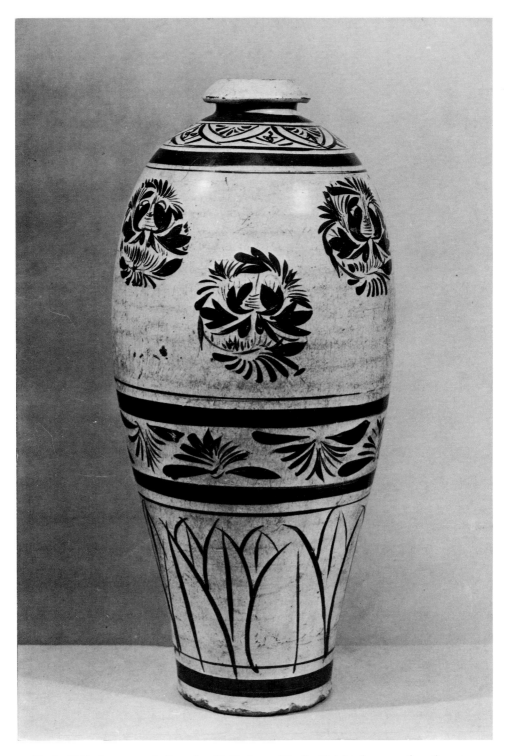

Fig. 87. Tz'ŭ-chou type *mei-p'ing* painted in black on white slip. Height 36.5 cm. 11th–12th century A.D. Bristol, City Art Gallery.

produced in China and includes carving, incising, *sgraffiato* with either one or two slips, slip painting, rouletting, polychrome lead glazing, overglaze polychrome enamelling, and glaze cutting, with occasional excursions into moulding. The motifs are at least as varied as the techniques, and include the full range of floral motifs, birds of almost every kind, animals, fish, waterweed, waves, landscapes and figures, as well as diaper patterns and ogival panels encircled by abstract scrolling designs, which ultimately have their source in floral designs. Because there is such diversity of technique and design it is most convenient to consider Tz'ǔ-chou in terms of the techniques employed.

SGRAFFIATO

This is perhaps the best-known technique and it persists from the late tenth century to at least the end of the fourteenth century. One of the two earliest kilns, Mi-hsien in eastern Honan, was certainly producing ware with this type of decoration by the beginning of the eleventh century, if not earlier, as the kiln is believed to have come into operation in late T'ang times.

Material excavated on the site indicates that the grey stoneware body was often covered with a thin slip coloured with haematite iron before the main application of the thick white slip. The decoration was then scratched and cut through the white slip, either to the grey stoneware body or just short of it, so that after the glazing and firing the body showed up either dark brownish grey, or red, the latter colour

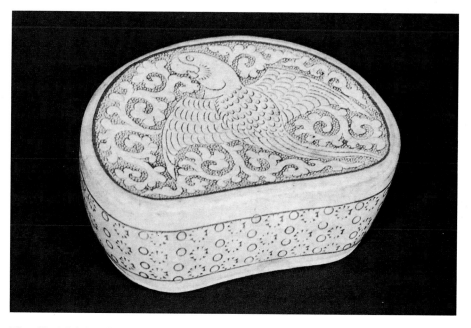

Fig. 88. Mi-hsien head-rest with *sgraffiato* decoration. Early 11th century A.D. Chinese Government.

being characteristic of the haematite slipped type. The background to the main decoration in early pieces was often 'ring-matted' using a piece of bamboo, a technique taken over directly from gold and silver metalwork and employed to throw the design up with strong emphasis on a flat surface (Fig. 88). The technique is common to all kilns, but is one often modified, especially in later

Fig. 89. Têng-fèng Hsien type vase with dished mouth and *sgraffiato* decoration. Height 39.7 cm. 11th century A.D. Washington, Freer Gallery of Art.

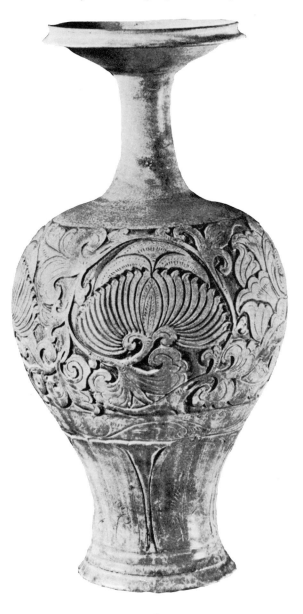

material, by substituting a striated ground made with a comb-like instrument for the more laborious ring-matting.

The logical step forward from this kind of textured ground was to cut it away altogether so that the decoration stood out even more emphatically against the dark ground. This was done at a large number of kilns, and at least one had its own very characteristic style. Fortunately the excavation of this kiln site has pin-

Fig. 90. Tz'ŭ-chou *mei-p'ing* with free painting. Height 35.4 cm. 12th century A.D. London, Victoria and Albert Museum.

Fig. 91. Tz'ŭ-chou truncated *mei-p'ing* with painted flower spray. Height 24.1 cm. 12th–13th century A.D. London, Victoria and Albert Museum.

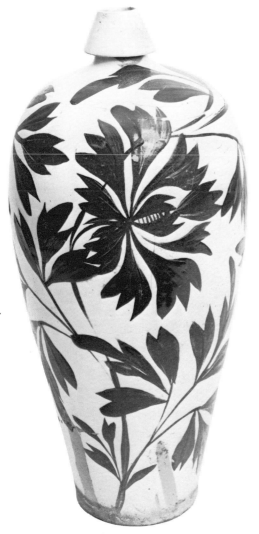
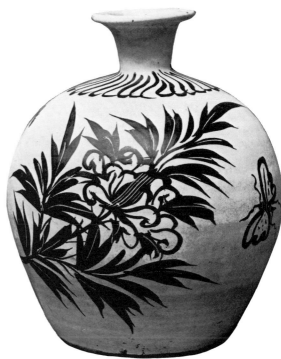

pointed one unique style which can be dated to the early period, as the kiln was one of several which suffered extinction at the end of the Northern Sung period early in the twelfth century. This was Têng-fêng Hsien in Honan, famous for its peculiar, sharp, deep cutting through the slip and for its unusual vase shape with long thin neck and dished mouth (Fig. 89). There were also a number of sturdy ewers based on a northern silver form with a wide straight shoulder, narrow cylindrical neck and a domed lid. The decoration of these is usually a rather strong floral scroll based on the peony. Floral decoration is generally preferred in the *sgraffiato* type, but in those pieces with a ring-matted ground the designs may include confronted animals, birds, and children, which echo the T'ang style in silver work, elements of which long survived in north China. *Sgraffiato* decoration is not usually found on the insides of bowls or dishes, but may occur on large basins; for obvious reasons the inequalities of surface even with a hard, high-fired glaze would tend to have practical disadvantages so far as cleaning was concerned. Nevertheless there is a group of basins and massive bowls, sometimes dark brown glazed outside, which have such decoration, usually with a striated ground. These seem to have come mainly from Yü-hsien in Honan.

SLIP PAINTING

Much more widespread and employed on all shapes was the painting of the white slip ground with a dark brown or black slip. The repertory of designs is vast and includes floral sprays and scrolls, birds, animals, figures, landscape scenes, and diaper designs, the last often used as fillers in odd corners. On small dishes, and sometimes on head-rests, inscriptions are used for decorative effect. Sometimes there is only a single character, but poems of varying length may be written with a casual boldness which is instantly attractive.

The technique was immensely popular and the density of colour varied from one kiln to another. Generally a neutral glaze was used, but green occurred quite often until about the thirteenth century, when turquoise glazing seems to have been introduced. When these glazes were used it was necessary to have a second firing because they would not stand up to a stoneware temperature.

There was some variation in the style of painting from one kiln to another and some pieces have been identified with specific kilns on this basis, but the prevalence of a common style usually makes provenance difficult to ascertain. Designs can be either free flowing over the whole surface, or confined to a series of bands. Both treatments are seen at their best on the numerous *mei-p'ing* vases, which were one of the most popular forms (Fig. 90). There are also detached sprays of flowers or bunches of lotus and other aquatic plants. These are particularly common on the form known as the truncated *mei-p'ing,* a shape fairly

Opposite: Plate III. Chün plate blue glazed and splashed with purple. Depth 18.6 cm. Late 13th century A.D. London, Percival David Foundation.

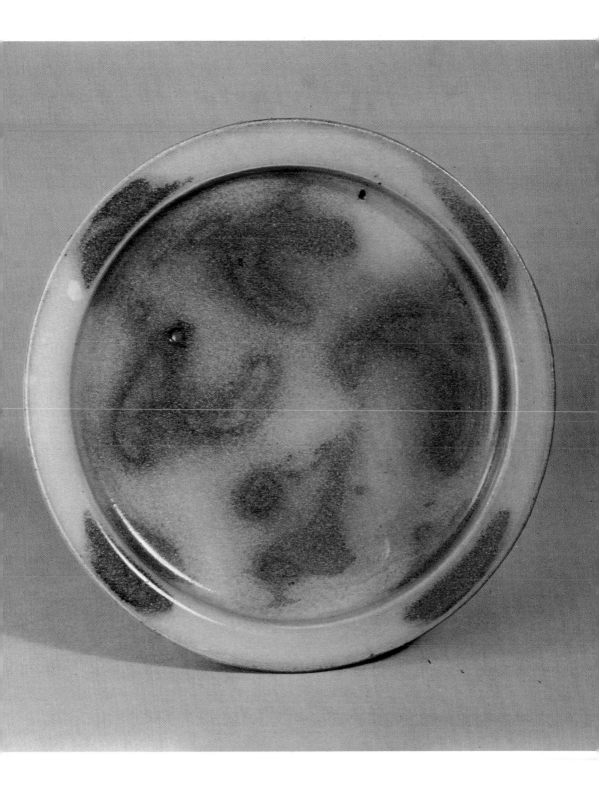

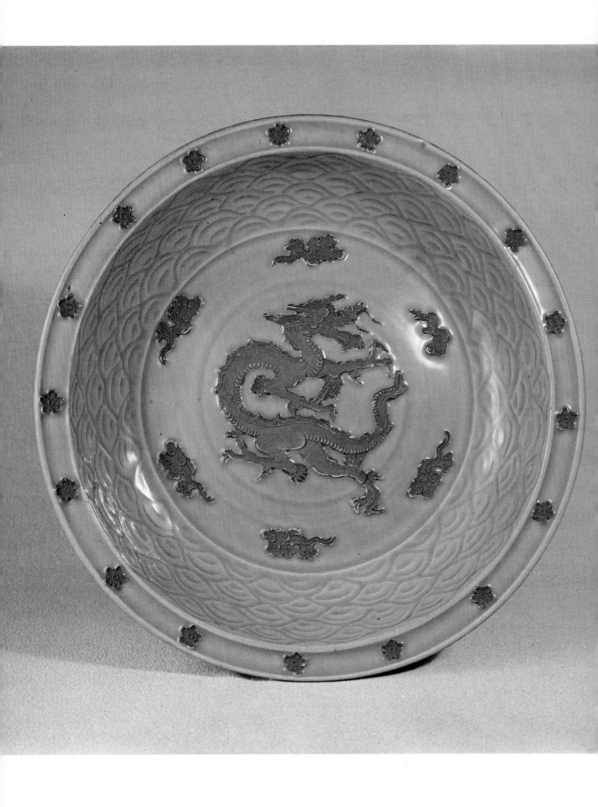

common in Tz'ŭ-chou type wares but rarely found in others, although known in Ting and in Northern Celadon (Fig. 91). Such detached sprays are also a frequent decoration painted on the vase often described as baluster shaped, which has an ovoid body, spreading foot and long neck expanding to a trumpet mouth, which may be deeply everted or turned down in a number of foliations.

From some time in the twelfth century onward many of the vases with black painted decoration were covered with a transparent green glaze coloured with copper oxide. These glazes, fluxed with lead, meant that the vessels had to be fired to a stoneware temperature before being decorated and were then fired a second time with the lead glaze to about 950°C. This type is particularly well known among the material from Hao-pi-chi and Yü-hsien.

Probably among the most important painted wares are those from Tz'ŭ-hsien itself. The ware from this district includes head-rests made by the Chang Company and bearing its seal. It was a family concern which specialized to a large extent in this type. The head-rests fall broadly into two groups, one rectangular with good flat sides, all surfaces admirably suited to sophisticated painting, and the other 'bean' shaped with an almost flat top surface, but rounded sides. On the rectangular type the top is painted with a landscape or a scene from some well-known anecdote. It reflects the painting style of the period and is often rather delicately executed (Fig. 92). On the vertical sides are animals and flower sprays treated with great boldness. The main scene on the top is often enclosed in a shaped panel, the spandrels at the corners being filled with loosely delineated peonies or pomegranates, and the whole framed by a meander pattern. The second group seems to have called forth a different style with bolder painting, often of only a single figure, while round the sides an abstract scroll decoration runs with great fluency. This same scrolling pattern is also seen on many of the sturdy jars. Some have covers which are painted at the same time as the body of the vessel so that the design runs freely over both parts. The design appears almost to be a hallmark of the Chang Company production and many sherds bearing the scroll have been found on the kiln site in Tz'ŭ-hsien.

PAINTED AND INCISED TYPE

A variant of the painted Tz'ŭ-chou type is that in which the application of the black is much more lavish. It is a thick layer of slip painted on in carefully calculated areas, and the details are then incised through to the white underneath. Sometimes the incising is bold, in some cases using a combing instrument, and at others it is finely carried out with a single fine point. The latter is more common in the later pieces, and continues into the fourteenth century (Fig. 93). In both cases the effect is bold and aesthetically pleasing. The technique is found mainly on jars

Opposite: Plate IV. Celadon plate with floated relief. Depth 43.2 cm. 14th century A.D. London, Percival David Foundation.

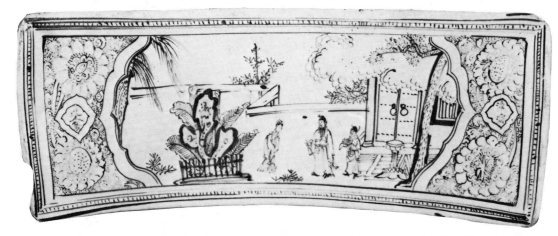

Fig. 92. Painted Tz'ŭ-chou head-rest. Length 43.2 cm. 13th century A.D. London, Victoria and Albert Museum.

of many sizes and shapes, tall vases, and on some head-rests. The glaze is usually colourless, but there are some green lead glazed examples in the twelfth and thirteenth centuries.

ROULETTED TYPE

The rouletting technique, which seems to have lapsed for many centuries, was used once more on a limited number of pieces. These were mostly deep cylindrical or slightly rounded deep bowls or barrel shaped jars, some of which have lids. On these the stoneware body was first covered with a white slip almost to the base, and then with a black slip, which generally stopped well short of the lower limit of the white. The roulette, which was of the simplest possible kind, consisting only of small ridges, was then rolled round in a slightly spiralling movement from top to bottom, with some overlapping (Fig. 94). Thereafter a colourless glaze was applied and the final result was a striking black and white patterning of the utmost simplicity. The Japanese attribute these pieces to Hsiu-wu in northern Honan, but it seems likely that they were also made at centres in the area south of the Yellow river such as Yü-hsien.

POLYCHROME LEAD GLAZING

In the post-T'ang centuries it was mainly at the kilns making the Tz'u-chou type ware that polychrome lead glazing survived. Such ware is more usually found in the north-eastern kilns, and in the Liao territory, the wares from which are discussed below. In the examples from the north-eastern Tz'u-chou kilns the body was generally pinkish or reddish earthenware, and, as was the common practice with the stoneware, it was often slipped before being decorated. The

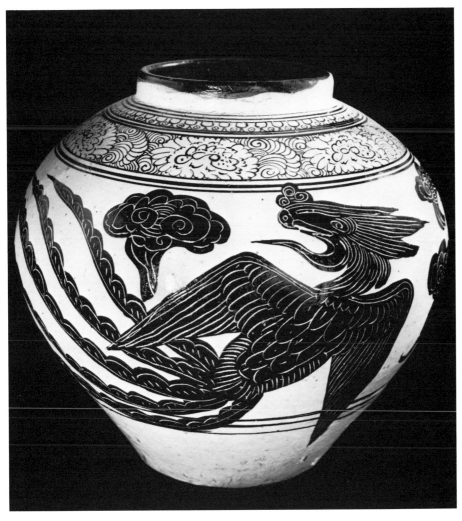

Above: Fig. 93. Tz'ŭ-chou wine jar with painted and incised design. Height 36 cm. Late 13th or 14th century A.D. Chinese Government.

Below: Fig. 94. Tz'ŭ-chou jar with rouletted surface. Height 10.7 cm. 12th–13th century A.D. Japan, Private Collection.

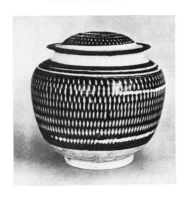

glaze colours are similar to those of the T'ang dynasty, but cobalt blue does not occur. The amber colour remains, but is sometimes brightened to a more distinctive yellow, which suggests the presence of antimony. On a very few examples there is brownish red which contains haematite iron. As we have already seen this was sometimes used as a covering to the body before the application of the white slip in the *sgraffiato* wares. The dating of the introduction of the brighter yellow and the red in this polychrome ware is very uncertain as little work has been undertaken on this aspect of Tz'ŭ-chou ware.

The only shapes on which the polychrome lead glazes were used were head-rests of various types, small bowls, and a few vases. The decoration was incised and then painted with the different colours. Floral designs and diaper patterns are among the most common, but on some of the head-rests, where the flatter surfaces were more convenient to work on, ducks in a pond, and scenes with children in landscape are found, the latter often being painted on a small scale and thus resembling more closely the central group of black painted head-rests.

POLYCHROME OVERGLAZE DECORATION

The latest technique to be introduced in the Tz'ŭ-chou stoneware was that of polychrome overglaze decoration using lead fluxed glazes. It was a technical advance which was to lead to interesting developments in the Ming and Ch'ing dynasties in later centuries. It is particularly important to recall at this point that polychrome effects under the glaze on high-fired stoneware are extremely limited on account of the thermal reaction. Bright colours are best produced using the low-fired glazes fluxed with lead. There is thus a conflict which has to be resolved if the bright colours are to be used on the high-fired wares.

The potters resolved this difficulty in the late twelfth century or early thirteenth century, when they took a white slipped stoneware piece, covered it with a transparent colourless glaze and fired it to the stoneware temperature in the usual manner. Then, after taking it from the kiln, they painted the glaze surface with coloured lead glazes and fired the piece a second time to the much lower temperature, between 800°C and 900°C, in a kiln which was fully protected from smoke and flame. Such treatment was sufficient to melt the lead glazes and fuse them to the main glaze without disturbing the equilibrium of the latter. This solution was to bring back into the technical repertory the lead glazes which had been in eclipse since the middle of the T'ang period. From now on the use of brightly coloured lead glazes for decorative purposes became fully established, and the colours earliest in use were green from a copper oxide, red from iron oxide (haematite) and yellow from a compound of antimony and iron. The last was less common than the red and green. At a much later stage black from a combination of iron and manganese was used, and a brown from iron oxide.

The most common decorative motifs in the early pieces, which cannot with certainty be dated before the beginning of the thirteenth century, were lotus

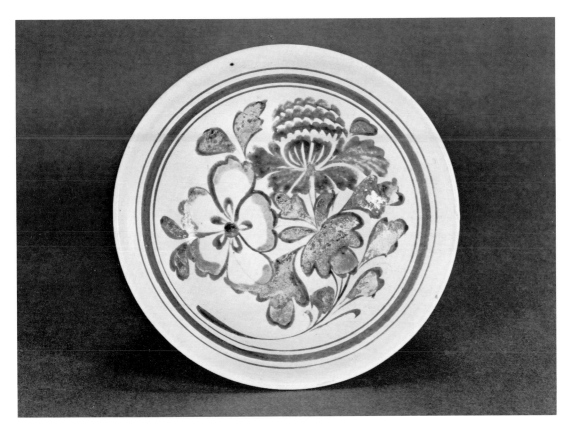

Fig. 95. Tz'ŭ-chou polychrome enamelled bowl. Diameter 8.9 cm. 13th century A.D. Osaka, Ataka Collection.

sprays, fish, birds in flight, peony sprays, mallow flowers and an assortment of Chinese characters. These provided a gay embellishment for the insides of bowls and the outsides of small jars (Fig. 95). To these were added, probably during the thirteenth century, small figures, perhaps intended as toys, with brightly coloured robes, which provide an interesting reflection of contemporary textile designs (Fig. 96). The hair and also some of the facial features are painted in a very dense black.

The Tz'ŭ-chou with this type of decoration continued over a long period, and by the late fourteenth century much larger surfaces were used such as those provided by the large wine jars, on which the decoration was often organized in roughly defined panels, bordered above by a floral scroll and below by a band of petals. On such large pieces the earlier floral decorations gradually gave way to landscape scenes with figures, some of which may be illustrations of popular stories. The technique seems to have remained a northern one, for it is not until the fifteenth century that it is possible to identify overglaze decorated pieces in the south, and then the body is a porcelain one and not a stoneware needing to be slipped.

The popularity of the type in the north was considerable and the bodies used varied from a fine almost white stoneware to a coarse dark brown ware, on which of course the use of a white slip was not only an advantage but a necessity. Precisely when and where the technique made its appearance and under what circumstances is a matter of speculation, but a Near Eastern origin cannot be ruled out. The centres which adopted polychrome decoration were clearly numerous, but so far the only kiln site certainly known to produce the type is that at Pa-ts'un in Honan. No doubt further excavations will bring other kilns to light.

CUT-GLAZED TYPE

This is a peculiar technique which constitutes a departure from normal practices. The striking effects produced are confined to a type with a grey body and a very dark brown or black glaze. The vessels were covered with a fairly thick glaze, which, while still damp, was incised and cut away from the body in bold designs in the same way as the *sgraffiato* slipped ware. In the firing, owing to the exceptional viscosity of the glaze, the incised lines and areas cut clear of glaze show the light body against the dark glaze; there is also a sharp contrast in texture between the high gloss of the dark surface and the dull, rough finish of the pale body. Most of the vessels on which this technique was employed were large pieces, such as wine jars and tall vases of both the *mei-p'ing* and pear-shaped forms (Fig. 97). Most characteristic are the massive globular jars with full rounded contour and small carinated mouth. The decoration is confined to bands on the upper part and tends to emphasize the robust quality of the swelling form, imparting to it an explosive character.

The designs are suitably large in scale and are organized as wide bands of floral scrolls, palmette scrolls and simple abstractions of foliage scrolls; there is a small number with fish and lotus, and one at least with a small boy among flowers, this being dated by an inscription to A.D. 1305 (Fig. 98). The technique does not seem to have been introduced until some time in the latter part of the twelfth century and it continued until at least the end of the Yüan period in the late fourteenth century. It is not precisely known where the type was made, but the Yü-hsien region in Honan is one likely area, while some of the simple incised examples probably came from the Pa-i kiln in northern Shansi.

Opposite top left: Fig. 96. Tz'ŭ-chou polychrome enamelled figure. Height 24.2 cm. Late 13th century A.D. New York, Metropolitan Museum of Art.

Opposite top right: Fig. 97. Cut-glazed stoneware vase of Tz'ŭ-chou type. Height 27.6 cm. 13th century A.D. Captain Dugald Malcolm.

Opposite bottom: Fig. 98. Cut-glazed stoneware bottle dated to A.D. 1305. Height 27.3 cm. London, British Museum.

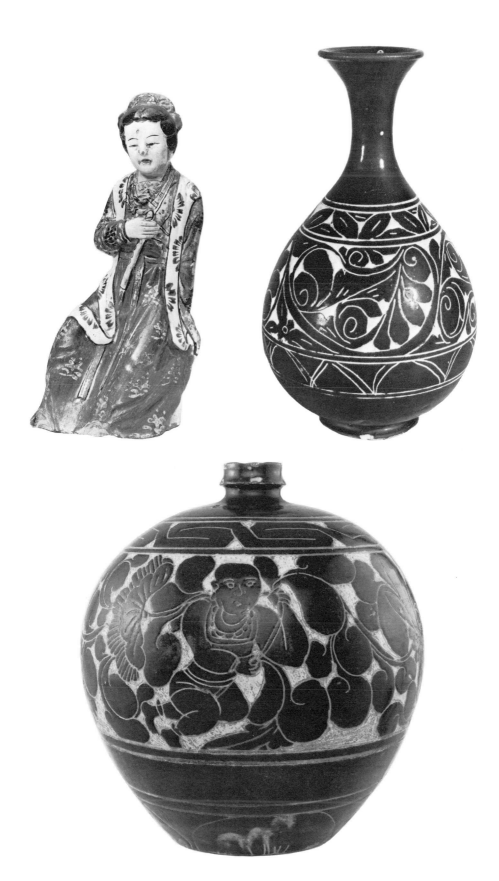

Black Wares

The black wares of north China are almost inseparable from the popular tradition of Tz'ǔ-chou, for not only are they similar in bodies, but are also made at many of the same centres. Moreover in most kinds of northern black ware the glaze is almost identical with that of the cut-glazed type described above. Nor do the similarities stop there, for most pieces are covered with a thick black slip before being given a transparent, and in this case, brown glaze. It is only in the decoration that distinctions can be made.

The body material is as varied as in the main stream of the Tz'ǔ-chou tradition, and the shapes too are as diverse, though often rather large. Bowls, ewers, wine jars and vases all have a place and continue from the late tenth century to at least the late fourteenth century. The glaze, like the slip which is more highly charged with iron oxide, includes a small amount of the same oxide, and by firing such pieces in an oxidizing atmosphere a dense black may be obtained. This in itself was evidently not thought particularly interesting by the Chinese potters and they tried varying the firing technique and the colour balance of glaze and slip. In so doing they introduced a number of attractive and intriguing decorative effects.

It was found, for instance, that by introducing a period of reduction towards the end of the firing cycle the excessive amounts of iron in the underlying slip could be made to precipitate out in a crystalline form to produce what is called 'oil spot', an attractive lustrous effect which became popular on small bowls and ewers (Fig. 99). The next step was slightly to reduce the iron content of the slip, paint highly abstract birds and flower sprays over it with a highly concentrated iron oxide, apply a transparent glaze and then fire using a similar reduction firing cycle. This resulted in the decoration standing out, sometimes elusively, against a lustrous dark brown background. A variant was to reverse the balance of slip and painting, so that the painted part contained less iron than the slip, a treatment which resulted in a rust brown decoration against an almost black ground (Fig. 100).

A different approach is the use of white slip in combination with dark glaze. A handsome example of this is a *mei-p'ing* with a floral decoration carried out very boldly in white slip on a dark buff body, the whole then being covered with a

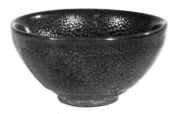

Fig. 99. Northern black ware bowl with oil-spot glaze. Diameter 9.2 cm. 12th–13th century A.D. Honolulu Academy of Arts.

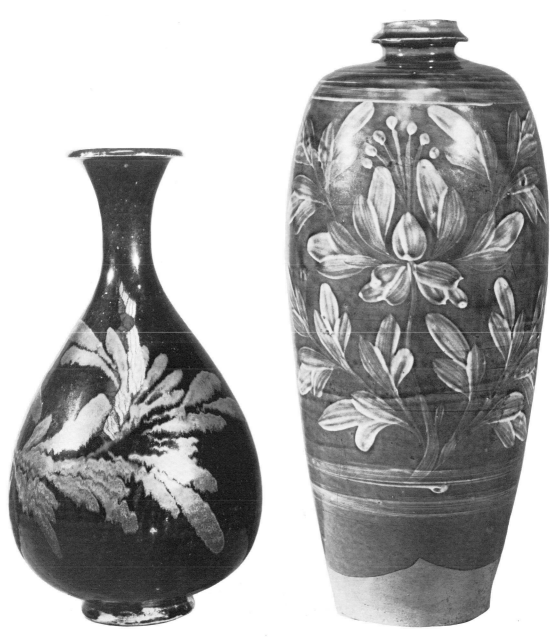

Fig. 100. Northern black ware vase painted with a bird in flight in brown. Height 27.5 cm. 13th century A.D. London, British Museum.

Fig. 101. Tz'ŭ-chou *mei-p'ing* painted in white slip under a transparent brown glaze. Height 34.9 cm. 13th century A.D. London, British Museum.

transparent light brown glaze (Fig. 101). But it was more usual to apply a black slip and then trail ribs down from top to bottom in white slip before covering with a transparent pale brown glaze. The brown glaze was less viscous than that on other types and so tended to some extent to run off the slip relief ribs, the result is that the ribs show up a light cream colour against a lustrous dark brown or black. The technique seems to have been popular on large jars, vases and ewers, and although in most cases the ribs are numerous and equidistant from one another, they are sometimes grouped in twos or threes (Fig. 102). A point of some interest is that this use of vertical ribbing is normally only found on relatively upright and cylindrical shapes. It is rare to find it on full swelling globular or spherical bodies; an instance of the Chinese potter's appreciation of what is aesthetically suitable to a shape.

One odd little group of bowls deserves special mention. These are small and low, about ten centimetres in diameter, often conical, but also known with slightly rounded sides. The body is usually pale greyish white and black glazed except for the foot and base. After glazing a band of the glaze was cut neatly away for up to a centimetre from the rim, both inside and outside. This was then coated with white slip and separately glazed with a neutral or slightly creamy glaze. The result after firing was a glossy black bowl with a wide white band round the rim; a handsome, if slightly startling, effect.

The kilns producing these different types were very widespread, as one must expect when a ware is popular, but the Yü-hsien region had a large output of various kinds of black ware, and some of the white ribbed type certainly came from there.

The dating presents almost insuperable problems, partly because the tradition of black glazing goes back into the T'ang dynasty, but also because of the wide distribution of the type among the kilns of north China. Production of black wares of various kinds continued well into the fourteenth century if not later. In addition it is necessary to remember that it was a popular ware, probably used in most households, so that, lacking the adulation of the aristocratic collector, nothing is recorded in the literature. In broad terms one can probably assume that the larger and more massive pieces are likely to be later, since it was not until very late in the twelfth century and in the thirteenth century that really large pots began to be made.

Liao Pottery

The Khitans, originating in the north-eastern territory of Manchuria, achieved a national identity and established themselves as an independent state during the latter part of the T'ang dynasty. They acquired a territory that included Manchuria, Inner Mongolia almost as far west as Beshbalik, and the northern parts of the modern provinces of Hopei and Shansi, which they appropriated on

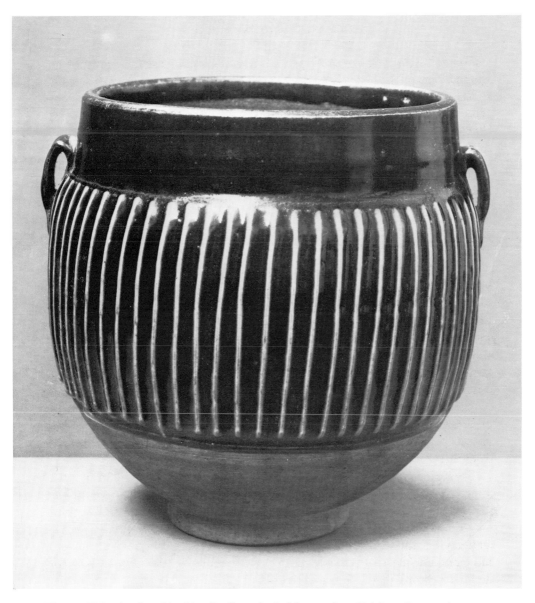

Fig. 102. Tz'u-chou jar with white slip ribs and a dark brown glaze. Height 17.8 cm. 13th century A.D. London, Victoria and Albert Museum.

the fall of the T'ang. In 929 they adopted the dynastic title of Liao and set seriously about the task of acquiring a veneer of Chinese culture. But although they accepted much from the Chinese the degree of acculturation was limited, and in their art they remained highly individual.[12]

Despite the alien character of Liao culture and the obvious divergences from the central Chinese ceramic tradition, it holds a position in the technical evolution which cannot be ignored in any history of Chinese ceramics. The Liao inherited the T'ang tradition of polychrome lead glazing together with some of the forms associated with the lead glazed ware. Subsequently they fed back what they themselves had developed from this inheritance, and it was this which was immensely beneficial to Chinese progress. Some of the kiln sites of the northern region are known, but few have been subjected to more than preliminary exploration, so we know nothing of where the technical developments took place. However, enough is known about the wares to distinguish the different types fairly easily,[13] although some of the chronology is still uncertain. There are three main types of ware: lead glazed earthenware, stoneware, and a porcellanous ware, the last mainly composed of small pieces. Most shapes may be found in all three kinds of body material.

The earthenware bodies are generally red or reddish brown, varying from a fine grained compact type to one of rather coarse, open structure. The firing was very often near the maximum for earthenware, so that some pieces are hard and resonant. The monochrome pottery is generally covered with a white slip to conceal the strongly coloured body, and this frequently shows as a narrow whitish band between the base of the vessel and the lower limit of the glaze.

The stoneware bodies may be coloured like the earthenware ones or be a pale greyish white. The pale body is usually finer grained than the coloured one and is much more compact. The porcellanous body is hard and thin and almost white; occasionally, like the earthenware and some of the stoneware, it is slipped.

The shapes of Liao pottery are distinctive and, among the closed forms, the wine flasks and tall vases are particularly unusual. The wine flasks include many based on a leather bottle. They have a bag-shaped body with a spout to one side at the top and a loop handle, which is sometimes finger pinched or made in the form of a twist of rope (Fig. 103). Some of the flasks are rather tall and have applied slip relief ribs and other ornament, others are squat and rotund, and again may have relief ornament. A superior type of this flask is represented by a few with a stopper for the spout and two holes for suspension in place of the loop handle. Examples of this kind are tall, less obviously bag-shaped, and may have incised scrolling decoration on the sides.

The vases, mostly of inverted pear-shaped form with a long neck, can be divided into three groups of which the most characteristically Liao is the cock's head vase. The neck is usually long and cylindrical with horizontal ribbing and it ends in a bird's head surmounted by a cupped mouth. In profile this somewhat resembles a cock's comb (Fig. 104). Some of these have incised floral decoration on the body, either a roughly sketched spray or a more carefully executed scroll. There seems to have been a strong liking for cupped or dished mouths to the tall vases, and they are found in green or yellow or white; the white ones sometimes with discreet touches of green. Vases with the true dished mouth are usually of very good quality and are found mainly in the stoneware and porcellanous ware. In shape the porcellanous ones closely resemble the Tz'ŭ-chou type manufac-

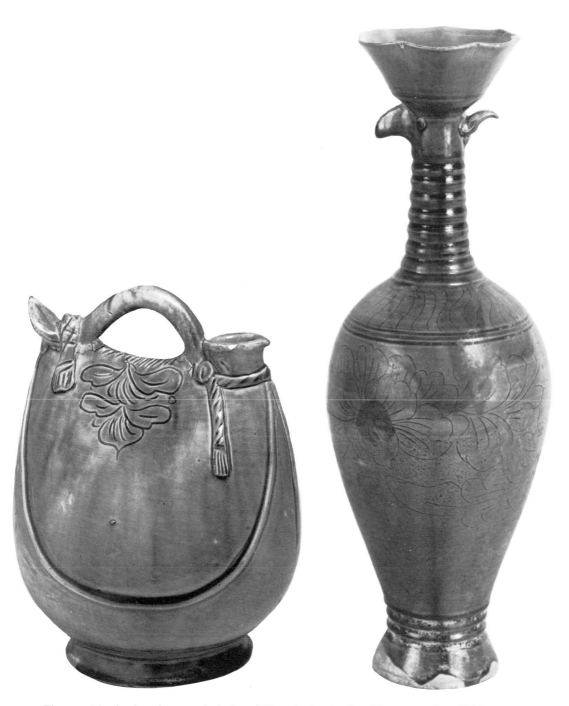

Fig. 103. Liao hard earthenware flask shaped like a leather bottle, with a green glaze. Height 23.5 cm. 10th–11th century A.D. Asian Art Museum of San Francisco, Brundage Collection.

Fig. 104. Liao vase with cock's head top and incised decoration; green glazed. Height 38.2 cm. 11th century A.D. Tokyo, National Museum.

tured at Têng-fêng and there may be some kind of influence from one to the other, but in which direction is not known.

The third type of vase is much rougher and, while the body is still the same inverted pear, the neck is wider, long and expanding to a straight lip. These are normally found in hard earthenware, slipped and covered with a green or warm amber brown glaze.

Ewers attributable to the Liao are varied, some depending directly on Chinese T'ang pottery and others on the metalwork traditions of the north common to both China and Liao. Others appear to be Liao inventions like the tall melon-shaped type with a high looped handle; there is also a gourd-shaped type with a rather small upper bulb. The tall melon-shaped ewers are well finished and have a porcellanous body, but the gourd-shaped ones may be in any of the three ceramic body materials.

Well-rounded jars with a wide straight mouth, or with a small neck rolled at the lip, occur equally in earthenware and stoneware and may have incised decoration or polychrome glazed decoration, or both. Stoneware examples are usually covered with a white glaze and if painted it is generally with florets or grouped dots. The latter type is well finished and reminiscent of some of the Tz'ŭ-chou. More closely and obviously connected with Tz'ŭ-chou, probably directly

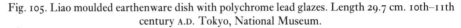

Fig. 105. Liao moulded earthenware dish with polychrome lead glazes. Length 29.7 cm. 10th–11th century A.D. Tokyo, National Museum.

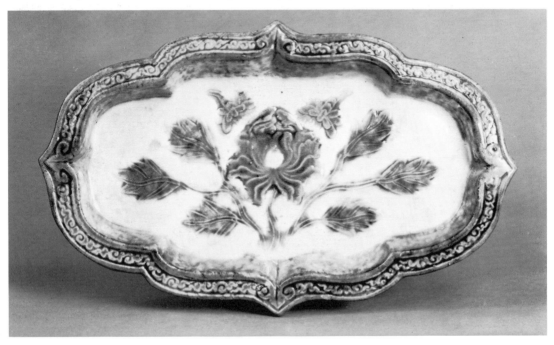

imitating the type, are some *mei-p'ing* vases and stout jars with bands of incised floral decoration with combed detail reserved in white against a dark brown background band.

The range of dishes and bowls is large and many are unusual. They are found in lead glazed earthenware and in porcellanous material. The shapes of many bowls and dishes are dependent on late T'ang metalware, or on silver forms which the Liao people themselves evolved. The simpler rounder shapes with only incised decoration or none at all are thrown on the wheel, but the more eccentric ones were constructed over moulds (Fig. 105). They are generally polychrome glazed.

It was this technique, which, with the incorporation of decorative motifs in the moulds, was to be the most important innovation and was to have the most influence in China about the beginning of the twelfth century. The decorations were usually floral, often rather stiff, but there are also some dishes with fish among waves and some with lotus blossoms. The earthenware examples occur in monochrome green or amber brown, and also in polychrome. The polychrome ones are generally slipped, for on these the colourless glaze is used to produce white, which would not otherwise be possible on a coloured body.

The porcellanous wares, which are less numerous than the earthenwares and

Fig. 106. Liao lobed porcelain bowl. Diameter 13 cm. 11th century A.D. London, Percival David Foundation.

Fig. 107. Back of Liao porcelain bowl inscribed *Hsin-kuan*. London, Percival David Foundation.

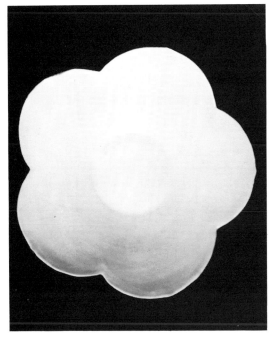
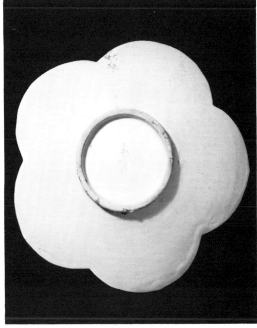

stonewares, are with few exceptions relatively small. They include the melon-shaped ewers referred to above, and some very thin, exceptionally white bowls of either conical or rounded form, some straight at the rim and others lobed or foliated (Figs. 106, 107). On the base of some of these is incised the character *kuan*, 'official', or the two characters *hsin-kuan*, 'new official'. These have been taken to mean that pieces so inscribed were intended for the Liao ruling house. It is not known where they were made, and it is not impossible that they may in some cases have come from the Ting kilns, since it is known that the Liao imported a certain quantity of material, and had in any case taken possession of the kilns for a short time in the eleventh century.

The study of Liao ceramics is still in its infancy, and the excavation of kiln sites, some of which were identified in the 1940s, has yet to be systematically undertaken. Finds from dated tombs discovered in the twenty years following the end of the war have added much to our knowledge of the range of shapes and indicate the dating of certain pottery forms, but much remains to be done. The contribution of moulding as a method of constructing whole pieces was of the greatest importance, since it opened the way for the development of an industrialized production. This would have amazed the Liao people, and it put China far ahead of any other country.

CHAPTER SIX

South China from the Tenth
to the Fourteenth Century

The Yüeh kilns, as we have already seen, were not only prolific, but the quality of their products was also sufficiently distinguished to stimulate potters in other areas, especially in Chekiang, to manufacture comparable pottery. During the tenth century many new kilns opened in the south and others already in existence, such as those in the vicinity of Wên-chou on the coast, tried to improve their wares. Nevertheless progress towards the kind of refinement seen in the north during the period of the Northern Sung dynasty, that is up to about A.D. 1127, was slow, mainly because the patronage of the southern kilns was less wealthy and sophisticated. This lack of superior patronage affected kilns producing other kinds of pottery, such as those at Chi-chou in southern Kiangsi, Chien-yang in Fukien, and ultimately the most important of all, those in the region of Jao-chou in northern Kiangsi, all of which catered for the local domestic markets of south China, and to some extent for the overseas trade to South-East Asia and the Philippines.

Since they had lacked sophisticated patronage, most of the southern kilns only attained their apogee during the late twelfth and thirteenth centuries, when the Sung court settled at Hangchou in northern Chekiang following the flight from K'ai-fêng in 1127. This placed the court in a new proximity to the southern kilns, on which they were henceforth compelled to rely for the satisfaction of their needs. During the following centuries the kilns flourished not only as the result of the court and the new metropolitan patronage of Hangchou, which became a wealthy and extravagant city, but also as the result of foreign patronage. The government, recognizing the need for high revenues to ward off the threat from the north, now did much to encourage the overseas trade, and foreign merchants took advantage of this to make constant and often heavy demands on the potteries, for Chinese ceramic wares far surpassed any produced elsewhere.

Of the wares which enjoyed both types of patronage, it was Lung-ch'üan type celadon which gained pre-eminence in the period up to the middle of the fourteenth century. The related Kuan ware was intended primarily for the court and for the wealthier members of society. The Chi-chou ware was mainly for local consumption, but was also popular as a less costly export ware in South-East Asia and the Philippines, while the Chien-yang ware, again for local use, enjoyed great popularity with the Japanese. The Jao-chou kilns, which made the *ch'ing-pai* type for both domestic and foreign use, became so much more important in the fourteenth century that they surpassed all other centres with the possible exception of Lung-ch'üan. It is therefore convenient to discuss these different centres in this order, for the products of Jao-chou lead on into the later traditions.

Lung-ch'üan

The stoneware and porcellanous ware which is usually named Lung-ch'üan, or southern celadon, was the product of a great number of kilns in central and

Kiln sites of south China from the tenth century.

southern Chekiang and the extreme north of Fukien. Lung-ch'üan, which gives its name to the Chekiang celadon wares, was the chief market town and was situated on the Hsi river. Also of major importance as a market centre was Ch'u-chou, whose earlier name was Li-shui. This city lay farther north at the point where the Hsi river was joined by the Chiao and Han rivers. Some of the kilns producing the finest quality ware lay well to the south, high up in the steep mountain valleys characteristic of the southern half of the province. Among these the best known and most recently investigated are Ch'i-k'ou, Ta-yao and Chin-ts'un, the last being over the provincial border in northern Fukien. Without documented material it is difficult to distinguish the products of the various kilns, but in the later stages it is clear that some began to specialize in certain shapes and decorative techniques, for it is possible to group the later ware on the basis of technique and style.

The body material varies, apparently at all kilns, from a heavy, compact grey stoneware to an almost white porcellanous material. Except in the finest whitish bodied pieces the exposed foot burns a bright reddish brown, a characteristic which easily distinguishes the southern type of celadon from that of the northern provinces. The glaze is opaque grey green or grey blue, and despite its opacity the whitish bodied type may be translucent if thin enough. The glaze owes its colour to a small amount of iron oxide and a reduction firing cycle. The actual tone of the glaze, whether more green or more blue, is dependent on both the temperature and the stage at which reduction is begun. The opacity is caused by the presence of plant ash and a close bubble structure which tends to scatter the light. The firing temperature is reported to fluctuate between 1,180°C and 1,280°C. The greener pieces were usually fired in the upper end of the bracket, between about 1,250 and 1,280°C.[1]

The kilns were of a standard down-draught design, but, instead of each standing in isolation like the horseshoe shaped type of the north, the south-eastern kilns were built in a series of interconnected chambers each a step higher up the hillside, climbing to a considerable height; a type of construction referred to by the Chinese as dragon kilns (see drawing on page 148). The number of chambers would vary according to the space available on the hillside, but the ones excavated at Ta-yao appear to have had approximately ten to twelve chambers, and a rough estimate made by the Chinese archaeologists suggests that these kilns could fire from 20,000 to 25,000 pieces in a single setting. This gives some indication of the size of the industry at this time.[2] The fire box and main stoke-hole was at the foot of the slope and there were additional stoke-holes at intervals up the slope on one side, and peep-holes on the other side, so that the temperature and state of the firing could be checked at regular intervals throughout the firing period. The kilns were fired from the lowest level first, the uppermost chambers being fired last and finishing last. The system had its advantages and disadvantages, for while control of reduction was relatively easy, the ware in the lower chambers was less good

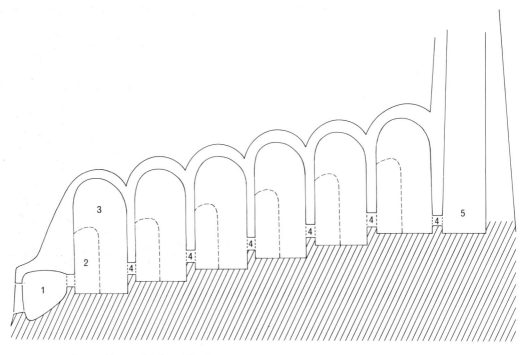

Lung-ch'üan 'dragon kiln': 1. Fire box; 2. Entry to chamber; 3. Firing chamber; 4. Fire vents; 5. Chimney.

quality than that in the top ones. This was due to the shorter time taken to raise the temperature at the lower end compared with the upper end, where the warming up period was extended and very even. Thus the finest and most expensive material usually came from the upper chambers. All the pots were fired in saggars, some of which must have been massive to accommodate the many very large pieces which were made from about the middle of the thirteenth century onward.

The shapes were those common to most kilns, with bowls of simple well-balanced form predominating. There were also vases of various kinds including the so-called mallet vase, with a stout cylindrical body, straight sloping shoulders and long narrow tubular neck with a widely flattened mouth rim (Fig. 109); handles in the shape of fish, or dragon or phoenix forequarters were usually added to the neck. Archaic bronzes, which at the time were immensely admired by the scholar class, provided a special source of inspiration and are more frequently found in the Lung-ch'üan ware than any other, the *li* tripod, *kuei* (Fig. 108), *tsun* and *ku* shapes proving most popular. Better adjusted to foreign taste were the large basins, massive dishes and plates, and wine jars, often with lids (Fig. 110), which began to be made in increasing quantities from the later years of the thirteenth century, once the prosperity of the kilns had become securely established.

The wheel was generally used and large vases were often constructed of several

148

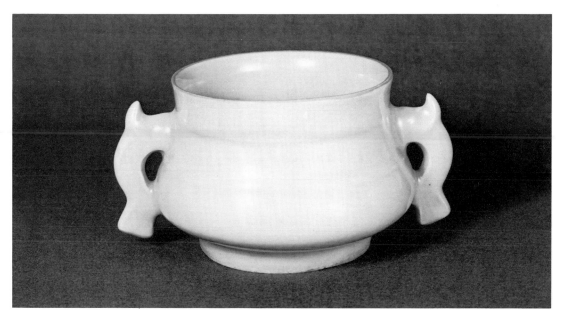

Above: Fig. 108. Lung-ch'üan celadon *kuei* form. Diameter 18.5 cm. 13th century A.D. London, Percival David Foundation.

Below left: Fig. 109. Lung-ch'üan celadon mallet vase. Height 30.7 cm. 12th–13th century A.D.

Below right: Fig. 110. Lung-ch'üan wine jar with carved decoration. Height 27.6 cm. 13th–14th century A.D. Philadelphia, Museum of Art.

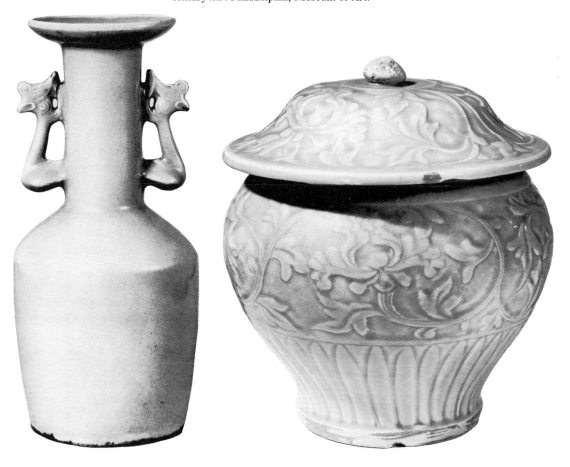

thrown parts stacked one on top of another and luted together. The *ku* and *tsun* shapes are examples of such stacked pieces, but there were many others, including a small number of ewers based on Near Eastern metal forms. Such forms were inevitably an important source of inspiration, since so much was exported to that area (Fig. 111). More eccentric shapes such as the *li* tripod might also be made of thrown parts luted together in various ways. The *li* was usually made as a bowl with a wide straight neck and flattened rim, and the three separate, partly hollow legs were very neatly luted on to the base, with a small air vent at the top of each on the underside as a necessary precaution against the explosive shattering of the piece in firing. Moulding was less common in Lung-ch'üan ware than in some others of the period, but when used it was often for mass production of quite simple shapes like globular jars, which were made in two parts luted together round the middle; sometimes decoration would be included in the mould. Such pieces were often fired without any attempt being made to tidy up the base, so that the foot-ring is only vestigial and the surface rough. The really large plates and dishes were normally made over a mould and the cutting of the foot varied from one piece to another. For pieces with a straight rim it seems likely that the fast wheel and template was used, while sufficient clay was left on the base area to make the cutting of the foot-ring a simple matter. If this were not the method, it would be difficult to account for the extraordinary consistency in size and thickness of this very numerous class. For pieces with a foliate rim the use of twin moulds was a necessity and here again remarkable consistency is found.

Decoration, if used at all, was at first confined to simple carved lotus petals round the outside of some of the bowls. Evidently the sensuous appeal of the colour and texture of the glaze on the extremely simple forms exerted so strong an attraction as to inhibit the decorator, and there is no doubt that deliberate attempts were made to produce a glaze that resembled jade in both colour and texture. Gradually, however, carved decoration was increased and became more elaborate. In the fourteenth century it was often extremely bold, although it did not at any time disrupt the contours, being perhaps consciously subordinated to the form (Fig. 113). Only in a few very late pieces dating from the fifteenth century does the decoration exceed the bounds of good taste.

From about the middle of the thirteenth century sprig-moulded elements began to appear, starting with a pair of fish rotating round a conceptual centre in the bottom of a dish. To this motif were added peonies or pomegranate flowers and leaves on vases and large drum-shaped jars. Dragons vigorously pursuing flaming pearls appeared on the bottom of massive plates. All these were sprigged directly to the body and the thick glaze lies over them, undulating slightly, but allowing the design to show through clearly, especially where the glaze lies more thinly over the finely modelled relief and shows the pale colour of the body. A later development in the fourteenth century was the continued use of sprig moulds, but with the decorations laid on top of the unfired glaze, a practice only possible on

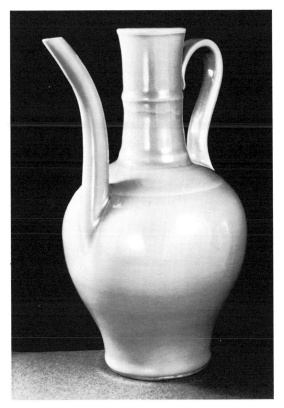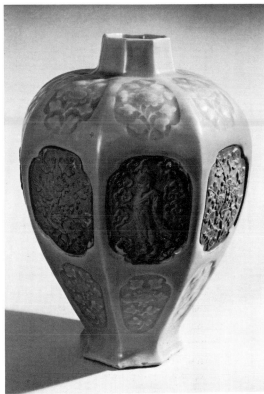

Fig. 111. Lung-ch'üan celadon ewer of Near Eastern metal form. Height 27 cm. 14th century A.D. London, Percival David Foundation.

Fig. 112. Lung-ch'üan celadon *mei-p'ing* with resist decoration. Height 24.5 cm. 14th century A.D. London, Percival David Foundation.

pieces whose decorated surface would lie in the horizontal plane in the firing. This would seal the unglazed relief to the glaze, and because the clay body burned reddish brown where exposed, the result was a contrasting colour and texture against the grey green of the glaze (Plate IV, opposite page 129). On a sloping or vertical surface this technique of floating a relief on the glaze was impossible because the weight of the relief would cause it to slip or distort as the glaze melted in the firing. It was an attractive, but purely ornamental effect, the reliefs often being so large that the piece would have been useless for practical purposes. In some cases the clay of the sprigs was coloured, or coloured slips were used. An example of the latter may be seen on a number of small dishes with a rock, prunus spray, and crescent moon, a design particularly familiar in the thirteenth and fourteenth centuries.

In order to obtain the same kind of effect on a sloping or vertical surface a different technique had to be evolved, and it is of some interest that the kilns making pieces using the different technique did not employ the floating technique, or *vice versa*. The solution to the problem of slipping or distorting was to mould the whole piece with the decoration incorporated in the mould. Before glazing, those parts intended to be burned reddish were painted with a resist medium, either wax or grease, to which the glaze failed to adhere. In the firing the resist would be burned off, leaving no trace, and the final effect would be similar to that of the floated type (Fig. 112), and could similarly be coloured if that was desired. In one or two cases the unglazed sections appear to have been gilt, a practice which would scarcely enhance this type of decoration in modern eyes.

One further decorative technique should be mentioned; like the foregoing it failed to survive beyond the end of the fourteenth century. This was to add spots of high percentage iron oxide to the surface of the body before glazing, so that dark brown spots occurred at intervals on the green surface after the firing. The higher percentage of iron ensured that even in reducing conditions the dark colour resulted. This seems to have been a spontaneous introduction of a technique originally used in the proto-Yüeh of the fifth century. Pieces decorated in this way are called *tobi-seiji*, 'spotted green wares', by the Japanese. In a few exceptional cases copper oxide has been used to give red spots on the grey green ground.

The dating of Lung-ch'üan celadon is not particularly easy for there is little real help to be gained from the character and colour of the glaze as so often suggested by the Japanese. Broadly it can be said that the smaller and simpler pieces, with little or no decoration, and a finely finished foot-ring, are earlier than the larger and heavier pieces, which are sometimes elaborately decorated. The decoration in fact tends to become heavier, bolder and more elaborate as time passes. The foot-ring also becomes thicker and less well finished. In the fourteenth-century vases and jars, and occasionally the dishes, the whole base is cut out, and the aperture thus formed is closed with a small dish, or a relief moulded plaque in the form of a flower head, and then sealed in place with the glaze. At first sight this appears a senseless arrangement, but evidently there were problems of shrinkage in drying to be overcome, and the solution was to put the dish or flower relief in place immediately prior to glazing.[3] Also characteristic of the later plates and dishes is the practice either of glazing over the whole foot-ring and then leaving an unglazed ring on the base for a setting stand, or leaving the whole base unglazed; the marks of the fireclay setting stands or rings can often be seen as black stained areas on the base.

Kuan Ware

Closely related to Lung-ch'üan is Kuan ware, 'official' ware, which was indistinguishably imitated by some of the Lung-ch'üan potters. Like Lung-ch'üan celadon the glaze is coloured with an iron oxide and fired in a reducing atmosphere, but it has certain peculiarities which distinguish it decisively from its greener relative.

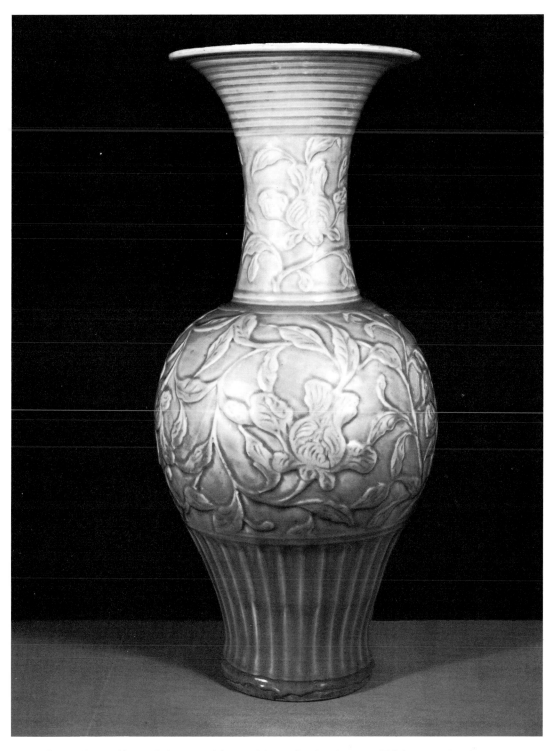

Fig. 113. Lung-ch'üan celadon vase with carved decoration dated to 1327. Height 72 cm. London, Percival David Foundation.

The manufacture of Kuan appears to have been inspired by the Sung court's desire to find a substitute for the high quality ware of Lin-ju Hsien and Ju-yao with which it had been familiar in the north. The materials in the south were necessarily different, so that the new ware, which can hardly have appeared before about the middle of the twelfth century, had nothing in common with any northern ware, apart from the iron content of the glaze; it was in fact something quite novel.

According to tradition the imperial household set up a kiln under the direction of the Hsiu-nei-sŭ, the Imperial Household Department of Buildings, in the palace precincts at Hangchou, to make the finest quality material. No site has ever been discovered, nor have the products been identified with any certainty. On the outskirts of Hangchou, however, during road building operations in 1929 a kiln known as Chiao-t'an, Altar of Heaven kiln, was discovered, and our knowledge of Kuan is largely based on the materials recovered from the rather unsystematic work carried out on this site, work which it must be confessed was more in the nature of plundering than of excavation. As the result of more recent excavation in the Lung-ch'üan region it is now known that at least two of the kilns further south, Ta-yao and Ch'i-k'ou, also made what has been defined as Kuan and is indistinguishable from the Chiao-t'an material, though some of the shapes are said to differ. At Chiao-t'an not only was much waster material and kiln furniture discovered, such as spurred stands and saggars, but a deposit of dark clay was also identified. Unfortunately little attempt was made at the time to analyse the raw material and the evidence that such work might have yielded has been lost.

The traditions handed down in the literature make it clear that the new ware was greatly admired and valued, and also that it was available in certain different qualities. The differences in quality are in fact quite easily defined, with a delicate pale grey-blue glaze, widely crackled on a very thin black body as the finest (Fig. 114). The second quality was duller and greener in colour, more closely crackled and still on a black body, while the third quality was almost a pale grey brown with a very dark close crackle on a dark grey body, somewhat thicker than the black one. It tended to burn a purplish brown on the foot-ring and to show dark at the rim where the glaze ran thin (Fig. 115).

The variations in crackle and glaze colour were evidently achieved by changes in the firing cycle, that is by varying the temperature at which reduction was introduced. The crackle itself is due to a difference in the coefficient of expansion between the body and the glaze, so that in cooling the tensions created caused cracks to appear. The effect is normally regarded as a serious fault and potters try to avoid it, because not only does it imply a badly constituted ill-fitting glaze, but it also weakens the body structure. In modern kiln practice special types of glaze

Opposite: Fig. 114. Kuan ware vase with wide crackled grey blue glaze. Height 18.1 cm. 13th century A.D. London, Percival David Foundation.

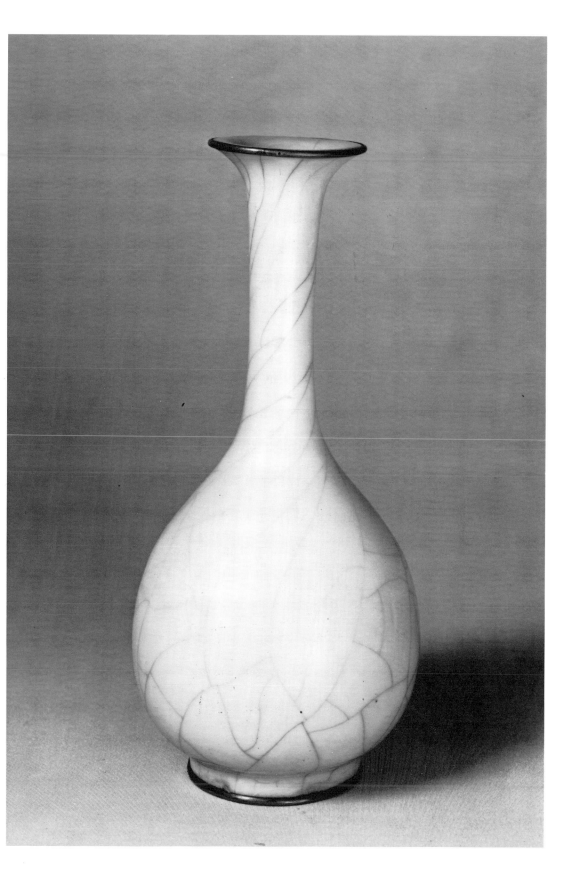

have been developed, which produce the same sort of visual impact without the practical disadvantage. The Chinese effect was almost certainly accidental in the first instance, but the potters learned to exploit it for its aesthetic effect. One of the means by which it could be induced was by applying the glaze in several layers, one after another, before firing. Examination of sections of sherds under a magnifying glass show up to four or five such layers. Examination also shows that in the best quality specimens the total thickness of the glaze was greater than that of the body, which is like a thin slice of clay sandwiched between two thick glassy walls. The difficulties in firing such material successfully must have been phenomenal and such as would daunt most potters. The wastage must have been enormous with pieces shattering and warping in every firing, quite apart from those which failed to emerge from the kiln with the right kind of colour.

The shapes are generally simple, the contour of thrown pieces displaying a smooth natural curvature with only rare additions, such as handles for the copies of archaic bronze *kuei*, which were as popular in Kuan as in Lung-ch'üan celadon (Fig. 116). Bowls, dishes, saucers and brush-washers were the most common shapes together with a few vases of sophisticated character and some copies of the ancient bronze *hu* vase form. It was only in the fourteenth century that some of the Kuan ware became large, heavy and sometimes angular, with decoration in low relief disrupting the smooth flowing line of the body (Fig. 117). Such angular pieces were naturally constructed in moulds, the different parts being luted together, with any imperfections in the joins camouflaged by the thick, opaque glaze. Among such examples are a number in imitation of the ancient ritual jade shape, the *tsung*. These were made either by slab moulding each of the four sides and the base and mouth, or by throwing a cylindrical central section and luting on four moulded angular elements; the latter method meant that the piece became exceptionally heavy.

The interest in archaic bronzes and jades is an important aspect of Chinese taste in the Southern Sung period and is very largely due to the antiquarian interests of the scholar class. These embraced the bronzes and jades of both Shang and Chou times together with the study, often very systematic, of the early inscriptions. Catalogues, with woodcut illustrations, such as that of the collection of the emperor Hui-tsung, *Hsüan-ho Po-ku t'u-lu*. were printed from woodblocks and enjoyed some popularity among the literati, whose members undoubtedly responded by seeking imitations of the ancient forms in the ceramic medium. It is

Opposite top: Fig. 115. Kuan ware bowl with close crackle and pale brownish grey glaze. Diameter 19.5 cm. 13th century A.D. London, Percival David Foundation.

Opposite centre: Fig. 116. Kuan ware *kuei* with pale greenish grey glaze. Diameter 16.4 cm. 13th century A.D. London, Percival David Foundation.

Opposite bottom: Fig. 117. Kuan ware *kuei* with grey green glaze. Diameter 27.4 cm. 14th century A.D. London, Percival David Foundation.

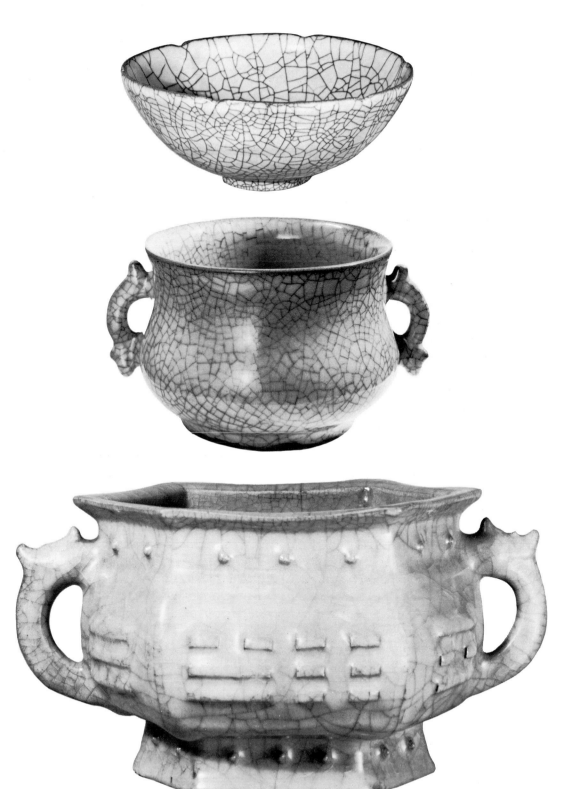

Kuei

157

significant that such forms are extremely rare in northern ceramics, and in the period of the Northern Sung dynasty as a whole; they appear to have been a late southern phenomenon only and as such very limited in their appeal.

It is not known how long Kuan and its Lung-ch'üan imitations went on being made, but it seems likely that it was at least until the end of the fourteenth century, for Ts'ao Chao in *Ko-ku yao-lun* writes of it as a contemporary ware. The late seventeenth and eighteenth centuries saw a revival of interest in the type and many superlatively good copies were made at that time, some of them so good that only close technical examination can distinguish the later copies from the originals of the Sung and Yüan periods.

Chi-chou Ware

Very different from the two former wares were those usually named Chi-chou yao, after the county town which was the market centre in southern Kiangsi for the products of a small group of kilns situated lower down the Kan river at Yung-ho. These kilns, whose rubbish heaps are numerous and in some cases very large, produced a varied and interesting assortment of material, often ingeniously decorated using techniques found nowhere else in China. The kilns are reputed to have begun operations in late T'ang times, reached their apogee in Sung and then begun to decline as the potters drifted north to the increasingly important centres around Jao-chou in the late thirteenth century. The kilns are said to have finally closed down in the fourteenth century after some so far unidentified natural disaster.[4]

The body material varies from a greyish white porcellanous material to fine and coarse grained buff and grey stoneware. The glazes are equally varied from a neutral transparent glaze suitable for the porcellanous material to opaque celadon type glazes and yet others with a higher iron oxide colourant which produced yellowish brown, dark brown, and black. The decorative techniques, however, display an unequalled diversity including double glazing, slip painting in pale slips on a blackish ground, dark brown painting on a cream coloured slip ground, decorations using leaves and paper-cuts, a most unusual variant of the cut-glaze style of decoration, and a limited amount of moulding.

The shapes include the usual range of small bowls, both conical and round walled, with the base left unglazed, small vases and jars, some with lids, which may be shaped like inverted lotus leaves, and ewers. Late examples of vases may be rather large and of unusual shapes such as would involve being made in a series of parts luted together.

The best known Chi-chou types are undoubtedly the leaf decorated pieces, which the Japanese call 'leaf *temmoku*', and the paper-cut pieces. These two types of decoration occur only on the insides of bowls, the outside is either plain black or

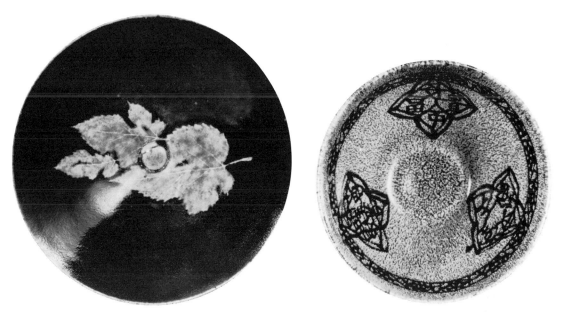

Fig. 118. Chi-chou leaf *temmoku*; black glaze with a pale yellowish brown leaf. Diameter 15 cm. 13th century A.D. Baur collection.

Fig. 119. Chi-chou paper-cut decoration. Diameter 12.6 cm. 12th–13th century A.D. Tokyo National Museum.

mottled with a second application over the black of a pale yellowish glaze, producing a tortoise-shell effect. The leaf type of decoration is literally this. A single leaf or a small spray of leaves was stuck down with a light adhesive to the unfired body. The glaze, heavily coloured with iron oxide, was then applied to the whole surface completely covering the leaf (Fig. 118). In the oxidized firing that followed, the leaf was burnt out in the glaze leaving the pale shadow of its existence as a light yellowish brown stain, the carbons having been completely burnt out in the oxidized firing. Because of the high iron content the glaze remains elsewhere a dark brown or black.[5] The body material of this type is a coarse gingery brown stoneware.

The paper-cut pieces are decorated in a similar manner, but are fired in a reducing atmosphere, so that the carbons, in what was probably at first a black carbon coloured paper, are not burnt out. The decoration remains in black or very dark brown against a brownish flecked, pale buff glaze. The design includes good wishes, composed of three or four characters, such as 'Long life, prosperity, wealth and peace', or 'Long life, emoluments and honours', and other designs of birds in flight, prunus sprays, and florets of various kinds, with scroll bands running round just below the lip in most instances. The body material is a coarse grey stoneware, the grey colour resulting from prolonged and fairly intense reduction in the firing (Fig. 119).

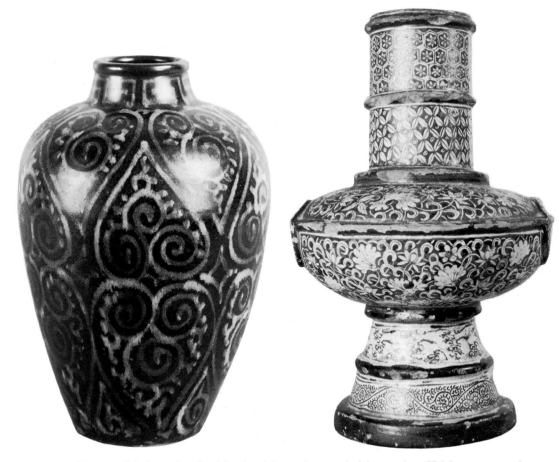

Fig. 120. Chi-chou pale yellowish painted decoration on a dark brown glaze. Height 23.1 cm. 14th century A.D. Tokyo, National Museum.

Fig. 121. Vase painted in brown against a white slipped ground under a transparent glaze. Height 25.4 cm. 14th century A.D. Mrs Lehmann.

Similar in body to the leaf *temmoku* is the dark glazed type with pale yellowish or whitish slip painting direct on the unfired glaze. The bowls are generally decorated inside with a very roughly executed prunus branch and crescent moon. There are a few examples, related to some vases and ewers similarly decorated, which have a carefully calculated scrolling design filling the whole surface (Fig. 120). These pieces can be dated to the late thirteenth century by analogy with a repoussé silver vase dating to the second half of the century.[6] The design is reminiscent of the stitched felts from Central Asia and Mongolia, and may indeed have been introduced into north China by the Mongols themselves in the earlier years of the thirteenth century, when they were beginning their invasion of the Chinese empire.

The reminiscence is even stronger with the creamy slipped ware painted in black or dark brown, and these pieces are certainly datable to the Mongol period, continuing as they did into the fourteenth century. A number of motifs common

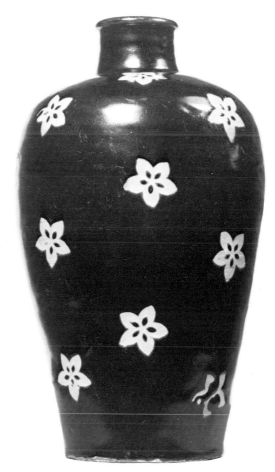

Fig. 122. Chi-chou vase with paper resist decoration. Height 26.2 cm. 14th century A.D. St Louis Art Museum.

to the whole range of decorated wares in the fourteenth century are to be found on the sometimes rather large pieces from Chi-chou. A few of these are somewhat surprising shapes (Fig. 121). The body of the slipped type is a fine grained buff stoneware with darker speckles. The slip is very thin and slightly off-white. It is painted in a consistent deep brown also rather thinly, but with meticulous care on some of the more elaborately decorated pieces. The glaze is unusually thin, colourless and almost wholly lacking in brilliance.

The variant form of the cut-glazed decoration, is found in both the white ware and in the brown or black glazed wares. The latter have the standard buff body of compact character, but the white is variable in that it may be coarse, sugary, fragile, and light in weight in relation to size, or it may be a well-constituted porcellanous body. In the northern type with cut-glazed effects the raw body cleared of glaze emphasized the decoration. In the Chi-chou type the arrangement is reversed; the decoration is only in the cleared areas against the dark glaze, or against the pale bluish toned transparent glaze of the whitish bodied pieces. The decoration is executed by using paper-cuts, which are lightly stuck to the raw body with a small tag sticking up at one side (Fig. 122). As soon as the glaze has been applied and before it has had time to dry properly the craftsman pulls at the edge of the paper-cut with one long fingernail, and glaze and paper-cut come away leaving that part of the body free of glaze. Because the glaze was viscous it did not run down over the unglazed areas in the firing. Occasionally additional details were painted in on the brown glazed pieces, using a brown pigment, or deep incisions were made to give greater emphasis, the latter practice being more common on the white type than on the dark ones.

Finally moulding for both manufacture and decoration seems to have been limited in Chi-chou pottery to white bodied pieces. Those with porcellanous bodies were mainly conical bowls with the popular decoration of prunus and crescent moon in low relief, covered either with a neutral glaze, or with a pale greenish celadon type glaze. The other rather lightweight sugary bodied kind of material was used for what must have been tomb ware. These were mainly vases with a globular body, high foot and long wide neck. They were constructed in four parts pressed out in roughly circular moulds in which were incorporated diaper patterns, florets, phoenix and dragons. The glaze was usually transparent, faintly tinged with blue, or a dirty brown. In neither case was it a good fit and most pieces demonstrate this in the way the glaze peels off, especially along sharp edges and over the higher parts of the relief decoration.

Chien

High up in one of the mountain valleys in northern Fukien were the kilns which produced the best-known black ware of south China, the Chien ware with its hare's fur glaze transmutation.[7] Like the Chi-chou pottery, it was intended for local domestic use, and must have found a place in most households, and it certainly was used locally in the Ch'an Buddhist monasteries, because this was how the Japanese came to acquire so many examples. Their monks used to visit the more distinguished monasteries in Fukien to learn the mysteries of Ch'an, or, as it is perhaps better known, Zen Buddhism, and when they returned home they took with them the bowls and other utensils with which they were provided. It is not known when the kilns began operations, or when they ceased, but it seems likely that production was limited to the period from about the middle of the eleventh century to some time early in the fourteenth century. Because of the standardized forms, which are confined to tea bowls of various sizes and only a few shapes, it is virtually impossible to date any specimens more nearly than to the Sung period.

The material is a very hard, coarse grained, but well compacted dark brown or blackish stoneware. It is covered inside and about two thirds of the way down the

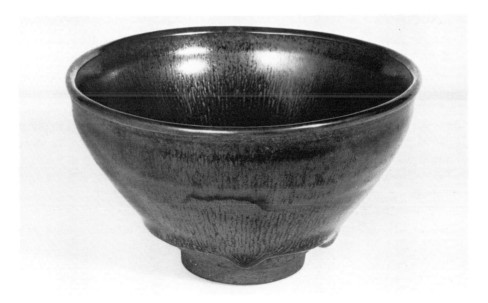

Fig. 123. Chien-yao hare's fur bowl. Diameter 12.2 cm. 12th–13th century A.D. London, Percival David Foundation.

outside with a thick glaze coloured with iron oxide in varying percentages, from about two per cent to ten per cent or more according to the colour and glaze effect desired. Low iron content yielded a pale glossy, yellowish brown, often transparent, glaze, while the high percentage produced the true streaked hare's fur effect, with the metallic iron being precipitated out on the surface as the result of a short period of reduction (Fig. 123). The low viscosity of the glaze encouraged the streaks as the glaze ran down in melting towards the foot to congeal on cooling into a thick welt or in black treacly globules; it also tended to pool thickly inside the bowls. The disadvantage of such a glaze, which probably had a short firing range and so melted rather suddenly at a particular temperature, was that it ran down so fast that the coarse grain of the clay body was inevitably revealed at the lip where only a very thin covering remained. For this reason the rough edge was often bound with silver by the Japanese, who found the roughness singularly unpleasant to the lips when drinking tea.

The bowls were fired in saggars stacked one on top of another, one bowl to each, and each bowl placed on a small fireclay button to raise it off the bottom. The arrangement was simple and probably in most cases satisfactory, but disasters were evidently not unknown, for the waster heaps revealed examples of bowls stuck to the button by the glaze, and also bowls and saggars fused into a single piece. Nor was it altogether unusual for a bung, or stack to become slightly tilted in the firing, so that the pooled glaze inside the bowls inclined towards the side tipped farthest over.

Jao-chou, *ch'ing-pai* and the Rise of Ching-tê Chên

The prefecture of Jao-chou in northern Kiangsi province close to Po-yang lake included a great number of centres, which became important in the production of pottery of many kinds from early Sung times at the beginning of the eleventh century. It was, however, Ching-tê Chên in the county of Fu-liang to the east of Jao-chou city, which became pre-eminent, largely on account of the easily accessible and virtually inexhaustible supplies of raw materials.

The early history of the kilns in the prefecture is unfortunately largely unknown, and it has only recently begun to come under the scrutiny of Chinese historians and archaeologists. All that is known for certain at the present time, and from the records, is that the kilns of what is now Ching-te Chên originated in pre-T'ang times in the fifth or sixth century, and that even in the three hundred year span of T'ang they were only operated when the demands of agriculture did not make prior claims on the local population. It was not until the Sung dynasty in the late tenth or early eleventh century that they became more active and securely established in regular production. According to Chiang Ch'i in his 'Appendix on the Ceramic Industry', an essay which was composed about 1322 and included in the local history of that date, the kilns in the Sung period were privately owned and operated by families whose sole concern it was to manufacture pottery. Thus by Sung times the change from casual to systematic organization had begun, and craftsmen properly trained in all aspects of potting had begun to replace the labourer from the field, who was sufficiently handy to apply himself to another skill in his spare time. From this time on an organized ceramic industry may be said to have evolved. A highly skilled labour force was developed with complex ramifications in the mining of materials, porterage, general transport and trading. In the early stages the output was aimed mainly at the local markets in south China, with a proportion of the production finding its way overseas to the Philippines, South-East Asia, Indonesia, India, and the Near East, to both the Persian Gulf ports and those of the Red Sea, and thence to Cairo. The products of Ching-tê Chên and other kilns in the Jao-chou region do not seem at any time in the Sung period to have attained imperial favour, for they find no mention either in the historical records or in the antiquarian handbooks produced for the wealthy connoisseurs.

Definitive evidence that any of the kilns in the prefecture of Jao-chou, let alone Ching-tê Chên, produced the first true porcelain, in the sense defined in the introduction, is totally lacking. Nevertheless the probability is that it originated in this region rather than in the north or east. By the beginning of the eleventh century the kilns of Jao-chou, as well as others further south and east in the province of Kiangsi, were already producing an extremely refined porcelain made from the local resources of kaolin, the white rather aplastic clay, which takes its name from Kao-ling, High Ridge, the hillside from which it was excavated, and from *pai-tun-tzǔ* (petuntse, or little white bricks), the white, highly felspathic material mined in the vicinity. The latter was crushed, washed, and dried to make the little white blocks or bricks suitable for easy transport to the potteries. The two ingredients were combined in suitable proportions, and when glazed and fired produced the delicate white porcelain with a glassy fracture, to which the name *ch'ing-pai,* 'clear white', is given. The Peking dealers' name for it from early in the twentieth century was, and to some extent still is, *ying-ch'ing,* 'shadow blue', on account of the slightly bluish cast of the transparent glaze. The name *ch'ing-pai,* however, must take precedence, as this is the name that occurs earliest in the Chinese literature.[8]

The glaze was prepared by fritting re-crushed *pai-tun-tzǔ* with layers of brushwood and leaves; the fritted material then had to be ground down to a suitably fine particle size before being mixed with water to a thin creamy consistency ready for application to the unfired body.[9] The slight bluish tone in the fired glaze is due to traces of iron oxide in the raw materials. This tends to colour the fired glaze, if there is any reduction in the firing cycle. The slight bluish tinge is characteristic of almost all the porcelain produced in this southern region until quite a late stage in the development; indeed it was not until the eighteenth century that the search for absolute whiteness of body and total neutrality of glaze became a conscious one. Up to that time, although some pure white material with a completely colourless glaze was produced, it was exceptional and the bluish tone in the glaze remained normal.

The pieces were usually fired on the foot or base, and if on the base the piece was generally set on a ring support. The blackish or reddish brown stain from this is often visible on the unglazed part of the base. At a later date, probably in the late twelfth century the practice of firing bowls upside down, like the Ting, was introduced, but this often proved unsatisfactory as the bowls and dishes were apt to sag in the middle.

The main problem facing the potters using the new type of body material was that it tended to crumble, since it did not have the same plastic quality found in earthenware and stoneware clays. This meant that in using the wheel they either had to throw small pieces, or throw large pieces which were rather thick. At first it was the practice to throw small ones, which required the minimum of subsequent shaving and finishing, so that either one finds small simple bowls, or larger pieces constructed of several parts neatly luted together. Gradually as the skill in shaving the outside wall improved, bowls and vases became larger. The repertory by the end of the eleventh century included bowls of various sizes (Fig. 124), vases, often of great elegance, and a variety of ewers, some of which were based on metal prototypes, while others were shaped like melons or gourds with multi-lobed bodies (Fig. 125). Among the more unusual shapes were lamps, which were rather heavily constructed, and incense burners with a heavily made base surmounted by

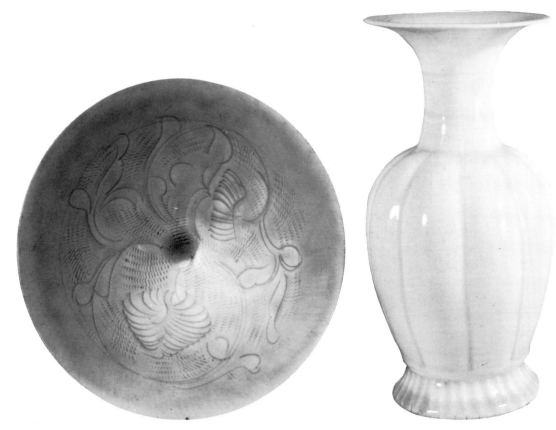

Fig. 124. *Ch'ing-pai* bowl with dotted combing. Diameter 14.6 cm. 12th century A.D. London, Victoria and Albert Museum.

Fig. 125. *Ch'ing-pai* vase with melon-shaped body. Height 17.8 cm. 11th–12th century A.D. London, Percival David Foundation.

a detachable, reticulated domed cover. Pieces like these more unusual ones can be dated to the period before the middle of the thirteenth century, but the more common bowl, dish and saucer forms, as well as the vases, continued over a very long period with relatively little variation in the basic contour, so that for dating we are largely dependent upon the decorative techniques and stylistic criteria.

The earlier of the two decorative techniques employed was incising, with limited carving and the use of a combing instrument. The combing effects, however, are quite different from those found on other wares, for, instead of the lines being continuous, they are broken so that the appearance is of dotted lines, an effect described as 'dotted combing'. In *ch'ing-pai* the use of incising and very light carving continued until well into the fourteenth century.

Moulding as a decorative technique was added, as it was to other wares, only at a later date. In the *ch'ing-pai* the addition of this technique was probably slightly later than it was in the northern wares, and is likely to have occurred in the middle or late twelfth century. As in other wares, the use of moulds is found primarily in

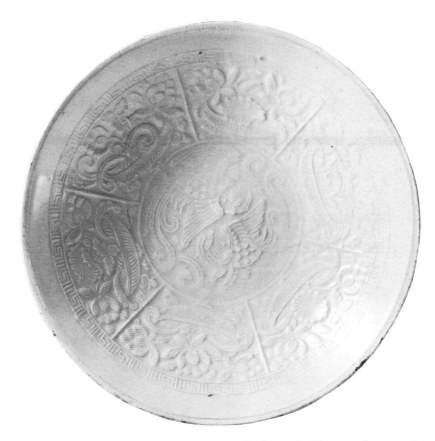

Fig. 126. *Ch'ing-pai* bowl with moulded relief decoration in panels. Diameter 18.1 cm. 13th–14th century A.D. Mrs Hans Popper.

bowl and saucer shapes, and these continued to hold an important place right up to the end of the fourteenth century (Fig. 126). Moulding was a singularly appropriate technique for the construction of forms made in porcelain, since the tendency to crumble was considerably reduced, and it made the manufacture of thinner pieces much easier and quicker. It was for instance easier to shave the outside of the bowl to a desirable thinness without fear of the piece breaking up, because the work could be done with the bowl in place over the mould. The moulded bowls are, in fact, remarkably consistent in thickness suggesting that the fast wheel and template may have been used, but the direct evidence of concentric rings slightly scoring the outside is lacking.

The decorative style of *ch'ing-pai* bears comparatively little resemblance to that of its nearest white relative, Ting, and few designs of the northern tradition in incised and carved wares of Ting are found in the southern wares, the treatment of whose surfaces is in some respects considerably less free. It is fairly rare, for instance, to find a free flowing lotus scroll running over the surface as one does in Ting, and a design such as ducks or geese swimming in a reed bordered pond is wholly unknown. Floral elements tend to be more static, being organized in

167

divisions of three or four on the inside of a bowl, with dotted combing in between as a filler (Fig. 124). On one small group of saucers the entire surface is occupied by a single fully opened lotus flower, the petals radiating from the centre; in one instance the original bowl made to fit has survived, and the outside walls of this and the cover are made to resemble the seed pod, with the seeds just protruding from the cover as a series of small bosses. Vases and ewers lend themselves to a different treatment and organization. There are bud-like elements on stems with sickle-shaped leaves against a dotted combing ground in early examples, while in later ones there is rather bold carving of floral motifs, sometimes with infants, against a striated ground, and with heavy scrolling decoration on the latest pieces.[10]

In bowls with moulded designs some resemblance to Ting may be seen, possibly because the technique may ultimately be derived from this ware. There are examples of the use of two phoenixes with flowers, rotating round the centre, with a key-fret border, albeit debased, which was a design also favoured in Ting. Moreover it was not until moulding was introduced that any of the *ch'ing-pai* were fired on the mouth rim instead of on the foot-ring or base. The rim of *ch'ing-pai* fired upside down was bound afterwards with a wide band of silver in place of the copper alloy used for binding Ting. Not many pieces survive with the silver rim completely intact, but fragments and traces of the bands may often be seen. Among the later moulded bowls are many with the surface divided into a central medallion surrounded by six radiating panels round the walls, the panels being alternately filled with a vase of flowers and a dish with growing plants, an unusual design found in no other ware. In quality the moulded *ch'ing-pai* is more variable than the incised examples, and pieces are quite commonly found with the glaze badly pitted, especially near the rim, or beginning to peel off over the high parts of the decoration in relief. The same fault may also be seen among the many small press-moulded boxes with floral designs on the top.

As time passed and the kilns, which were widely distributed, became better organized and known, changes began to take place which heralded the final steps in Chinese ceramic development from the technical point of view. The *ch'ing-pai* continued into the fourteenth century in its own right, but towards the end of the thirteenth century it gave birth to a number of variants. These are best considered in relation to the final innovations which were to take ceramics into the modern age.

CHAPTER SEVEN

The Last Great Innovation

In order to appreciate the implications of the last great innovation in ceramic technology, and to understand how the white wares developed in their later stages in the Jao-chou area, particularly at Ching-tê Chên, it is necessary to look at the events of the later thirteenth century, both before and after the final conquest of south China by the invading Mongols. The social and economic pressures and the military needs of the Southern Sung dynasty brought about changes which had a fundamental effect on the ceramic trade and industry. So important were these changes that their full impact was not fully realized until the fourteenth century, when the Mongol hold on China was completely secured.

Historical and Economic Background

After the Southern Sung had established the new capital at Hang-chou in northern Chekiang, the Chinese were under a constant, often hostile, pressure from the north. They had to maintain defensive military forces on the northern frontier with the Chin, and, following the total obliteration of these by the Mongols in 1234, against their potentially more dangerous successors. The life of the Southern Sung dynasty was slightly prolonged by disputes among the Mongols themselves, but in 1250 the final attack on the diminished Chinese empire was opened, and, although the campaign was long drawn out, the conclusion perhaps was inevitable because the Mongols had better control in the field.

In the face of the threat of invasions, the Chinese government was forced to exploit every possible means of increasing the revenue in order to maintain the army and administration. One of the most effective measures, and the one with the most far-reaching effects, was the institution of a series of Superintendents of the Shipping, combined with active government sponsorship of the overseas trade.

Three of the ports at which superintendents were established were Canton in the south, which for many centuries had held first place in the overseas trade, Wên-chou in Chekiang, which had in early Sung times been a place of some importance, and Ch'üan-chou in northern Fukien, Marco Polo's Zayton, which from the middle of the thirteenth century came to supersede Canton. From the second half of the thirteenth century the volume of trade passing in and out of China by way of Ch'üan-chou began to surpass that of all other ports and from the beginning of the fourteenth century until about the middle of the fifteenth century, Ch'üan-chou became the greatest mercantile city in East Asia. Trade indeed was of such dimensions as to draw comments from both Chinese and Arab geographers and historians, while the size and stability of the Chinese trading ships made a remarkable impression on all foreign visitors.[1]

The bulk of the trade, however, was carried by the Arabs and Persians, as the Chinese did not normally sail beyond the islands of Indonesia. The merchants were mainly Chinese, Persian and Syrian. In both Canton and Ch'üan-chou, the Muslim communities were large, well-organized, and subject to the control of their own elders. The wealth of these merchant communities and the luxury in which many of the Muslim merchants lived was famous, if not notorious, and is frequently found recorded in contemporary literature. The houses were furnished with the best that money could buy, with many objects imported from the Islamic countries to the west, as well as with Chinese goods. With communities of such wealth, and inevitably of influence, the merchant class began to emerge as an important component in society, able to influence Chinese manufactures and to some extent determine what should be imported and exported.

The imports of greatest value were spices, aromatics, ivory, selected hardwoods, and from the Near East metalwork, glass, crystal and superior textiles. The Near Eastern imports were the most influential in stimulating Chinese design and decoration. In exchange for these the Chinese exported silks of all kinds, and ceramics, the stonewares of both Chi-chou and of Lung-ch'üan and the fine porcelain from Jao-chou and other kilns of northern Kiangsi.[2] The more the trade grew as the result of government encouragement, the more the foreign merchants were prepared and able to demand, so that what the Sung government instituted for expediency's sake, the Mongols later continued for the sake of the wealth they could extract for their own personal enrichment. The effect of the original measure snowballed, the greater the encouragement given, the greater the revenue with increasing demands on the different industries involved. Thus it is not difficult to appreciate what happened in the ceramic industry during the thirteenth and fourteenth centuries.

Industrialization of the Potteries

The consequent increase in production, and the pressure exerted to maintain the increase in accordance with specific requirements to suit the foreign trade, led to profound changes at the kilns, especially those at Ching-tê Chên where production now began to be concentrated. It was during this period, especially under the Mongols in the late thirteenth century and through the fourteenth century, that the kilns in northern Kiangsi, in particular those of Ching-tê Chên, were transformed from privately owned craftsmen's kilns into a series of industrial complexes. The manufacture of porcelain in fact became fully industrialized and was financed by commercial syndicates who capitalized production and thus ultimately owned the kilns. The more demands were made on the kilns, the more expedient it became for the private owner to give up a somewhat insecure existence in favour of an assured future in a well-organized industry.[3] A highly skilled labour force came into existence with an economic distribution of labour within the kilns, which were now equipped for the mass-production of porcelain to a high standard.

There were different workshops for the different processes and firing was controlled in kilns constructed to properly established standards in size and hence capacity;[4] they were also taxed on the basis of their capacity. The firings were managed by kiln masters with semi-skilled labour, often on short term contracts, to help with the setting, stoking, and unpacking at the end. The kilns were of a multiple smoke-vent, down-draught type, known as bee-hive kilns, which were the ultimate descendants of the Shang-type kiln which so many centuries previously had been developed in Honan.

It should be noted that before such industrialization became possible it was essential that the actual techniques of manufacture should have reached a point at which the transformation from simple craft work could take place without a total disruption. Without moulding as a means of shaping and perhaps of decorating, without highly skilled throwers, the use of the fast wheel and template, and the construction of an efficient large capacity kiln, what was to be achieved in the Mongol period would have been inconceivable. It should further be noted that a large demand, combined with industrial techniques, inevitably had some effect on the quality of the finished objects. It was in this area of technique that adjustments had to be made before a degree of standardization was achieved.

Ch'ing-pai and its Development

In the earlier material of Jao-chou, in the *ch'ing-pai* for example, the extreme thinness of the walls of many of the vessels is a striking feature. But to obtain this quality using industrial processes required much time, great skill, and thus additional finance, all of which can hardly have endeared such refinement to the commercial syndicates. The use of moulding techniques, however, was now exploited and to some extent overcame the problem, for much thin lightweight material continued to be produced using a fast wheel and template. But alongside this there grew up a tendency towards heavier, often less well finished construction. Shapes were roughly thrown, and the minimum of shaving was used, while jars and vases were thrown in several thick parts, stacked one on top of another, and given only just sufficient finishing to conceal the joins. Decoration became cursive, but with a spontaneity of rhythm wholly consonant with the need for high speed production of standard shapes and sizes (Fig. 127).

The glazes during the late thirteenth and through the fourteenth century also began to change. The transparent glassy one with a faint bluish tinge continued, but frequently became less good, with a tendency to break up where it lay thin, or to be pitted where gas bubbles which had burst in the firing had failed to reseal in cooling. This was particularly noticeable near the rim of a bowl where the glaze ran thin. This glaze was gradually replaced by others which showed no such failings. A much better one was thicker, often somewhat opaque with a slightly matt surface, occasionally brilliant, but still with a pronounced blue tinge. Another good glaze was one of extreme brilliance, rather thick and of an egg-white consistency, indeed the Chinese term *luan-pai*, 'egg-white', admirably describes it. Between these two there are several that are intermediate and can conveniently be grouped under some such head as 'transitional white'.[5]

The bluish glaze with a tendency to opacity began to make its appearance about 1300, and is best seen on a number of large *mei-p'ing* vases with carved decoration organized in three bands round the body. The central band consisted of a vigorous three-clawed scaly dragon on a comb-hatched ground, with a band of lotus petal panels below and a sketchily drawn lotus scroll on the shoulder. In its less brilliant, more opaque manifestation the glaze is frequently seen on ewers, small bowls with modelled dragon handles (Fig. 128), and on vases decorated with thickly applied slip. It also occurs on an innumerable succession of small ewers of rectangular cross-section, pressed out in two-part moulds in which the decoration was incorporated, and luted together vertically with the spout and handle partly concealing the joins. These were mass-produced for the Philippine market, where many have been found in the last decades, together with small jarlets of various shapes, some with applied beaded relief and slip decoration.[6]

The use of beaded relief decoration is peculiar and it seems to have made its appearance at about the same time as the slightly opaque bluish glaze. Its most surprising use is on a number of massive Buddhist figures of seated Bodhisattvas, where the beading occurs as part of the jewelled ornament with which these saintly figures were commonly adorned.[7] The figures are mostly about fifty centimetres high and are heavily constructed, but there are a few smaller ones

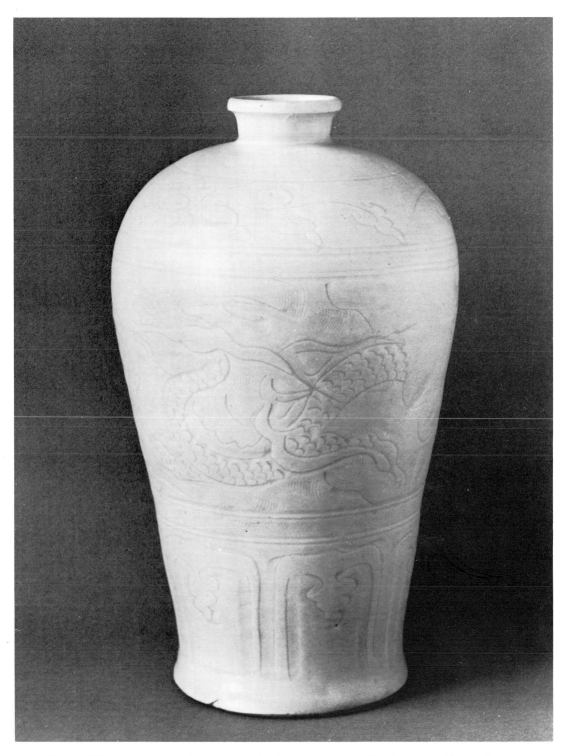

Fig. 127. White porcelain *mei-p'ing* with incised and carved decoration. Height 27.3 cm. Early 14th century A.D. Kempe collection.

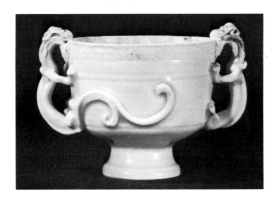

Fig. 128. White porcelain cup with modelled dragon handles. Diameter 8.1 cm. *c.* 1300. Honolulu Academy of Arts.

about twenty centimetres high. To the same group belong a number of bottle-shaped vases, either circular or hexagonal in cross section. These are exceptionally odd, since they include not only relief beaded decoration, but also flower sprays, chrysanthemum and peony being preferred, which are sprig-moulded and attached to the body, either in recessed panels of ogival shape, or on the smooth surface with small plugs of clay (Fig. 129). Both figures and vases date from about the first quarter of the fourteenth century. The earliest dated example is a figure bearing a date equivalent to either 1298 or 1299 in the Nelson Gallery in Kansas.

The opaque type glaze culminates in a series of bowls and small dishes, which are characterized in most cases by two characters, inscribed in slip on diametrically opposite sides on the inside wall. The two characters are *shu* and *fu*, and hence the ware is named Shu-fu. The combination of these two characters has been interpreted in a number of ways, the most generally accepted being 'Privy Council'. It is traditionally believed that this type was made for the imperial Mongol household, but proof is lacking. The moulded decoration on the inside is limited to two designs, one of which is of geese in flight among clouds, and the other a stylized lotus scroll with double *vajra*, or Buddhist thunderbolt, in the centre (Fig. 130). The bowls are usually heavily constructed, with a foot-ring with a diameter small for the size of the piece, but thick and squarely cut. The small basal area within the foot-ring is convex and may in some examples rise to a small point in the centre. The base is always unglazed, and may burn a pale reddish tone. The glaze, which is viscous, often displays a tendency to form a thickened welt just below the rim both inside and outside, a feature due to the method of glazing; the glaze when applied was evidently allowed to run towards

Opposite top: Fig. 129. White porcelain vase with applied relief flowers and beading. Height 27.7 cm. Early 14th century A.D. London, Victoria and Albert Museum.

Opposite bottom: Fig. 130. Shu-fu bowl with scroll decoration in relief. Diameter 20.8 cm. 14th century A.D. London, Percival David Foundation.

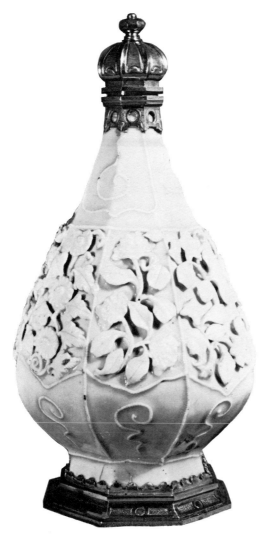

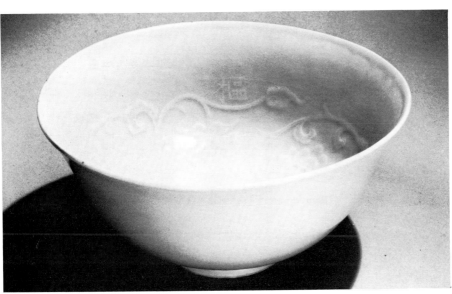

the rim after dipping. It was a characteristic which occurred first on an important piece of transitional white ware, which is inscribed and is datable to 1328. The piece is a dish made over a mould incorporating a decoration of two phoenixes in flight round the inside wall and two others in the centre. The glaze is midway between the true *ch'ing-pai* glaze and the fully developed Shu-fu one, and almost certainly antedates the Shu-fu, which probably did not appear until about the middle of the fourteenth century. The dish is also important because it introduces a new form, with its rounded sides, straight rim, and wide base. The form is of great interest because it was to remain popular from this date right down into modern times.

The other glaze, the egg-white one, was also used on dishes of this kind, and on a few vases, but it was not to achieve the popularity of the blue toned one. The reason for this is uncertain, but it may well have been a technical one which made it too expensive to fire satisfactorily in large quantities. Such pure whiteness was difficult to achieve because of the natural iron content of the glaze materials, and it is possible that the right result could only be obtained by a perfectly controlled neutral firing, that is, one in which neither oxidizing nor reducing conditions were allowed to prevail.

It was the thick, slightly bluish toned glaze with a variable opacity which was to remain predominant, and which became the medium for the entire range of porcelain from Ching-tê Chên and other kilns in the Jao-chou area. It was also the glaze to be used on all the porcelain on which there were painted underglaze blue or copper red decorations. This underglaze painting was the last great innovation in Chinese ceramic history, and it requires some explanation as to its introduction and the technique of its use.

Underglaze Painting on Porcelain

While copper had already been in use for about a hundred and fifty years in Chün wares, and its reaction when subjected to a reducing cycle in the kiln was known, cobalt blue was a new addition to the decorative repertory. Cobalt blue had been imported in T'ang times, as has been noticed in an earlier chapter, but at that time it was used in a lead glaze as a glaze colourant. The new introduction was as a pigment for decorative purposes, and thus fundamentally different. The introduction is unlikely to have occurred before about the end of the first quarter of the fourteenth century, despite suggestions that it was first employed in the Sung period. In any case no piece of Sung blue and white has ever been identified, and there are cogent arguments against the use of blue at so early a date.[8]

In the Near East cobalt blue had long been used for the decoration of earthenware, and particularly in Persia during the thirteenth century, when it was often used on tiles under an alkaline glaze. In the Persian earthenwares the blue had an unfortunate tendency to run, and this fact may have led the Persian merchants to investigate the possible use of the cobalt pigment on the very different ceramic ware of China. In any case the Chinese porcelain was enormously admired and valued since it was infinitely stronger and more serviceable than any other pottery then being made, and for which there was consequently a ready and assured market.

The ore from which the colourant was obtained, an arsenide, almost certainly came from mines near Kashan. The material was either roasted to provide a reasonably pure oxide of cobalt (zaffre) or was fused with glass to give a deep blue frit (smalt).[9] It is not known in which of these forms it was transmitted to China by the Persian merchants. At this period the pigment was transported by the sea route from the Persian Gulf by way of Acheh at the north end of Sumatra, and thence probably direct to Ch'üan-chou, which by the end of the first quarter of the fourteenth century was the chief port. As we shall see, the introduction of this colouring oxide, called *sulimānī*[10] by the Near Eastern merchants, inevitably meant that it was the Near Eastern market which had, in the first instance, to be catered for, rather than that of China. But first there were technical problems to be solved.

The chief difficulty in the decoration of porcelain is that there are only three colouring oxides able to withstand the high temperatures required, that is, from 1,280°C upwards. One is iron oxide, and another is copper oxide fired in reducing conditions, and about both the Chinese were already well informed. The third colour is cobalt oxide, of which at this point the Chinese knew nothing, the tradition of T'ang having long since been forgotten, besides being irrelevant in the context of porcelain. In the twentieth century this restriction to three colours has, within certain limits, been overcome, but the mastery by the Chinese of underglaze painting in cobaltiferous oxides was a technical step forward of great importance.

The oxide was almost certainly fritted with glaze material and then ground down before being mixed with water and painted directly on to the unfired body, which tended to absorb a little of the colour and thus in some sense fix it. This reduced the likelihood of running in the firing, an almost perennial problem for the Islamic potters. After painting the glaze was applied and the wares fired to temperatures between 1,280 and a little over 1,300°C, to produce a superb blue decoration against a white ground with a faintly blue tinged glaze of considerable thickness, of the type already in use on the white ware of Ching-tê Chên. The success of the early pieces was largely due to the viscosity of the glaze and its remarkable stability, unlike the glazes of the Near East, which lacked both viscosity, and chemical and thermal stability owing to their different constitution. In early Chinese examples, however, lack of familiarity with the intensity of colour to be derived from very small quantities of the colourant led to the appearance of black or reddish brown scaly blemishes on the surface in some areas of the decoration. This was caused partly by excess of cobalt, which also acts as a flux, rising through the glaze covering in the firing and becoming oxidized on the surface, and partly by what must have been coarse grinding of the fritted colour. Despite this fault there seems no doubt that the new ware was enormously admired by patrons overseas. It was a fault which took many years wholly to overcome, perhaps also because the proper grinding of the glaze materials as well as the cobalt was a factor not at first recognized.

Although the bulk of the blue and white produced in the fourteenth century up to about 1368, the year of the Mongols' defeat at the hand of Chu Yüan-chang, the first emperor of the Ming dynasty, was for the overseas market, a proportion of the material was made for local markets in south China. The types for the two different markets are, with very few exceptions, distinctly different. The exceptional pieces include two famous vases made for a temple about seventy-five miles south-east of Ching-tê Chên. These, known as the David Vases, are dated by their inscriptions to a year equivalent to 1351, and on them depends the whole chronology of blue and white in the fourteenth century (Fig. 131). Without these pieces, based on contemporary bronze vessels, it would be almost impossible in the almost total absence of excavated material to plot the development of the most influential ceramic ware ever produced. Both the motifs and the manner of painting provide valuable keys for dating the vast quantity of fourteenth-century output, which was intended primarily for the Islamic market, although some of it went to Indonesia, India, South-East Asia and the Philippines.

Blue and White for the Overseas Market

The enormous output of material intended for the foreign trade, especially for the lands of Islam, can be divided into two main groups, the first comprising open forms such as plates, dishes and bowls, which far outnumber the second group composed of closed forms represented by vases of *mei-p'ing* form, *kuan* wine jars, and ewers. An intermediate group is composed of boxes of various kinds, which have been found mainly in Indonesia; they do not appear among any of the material known in Near Eastern collections.

The plates and dishes are of two types, both of them produced by mechanical means.[11] One type, the earlier in origin, has a flattened rim with bracket foliations, often a rather deep well, or cavetto, and a wide unglazed base (Fig. 132). The form is based on a Near Eastern metalwork prototype of precisely the kind which would have been found in a wealthy Muslim household in either Canton or Ch'üan-chou. It is worth noting that the form also appears in Lung-ch'üan ware at about the same time. Most of these dishes are large, varying between thirty-eight and forty-six centimetres in diameter, dimensions also found in the second type of dish, which was introduced slightly later, about 1350,

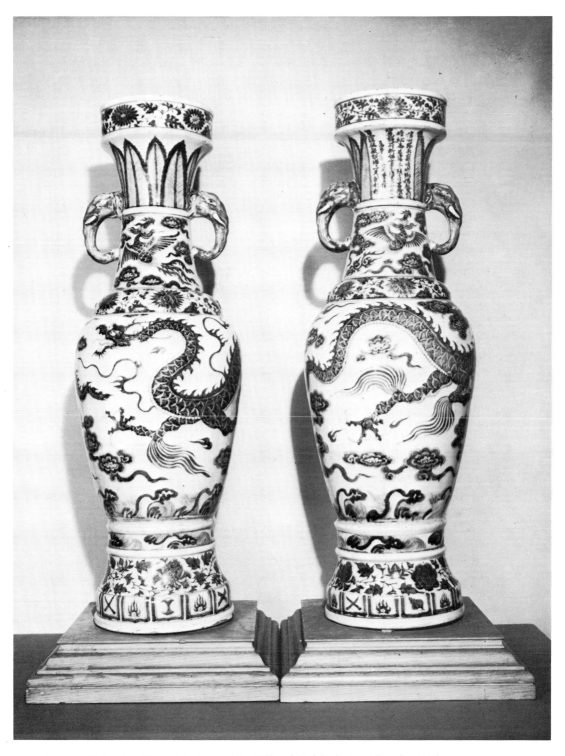

Fig. 131. Underglaze blue painted vases, 'David Vases'. Height 63.3 cm. Dated equivalent to 1351.
London, Percival David Foundation.

and which also had a flattened rim, but without foliations (Fig. 133). These, too, were mechanically produced and were a particularly persistent form.

The first type, because of its eccentric shape, could not be thrown on the wheel, but had to be made using two moulds, an inner and an outer, which were designed to fit together under pressure with the porcelain clay body between. The mould for the inside included some decoration, usually a peony scroll, which appeared in low relief in the well of the finished object, but which sometimes had florets or a narrow chrysanthemum scroll running round the narrow flattened rim as well. After being taken from the moulds, the base was shaved and the foot-ring cut before the piece was passed on for drying in preparation for the painting. One of the peculiarities of this type is that in the earlier pieces, that is up to about the middle of the century, the decoration was predominantly left in white against a blue ground, the relief elements generally having only small details touched in in blue, and sometimes not even that. It was only the central field that was freely painted in blue on white.

When the second type was made with the plain flattened rim, the fast wheel and template were used, and again the foot-ring was cut separately. On this type the decoration was predominantly blue on white, and the general impression is consequently less rich and elaborate than the twin moulded series, which have a splendour approaching flamboyance.

The organization of the decoration departs completely from any hitherto traditionally accepted in Chinese ceramics, and is based to a remarkable degree on that of Islamic metalwork.[12] Many of the earliest pieces such as foliate rimmed dishes, have a decoration based on a system of concentric rings or of conceptually interlocking arcs. In both cases the design is worked out on arithmetical two-dimensional principles of a kind quite alien to the Chinese concepts of design, in which elements move freely in space (Fig. 132). The complex enrichment of surface seen in the early blue and white has no parallel in contemporary Chinese art, which is characterized by a restraint amounting to understatement and a subdued, even sombre, colour.

The motifs employed to fill out the unusual organization were, however, purely Chinese in inspiration. There was only one exception, the so-called 'cloud collar' motif, which had its origins in Mongol Central Asia. This curious lappet-like motif is sometimes used in its proper form, or the four sections are disengaged and used independently in various ways (Plate V, opposite page 192, Fig. 134); in the independent treatment it most often occurs on plates and dishes. The purely Chinese motifs are numerous, those preferred among plant forms are the peony, chrysanthemum, camellia, gardenia, lotus, morning glory, blackberry lily, vine and gourd. Among birds, the phoenix, heron, peacock and pheasant are prominent, while the animals include deer, fabulous beasts such as the kylin and dragon, and a rather absurd-looking beast usually described as a lion. To these should be added symbolic elements and emblems, such as those of Buddhism and

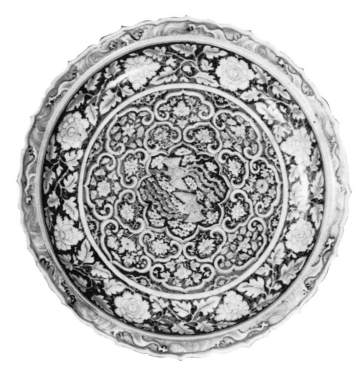

Above: Fig. 132. Blue and white painted foliate rimmed plate. Diameter 41 cm. Second quarter of the 14th century A.D. Istanbul, Topkapu Saray.

Below: Fig. 133. Blue and white plate with straight rim. Diameter 45.5 cm. Third quarter of the 14th century A.D. Washington, Freer Gallery of Art.

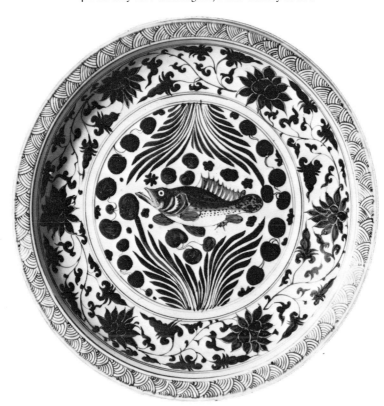

Taoism, and other auspicious emblems, often all mixed together on the same piece. Border patterns, which play an important role on dishes, include free-flowing wave patterns, one of great freedom and boldness and another rather weak and stereotyped, narrow floral scrolls, diamond diaper, segmented waves and classic scrolls.[13] All these elements are combined in an almost endless variety, the central field of the later large dishes being most freely treated.

The same type of handling is found on the straight rimmed dishes, but on these the alien influence in the organization of the design on the surface is less obvious than on the earlier type. Evidently by the time this variation of form was introduced and speed of output had been increased in response to demand, a series of pattern books was available from which the painters could choose appropriate decorations for the different areas, for there is less variation amongst this later group (Fig. 133). A significant difference between these and the earlier type is also seen in the back of the straight rimmed dishes. These are painted with a band of lotus petal panel motifs, instead of a stylized lotus scroll pattern encircling the outside of the rounded well like a wreath.

There is a period when the two forms of dish overlap, but the foliate rimmed type was temporarily abandoned some time between about 1355 and 1360, probably because the original moulds were worn out and too costly to replace, and because they were slower to use than the fast wheel and template employed for the straight rimmed type. When the foliated form reappeared it was to do so under different conditions and with certain modifications which will be described later.

Bowls of various kinds were also produced, but they were much less common before the middle of the fourteenth century, and the decoration on most of them adheres closely to the kind found on the straight rimmed dishes. One of the most popular designs in the central field was the lotus pond, with or without two ducks, a decoration also found on the later dishes. A large number of this type has been discovered in recent years in Egypt and Syria, in addition to those already known in the great collections of Topkapu Saray in Istanbul and of Ardebil, part of which is in the Iran Bustan in Tehran.

Among the closed forms were the *mei-p'ing* vase and the *kuan* wine jar. The *mei-p'ing* was small at the mouth, wide on the shoulder with a tall body narrowing to the base. The *kuan* was either a tall ovoid form with a short wide neck, or it resembled the *mei-p'ing* in the width of the shoulder, but had a wide mouth and a shorter, stouter body. In addition to these were a small number of ewers, whose methods of construction were somewhat varied. Pieces circular in cross-section were generally built up from a number of thrown parts carefully luted together one on top of another, but hexagonal and octagonal pieces had to be constructed in moulds. The shapes, so different from the straightforward plate and dish forms, were something of a challenge to the painters, and a number of different solutions to the problems of decoration were worked out. The most usual was to divide the whole surface into a series of horizontal bands of varying width, the widest and

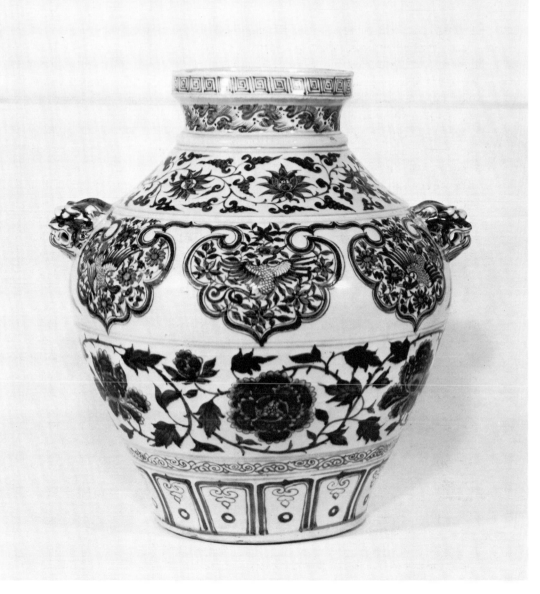

Fig. 134. *Kuan* jar in blue and white. Height 39.4 cm. Third quarter of the 14th century A.D.
Cleveland, Cleveland Museum of Art.

dominant one normally roughly central between top and bottom, with supporting
narrower bands above and below containing quite different decorative motifs. A
number of other solutions were found, some of them showing a tendency to disrupt
the contour, others wholly subordinate to it.

The motifs are usually those already familiar on the plates and dishes, but there
are some distinct from these, especially on pieces dating from about the middle of

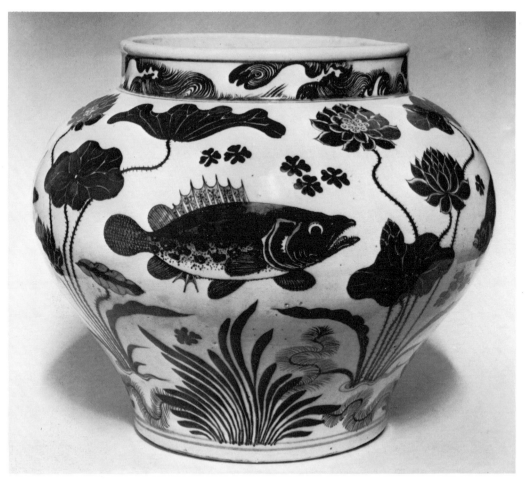

Fig. 135. Blue and white wine jar with fish. Height 29.8 cm. Mid 14th century A.D. New York, Brooklyn Museum.

the fourteenth century and just before. To these belong the ogival panels, with beaded relief borders and sprig-moulded floral patterns on some wine jars, painted in both copper red and cobalt blue within the panels, which are recessed into the walls (Plate V, opposite page 192). Ogival panels may also occur on hexagonal *mei-p'ing* with a background of knobbed classic scroll, a motif derived from the Mongolian stitched felts.[14] In a number of cases on both wine jars and *mei-p'ing*, the main decoration is illustrative of incidents from popular dramas of the period, executed with great verve and a remarkable rhythmic control (Fig. 136).[15] Probably the most popular major theme was the peony scroll, which was boldly handled in broad bands, especially round the large wine jars on which there was ample space to let the brush flow. There was one other type of decoration found on the wine jars and not commonly seen on dishes: handsome designs of fish in weedy ponds, sometimes only three or four different fish being depicted, but in a few instances several of the same species or different species (Fig. 135). In a few

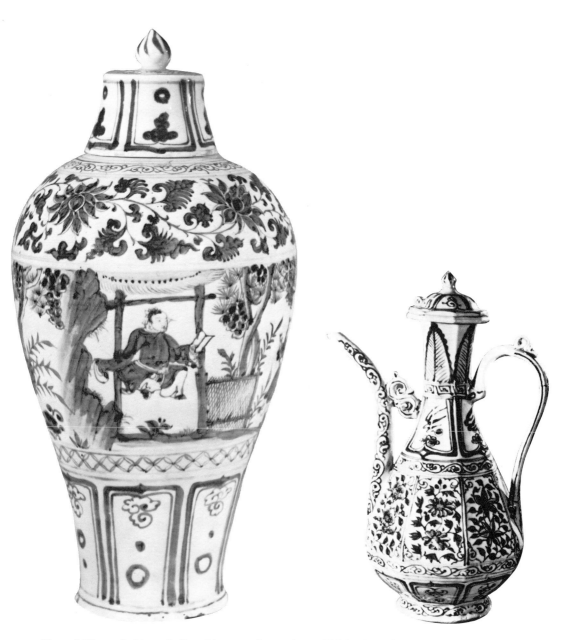

Fig. 136. Blue and white *mei-p'ing* with a scene from a drama. Height 38 cm. Second quarter of the 14th century A.D. Boston, Museum of Fine Arts.

Fig. 137. Blue and white ewer from Pao-ting, Hopei. Height 23.5 cm. 14th century A.D. Hopei Museum.

examples there is a shoulder band of floral scroll of some kind, but most fish decorations utilize the whole surface with perfect freedom.

The ewers, which at this time were few and far between, were dependent upon metal, glass or crystal forms from the Near East, and the octagonal faceted type characteristic of the period was decorated in a manner close to that known in Islamic metalwork (Fig. 137). The rhythm of the contour, as in Islamic metalwork, was broken by a counter rhythm provided by horizontally ordered bands round the vessel, but in some cases with the wide central band being additionally divided vertically into panels to fit the facets. The whole decorative scheme, which is also occasionally found on simple bottle-shaped vases of similar hexagonal or octagonal section, is alien to Chinese tradition and indicates the need to adopt an unfamiliar approach to the use and treatment of a surface to suit a specific market. By the middle of the second half of the century the uncertainties were either resolved in the initiation of a new style, to be discussed below, or the whole approach was abandoned.

Also destined to be exported, but to the Philippines and Indonesia, were boxes of various kinds and sizes. Of the two most important types one had a bow-lobed plan, the other a bracket-lobed plan. Both forms were based on purely Chinese originals made in lacquer and silver.[16] The lacquer prototypes were plain black and undecorated, but the silver ones were either elegantly traced with floral designs or had rather heavy repoussé decoration on the cover. In the porcelain examples, however, the painters drew on the vocabulary of decorative motifs already available for other shapes in the medium. Often the various auspicious emblems occur round the irregularly shaped sides, and in all cases a very freely painted scene appears on the central panel on the lid, the ducks in a lotus pond being particularly favoured. This suggests a date for these pieces of just after the middle of the fourteenth century.

Other shapes intended for the same markets, but more especially for the Philippines, were small jarlets of various kinds, which were embellished with beaded reliefs as well as flower sprays, and scrolls in either blue or red.[17] With these are also associated small gourd-shaped ewers constructed of four cup-shaped parts hurriedly pressed out in moulds and carelessly slapped together with the minimum of finishing. The decoration of the ewers was generally organized in two narrow bands, one running round each bulb, but there are some which are ornamented with groups of large dots in either red or blue scattered carelessly over the surface. These have until now been dated to the early part of the century, but careful analysis of the great quantity of blue and white of all kinds makes it clear that they should be assigned to a relatively late date in the fourteenth century.

Products for the Domestic Market

The somewhat careless construction and decoration of the pieces described above is close to that found in the relatively small number of blue and white, and red and white pieces evidently intended for the home market, which seems to have

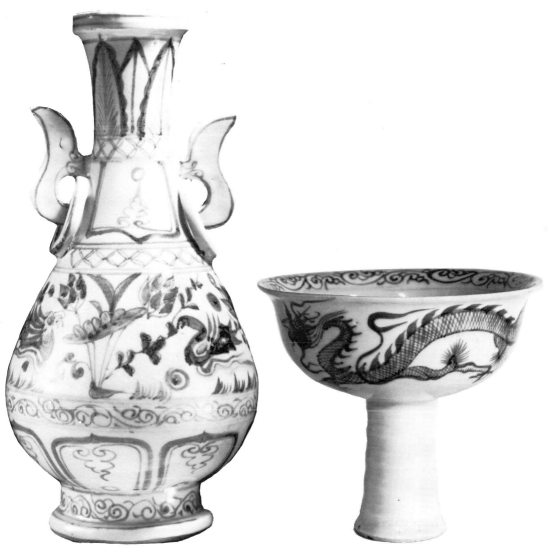

Fig. 138. Blue and white temple vase. Height 25.4 cm. 14th century A.D. Formerly Mrs Alfred Clark.

Fig. 139. Blue and white stem-cup. Diameter 13 cm. 14th century A.D. Cleveland, Cleveland Museum of Art.

absorbed pieces made for family altars and shrines. These are quite small compared with the massive pieces made for the Near East and rarely exceed twenty-six centimetres in height. In this group are altar vases and tripods, some of which have rather disordered decoration as though the painter, in a hurry to execute an unprofitable order, had little time or inclination to expend upon them the thought needed for the careful matching of the motifs, and the adjustment of their proportions to each other and to those of the object (Fig. 138). The small stem-cups which make their appearance in this group are better treated. The bowls

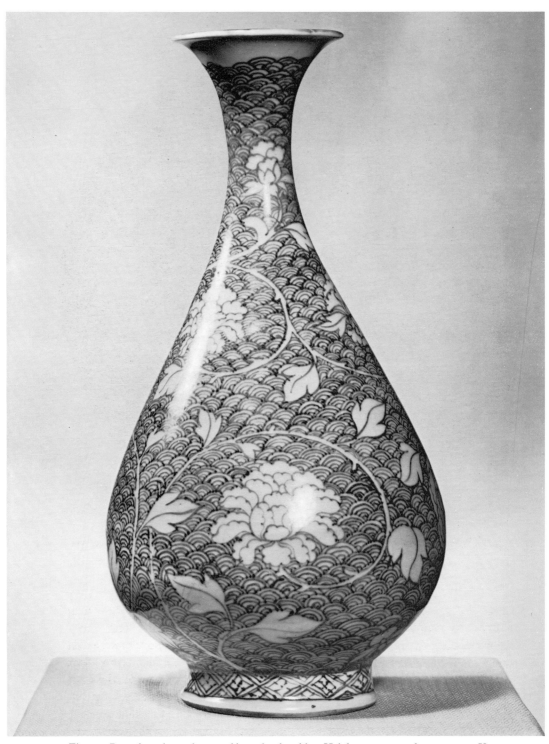

Fig. 140. Pear-shaped vase decorated in underglaze blue. Height 50.5 cm. 14th century A.D. Kansas, Nelson Gallery of Art.

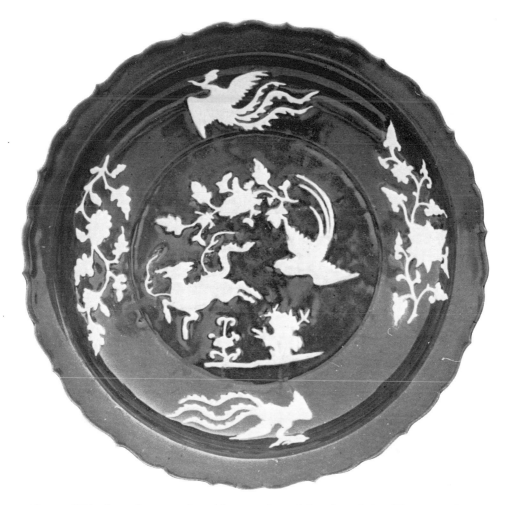

Fig. 141. White decoration reserved on a blue ground, on a foliate rimmed plate. Diameter 35.6 cm.
Mid 14th century A.D. Istanbul, Topkapu Saray Museum.

of the cups are pressed out over decorated moulds which incorporate designs of
four or five-clawed dragons running round the inside walls with great vigour
among clouds. The cups which had a small tapering shank on the bottom were then
luted into a tubular stem, sometimes shaped to resemble a bamboo stem, with ridges
marking the joints. The painting of these was chiefly on the outside, the most
favoured motif being two three-clawed dragons scribbled with a cursive energy
(Fig. 139); inside on the bottom of the cup it was usual to add a flower spray,
chrysanthemum or lotus being popular, but a few have the conch shell associated
with Buddhism.

To this small group may be added another consisting of bottle vases with an elegant contour and a narrow neck spreading to a trumpet mouth, and some small jars with lids, resembling the large *kuan* wine jars in shape. While the vases were generally painted with peony, lotus, or chrysanthemum in a free all-over design, there were a few with figures in landscape or peony scrolls reserved in white against a segmented wave ground (Fig. 140). The jars, like the vases, are found in both copper red and underglaze blue and the designs are similar to those of the altar vessels and found equally in both colours.

All these pieces for the domestic market were at one time thought to be early in date, but it now seems more likely that they were not made before the middle of the fourteenth century. There are certain decisive elements and treatments, which link them to the later manner of painting found on the large wine jars and on some of the dishes.[18]

Less easily dated, but probably fairly early is an unusual and attractive series of pieces, limited at present to a total of seven, which have what is called white slip reserve decoration (Fig. 141). The series includes one *mei-p'ing*, two large dishes with foliated rims, two small plates with narrow straight rims and a small spouted bowl. The technique of decoration is curious and only survived briefly. After the piece was made and allowed to dry, it was covered with a blue glaze to which was immediately applied a relief decoration in white porcelain clay; this was then quickly covered with a neutral glaze. The white relief was therefore firmly sandwiched between two layers of extremely viscous glaze, the under one blue and the upper one colourless. The result is a simple bold decoration in white against a rich blue ground.

The use of coloured glazes on the porcelains was extended at this time to dishes, deep bowls and small cups, all of which were made over moulds incorporating decorations of dragons, normally with five claws, round the inside. A copper red glaze was used as well as cobalt blue, and occasionally there are examples of pieces with a blue or a red glaze inside and a dark brown or black one on the outside. The copper red glaze, as a monochrome effect, was not always very successful, partly because of the firing temperature and the problem of beginning the reduction at the right time, and partly because of the thinness of the base glaze, a neutral glaze, overlying the copper coloured glaze. The use of a base glaze over the copper was essential in order to secure a good red, and if this was not thick enough the copper did not react properly in the firing. The failures in these respects resulted in a dull opaque, almost brownish red, but there are some pieces of good colour with comparatively little opacity. The type was evidently much favoured in the latter part of the century, and later the techniques required to secure good results were to be more seriously investigated.

If, at this point, we look back over the achievements of the thirteenth and fourteenth centuries, it will be seen that the period represents the culmination of a long series of developments, which were rooted in the tradition of the late sixth and seventh centuries when the concentration on high-fired wares began in earnest to the gradual exclusion of earthenware. The growth of stoneware traditions in the centuries following the establishment of T'ang was of great importance because the experience with the high-firing clay bodies led to a better understanding of glaze constitutions and firing techniques. Both these aspects of ceramic technology were vital for the potter to grasp before porcelain could be satisfactorily developed from the late eighth or ninth century.

It was probably the enormous market value of the pure white porcelain which led to the eventual shift from stonewares, with their coloured bodies and restrained glaze colours, to the hard white ware, the potential of which, in decorative terms, had still to be fully explored. In stonewares, during the centuries following the fall of T'ang in the tenth century to the collapse of Southern Sung in the thirteenth century, the decorative techniques had been exhaustively investigated, but the use of painting had been somewhat limited by the colourants capable of withstanding the temperatures needed to fuse the stoneware bodies. It was only in the Tz'ŭ-chou wares that the use of overglaze painting, with its brighter lead fluxed colour, had been tried, but the designs remained simple until the end of the fourteenth century and the market was limited mainly to the northern provinces.

The introduction of cobalt blue for the decoration of the already admired porcelain of Jao-chou, with its valuable overseas market, changed the potter's approach to the material and the direction in which it was to develop in the following centuries. It resulted in a gradual turn away from the hitherto sensuous attractions of stonewares, with their subtle glaze colours and textures and their simple forms, towards more elaborately structured vessels in which the austere simplicity of the earlier traditional shapes was sometimes lost. But most important of all it hastened the transformation of ceramic manufacture based on a craft tradition into a highly organized industry, and one in which the artist craftsman was to be less the potter than the decorator, and in which the potential of the material had been fully explored and the techniques largely mastered.

From the fourteenth century onward, the history of Chinese ceramics becomes one of art rather than technology, and it is the decorative style and fashion which take first place. Techniques in the history of domestic ceramics have changed very little and the innovations have for the most part been minor ones aimed at speeding production rather than changing its methods. The fourteenth century and the introduction of cobalt blue was the final step which brought Chinese ceramics into the modern age, and led to developments in Europe, both in the techniques involved in the use of clay materials and in the design and decoration, in an even wider area than that of ceramics.

PART THREE

DEVELOPMENT AND VARIATIONS

CHAPTER EIGHT

Imperial Patronage

In the centuries following the introduction of underglaze blue and copper red painting on porcelain, the ceramic history of China is mainly one of the exploitation of this technique combined in various ways with all those others which had been learned over the previous centuries. Thus from now on it is a history of ringing the changes rather than of radical innovation, and of gradual change in decorative style, with a concentration on porcelain to the almost total exclusion of stoneware.

The establishment of the new, native dynasty of Ming in 1368 under Chu Yüan-chang was to have marked effects on the ceramic industry. The chief long term consequence was to be a transformation of style and not a change in the level of production. In fact after an initial pause this built up steadily until about the middle of the fifteenth century. For the first time Chinese imperial and courtly taste was briefly to dominate common taste in the decorative arts.

One of the immediate effects of the collapse of the Mongols under the pressure of Chu Yüan-chang and other contemporary rebels appears to have been at least the partial closure of the kilns of Jao-chou. This was probably forced on the kiln masters and the syndicates owning the kilns because Chu Yüan-chang fought a large part of his campaigns against his rivals through the northern part of the province of Kiangsi before turning north against the Mongols. Hung-wu, as Chu Yüan-chang is better known in history, had seized Nanking as early as 1356, and from that date it became his strategic base for his campaigns in central China. When he proclaimed himself emperor and took the dynastic name of Ming in 1368, he retained the city as his capital. It became a secondary capital only in 1421

Opposite: Plate V. Wine jar with recessed panels, relief ornament and painting in underglaze blue and copper red. Height 33 cm. *c.* 1330. London, Percival David Foundation.

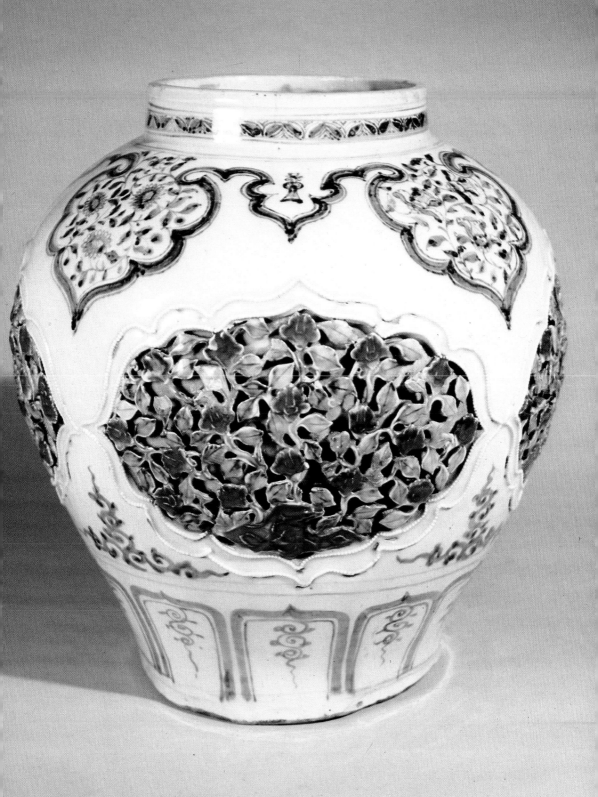

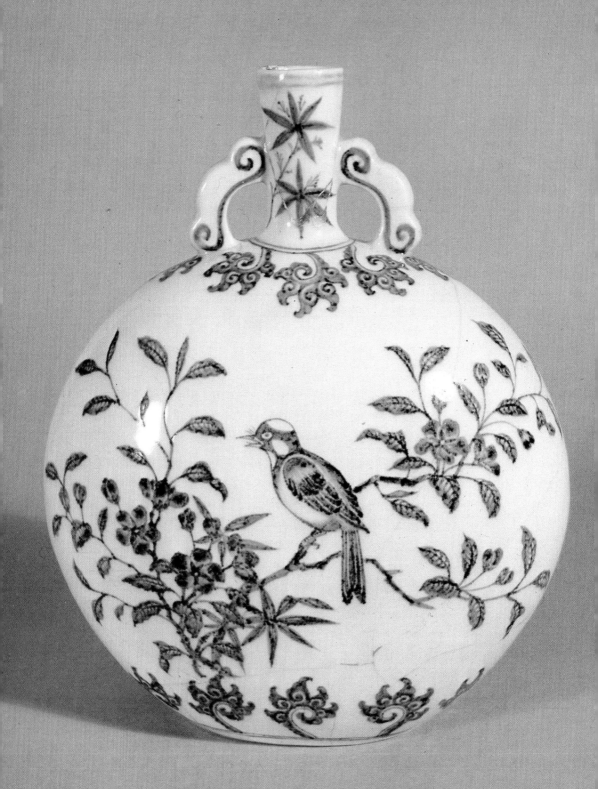

after the emperor Yung-lo had extravagantly rebuilt and extended Peking.

Hung-wu was an intelligent, if difficult and often barbarous character, who assumed autocratic powers and governed with great firmness. He very early announced his accession to the Chinese throne to neighbouring states, sending envoys with gifts to the rulers and seeking 'tribute' in exchange.[1] After this, and following a brief period when the ports were largely closed and foreign trade restricted, the further despatch of envoys abroad reactivated trade. At least two of these overseas visits were of great significance to the ceramic industry, because they are probably the earliest recorded examples of market research.

In the year 1374 an envoy, Li Hao, was ordered to take to the Liu-Chiu (Ryuk-kyu) Islands 20 pieces of silk, 1,000 pieces of pottery and 10 forged iron axes each for the rulers, and to take 100 pieces of silk, 50 pieces of silk gauze, 69,500 pieces of ceramics and 990 axes to trade for horses.[2] Nine months later Li Hao returned with 40 horses and 5,000 catties[3] of sulphur and reported that the silks had sold cheaply, but that the porcelain had fetched a high price.[4] So it was decided to take more porcelain and axes to trade for horses.

A further series of expeditions in 1383 to Siam, Cambodia and Champa were undertaken with initial gifts of 32 pieces of brocade for each of the kings, and 19,000 pieces of porcelain, no doubt with somewhat similar results.[5]

After these probings of the market the potters were forced not only to increase production, but to adjust to new markets, which by the last twenty years of the fourteenth century included the domestic market. They had to evolve a decorative style to suit these. In this double adjustment the potters were highly successful, as indeed they needed to be; it was inconceivable that they should give up the exciting and hitherto profitable blue and white.[6] Once they had succeeded in transforming the decorative style, imperial orders for a variety of wares flowed in along with those for the ordinary domestic and foreign market, and the demands made required an immense output of material of the greatest technical and decorative excellence.

After the dust and turmoil immediately following the death of Hung-wu in 1398 had settled, and his son Yung-lo had replaced his grandson, Chien-wên, in 1403 after violent civil war, the great era of Ming began. In the next twenty-five years the fame of China once more spread across the world as the eunuch admiral Chêng Ho led his remarkable expeditions south through Indonesia and then west to India, the Persian Gulf, the Red Sea and the east coast of Africa. The prestige accruing from these expeditions was enormous and Chinese silks and porcelains streamed westward into every country able to buy what was offered. The domestic trade too flourished as never before, and the arts began to achieve a unity such as could only compare with that of the T'ang dynasty five hundred years earlier. The

Opposite: Plate VI. Blue and white flask painted with a bird on a branch. Height 30.4 cm. Early 15th century A.D. London, Percival David Foundation.

emperor established a number of workshops and craftsmen of all kinds were employed to produce luxury goods to please the imperial taste.[7] Silk weaving, metalworking, lacquer working and the ceramic industry all benefited. Courtly interest in these products grew and the artistic achievements of the first part of the fifteenth century bear witness to new glories which echoed the splendours of T'ang.

When imperial orders were sent out for luxury goods requiring a high standard of craftsmanship, the order was often taken in person by an official from the Board of Public Works, as were the orders to the kilns at Jao-chou. The official taking the order would also take specially prepared drawings which the ceramic decorators were required faithfully to follow.[8] The system of ordering, however, had the grave disadvantage that much of the authority for it lay in the hands of the eunuchs, and over-ordering from the potteries certainly occurred. One eunuch was executed for selling off and giving away part of an imperial order,[9] while another on the delivery of the goods on one occasion, 'pretended he saw faults in the porcelain and had the whole order executed over again;' he almost certainly appropriated the first order for his personal use. Yung-lo was largely to blame for their increasing power, and although he could keep them in order a less capable ruler would inevitably fall victim to their influence. It was indeed the abuse of their position which was an important factor in the disruption of the rulership in the middle of the fifteenth century, after the death of Hsüan-tê in 1435. The eunuchs advised the young emperor Chêng-t'ung to take up arms personally in north China against the Mongols, who were in rebellion, with the result that he was taken prisoner in 1449. His place was taken by his brother Ching-t'ai, but in 1457 Chêng-t'ung escaped his captors, and to everyone's annoyance resumed the throne, with the title T'ien-shun. The expeditions against the Mongols had been costly and largely a waste of time, and now the same weak ruler had come back and imperiously ousted his substitute. When he died in 1464 he was succeeded in the following year by Ch'êng-hua and a more stable period followed.

The period of these disturbances, between the death of Hsüan-tê and the ascent of Ch'êng-hua, is known in ceramic history as the Interregnum, and it used to be believed that the kilns in Jao-chou closed down and were only reopened in 1457, but the evidence of the texts and of the wares is against this. Certainly production was reduced for a time, but it did not cease, and in the Ch'êng-hua period from 1465 to 1487 it increased steadily in quantity and improved to a phenomenal degree in quality. The technical and aesthetic standards attained during the Ch'êng-hua and succeeding Hung-chih periods were not again to be surpassed until the early eighteenth century in the Ch'ing dynasty.

The overseas trade underwent considerable fluctuation during the fifteenth century, for Chêng Ho's expeditions, which had begun in 1405, when he received his first commission from Yung-lo, came to an end in 1436, up to which time the trade showed a steady increase, but thereafter began to diminish. Much early fifteenth-century ceramic material found its way to western Asia and to Egypt through Ch'üan-chou, which was still the most flourishing port, but from the middle of the century until early in the sixteenth century, the porcelains, whether from Jao-chou, Lung-chüan, or the minor kilns diminished noticeably. Some of the provincial kilns in the south, however, seem to have continued supplying Indonesia reasonably well, if we may judge from finds in that area.

Transition to the Fifteenth-Century Imperial Style

The production of ceramic wares in the fourteenth century under the Mongols had been dominated in both quality and quantity by the blue and white and the Lung-ch'üan celadons. In the last thirty years of the century these two wares remained pre-eminent under the new dynasty. With the temporary closing of the ports, however, the potters were thrown off balance. When a degree of stability was recovered and the markets had begun to improve in the early decades of the fifteenth century, it was the blue and white porcelain of Jao-chou which was to reign supreme, and to remain so to the end of the dynasty. Lung-ch'üan celadon continued to be made, but the material, except during the first quarter of the century, became heavy and coarse, the standards of craftsmanship showing a marked decline in every process.

The reason for the achievement of supremacy by the Jao-chou kilns probably lies in the consistently high standard maintained by the craftsmen, the better organization of the kilns, and a sound financial backing. Moreover careful control of firing, such as the reduction cycle needed for celadon, was not so important. With cobalt blue as a decorative pigment it was almost impossible to make a mistake, although in one group which includes underglaze copper red pieces mistakes were made; but they were not as disastrous as the uneven colour from a mistake in the reduction for celadon. The uneven, often yellowish brown of so much of the later Lung-ch'üan material in the fifteenth century tells its own story of failure.

The problem for the Jao-chou potters was of readjustment to a new situation, and the need to modify the shapes and decorative style, which had been much influenced by the requirements of the Near Eastern market up to this time. They had to evolve something congenial to sophisticated Chinese taste.[10]

Initially the shapes underwent little change, and large dishes, vases, and jars continued in production. The straight rimmed dish, so easily produced in quantity, was a natural shape to go on making, but more surprising is the reappearance of the foliate rimmed type made using twin moulds. These are easily distinguished from the earlier examples by the way the foliations are carried down the well to the foot-ring. In two classic examples the foliations actually occur in the foot itself.[11] Most of these foliated dishes are massive, measuring about fifty

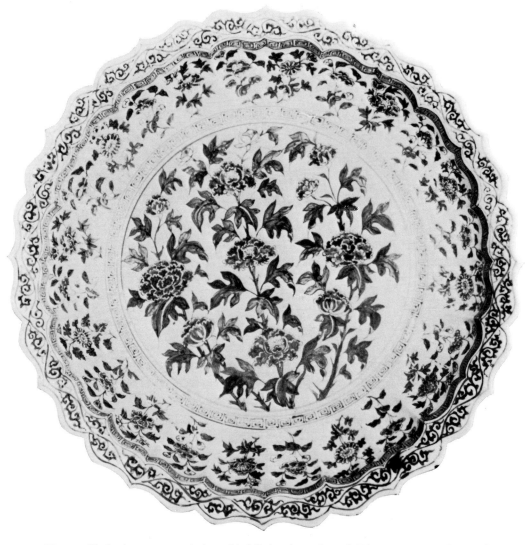

Fig. 142. Underglaze copper red plate with foliation down the well. Diameter 55.2 cm. Late 14th century A.D. Taiwan, Palace Museum.

centimetres in diameter, and in some instances more (Fig. 142). There were also several really large jars of unusual shape, with multi-lobed bodies and flaring mouths. These were not to last very long, probably because firing such huge pieces successfully was both hazardous and costly. At the other end of the scale, small deep bowls, small plates, and cup-stands made their appearance. The plates were invariably made with a straight rim, but the cup-stands had a foliate rim and a raised circular band in the centre. These two shapes were wholly consistent in diameter and thickness; the plates always about 19.7 centimetres and the cup-stands 19.1 centimetres, which indicates that they were mechanically produced.

One significant feature of this later fourteenth-century material is that the

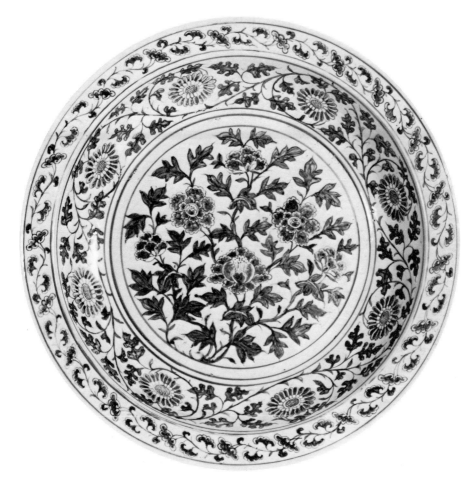

Fig. 143. Underglaze copper red plate with straight rim. Diameter 46.4 cm. Late 14th century A.D.
Chicago, Art Institute.

underglaze blue painted pieces are outnumbered by those painted in red. Neither colour is as a rule fired with complete success; the blue shows rather pale and greyish, while the copper red is uneven, often brownish, and has sometimes volatilized. The poor colour is partly due to the failure to fire at a high enough temperature, and on the red pieces partly due to poor reduction or too thin a glaze. The reason for the great number of copper red decorated pieces is likely to have been the shortage of cobalt blue following the closure of the ports. By the end of the century the situation had improved with the ports being reopened. It is probable that the shortage stimulated a search for native resources of cobaltiferous ores, but, although located in Yünnan, on present evidence this cobalt did not come into use until after 1426,[12] when it began to be mixed with the imported colour.

The potters, despite the difficulties with which they were faced, seem to have persisted and struggled with the problem of decorative style. The first step was to change the scale of the decorative elements in relation to each other and in

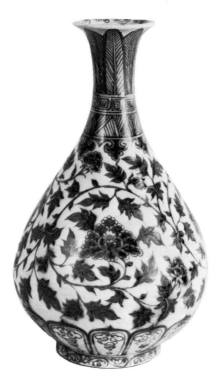

Fig. 144. Underglaze copper red vase. Height 33.7 cm. Late 14th century A.D. Tokyo, National Museum.

proportion to the whole (Fig. 143). For instance, the central field of a dish, which earlier had generally been decorated with a host of different motifs, now became the setting for a single motif, or at most four related ones, such as the flowers of the four seasons. These were enlarged to use the surface without overcrowding it, while round the well, floral scrolls, or sprays, were reduced in size and were carefully disposed so as not to take up every square centimetre of the available space. This had the effect of increasing the visual impact of the central theme. The most favoured motif seems to have been a large spray of peony or chrysanthemum, rather stiffly drawn, and springing from one side of the base. On ewers and vases of *yü-hu-ch'un p'ing* shape, a pear-shaped vase with narrow neck and spreading lip, a similar treatment is found, but floral scrolls are preferred. The scroll runs round the body, is very large in scale, and takes up more of the surface than in earlier vases. It also does so at the expense of the banding decorations above and below, which are drastically reduced, and play only a minor role (Fig. 144).

The next step was to replace the stiffly drawn spray on the dishes with a tree or shrub growing from a base line painted as a series of shallow banks. The shape of the dish also changed, the sides often curving up to a straight rim, and when there were no foliations on those with a flattened rim, the well was filled either with a naturalistically drawn floral scroll, often with different flowers, or with detached floral sprays, also naturalistically drawn, which might alternate with fruiting

198

sprays. If a flower spray was used in the centre, the number of flowers was reduced from four or more to two, with perhaps a pair of buds. To these should be added an exceptional group of massive dishes, about sixty-three centimetres in diameter, decorated in the centre with marvellous garden and landscape scenes (Fig. 145), with garden flowers and shrubs along the banks of a stream, and once or twice with pine trees. Round the curving sides are either flower sprays or neatly painted well-plenished flower beds. These would appear to have been made for special customers abroad, for they are recorded in the Ardebil Collection, in Topkapu Saray and in Japanese collections.

Fig. 145. Blue and white dish with loquat tree. Diameter 58.4 cm. Early 15th century A.D. Mr R. P. Griffing.

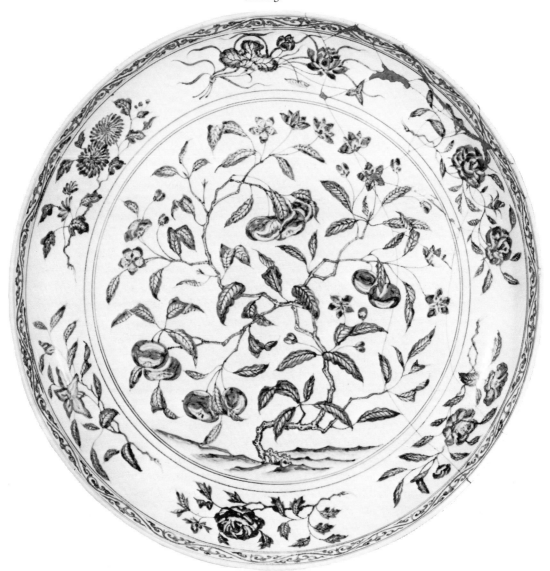

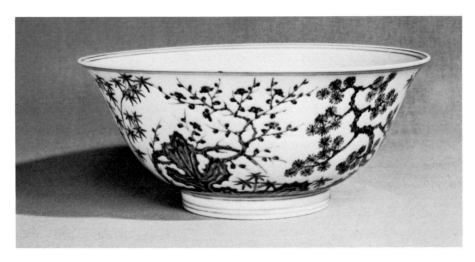

Fig. 146. Blue and white bowl with the Three Friends. Diameter 20.8 cm. Hsüan-tê mark and period. London, Percival David Foundation.

In the early part of the first quarter of the fifteenth century it was this style that aroused real interest, and the court began for the first time to seek the products of Jao-chou. By the end of the first quarter of the century orders were being despatched from the palace for the manufacture of plain white, blue, and red bowls and stem-cups for use on the ancestral altars of the princes.[13] Blue and white was undoubtedly being ordered too, but there is no record of a specific order before 1433.[14] By this time Jao-chou was the chief region for the production of high quality ceramics, and the order of 1433 indicates that the quantities must have been enormous, and also that the kilns were well able to meet the demands. For instance, the order required the manufacture of 433,500 pieces of porcelain to be decorated with dragons and phoenixes, in accordance with designs transmitted by an official of the Board of Public Works. How much of the order was to be in monochrome with moulded decoration and how much in blue and white is not made clear, but orders of similar proportions were to be made in the following centuries, and some are recorded in the later editions of the local histories.

The features which characterize the blue and white, the chief product up to the end of the Hsüan-tê period, are great strength in the control of line and the balance of the design in proportion to the whole surface. To these should be added the depth and intensity of the blue, which displays what the Chinese called 'heaped and piled' effects, due to increased concentrations of blue in carefully calculated places. The pigment was often so thickly applied that it broke through the glaze surface to oxidize almost black. There was also a tendency towards a type of glaze undulation referred to as 'orange peel' due to the rather coarse grinding of the glaze materials. These two effects were common to most of the early fifteenth-century wares up to the end of the Hsüan-tê period.

The decorations, which include dragon, phoenix, lotus scrolls, sprays and bouquets, fruiting vines, a multitude of flowers, and wave patterns, were evidently drawn out in pattern books and made easily available to the potters. Among the newer motifs introduced about the end of the first quarter of the century was the Three Friends, prunus, bamboo and pine, symbolic of beauty, integrity and long life with staunch friendship (Fig. 146). This group of three was often treated in a very painterly fashion, the different elements being freely disposed on the surface to create a naturalistic landscape scene. There were also fruiting sprays, which the decorators scattered freely round the outside of large bowls, and round the bodies of *mei-p'ing*. The fruiting sprays also occur in textiles at this time and the likelihood is that the palace artists made designs that could be freely adapted from one medium to another for items intended for imperial use.[15]

A certain number of porcelains were probably designed to special order from individual drawings. Such specimens, of which the flask illustrated (Plate VI, opposite page 193) is an example, are of the finest quality and are justifiably described as 'imperial'. In the Ming dynasty this term should always be understood as qualitative, and should not be assumed to mean that the pieces to which it is applied, were made in an imperial kiln. There was no imperial kiln in the Ming dynasty in the sense understood in the eighteenth century; there were government kilns, and these were not confined to Jao-chou, being found also in Honan and Hopei.[16]

By the Hsüan-tê period Chinese potters had largely freed themselves from the insidious influence of the Near East, and their products are so much more securely integrated into the native tradition that when an alien shape or decoration occurs it stands out very sharply. The alien origin is usually Persian or Syrian metalwork, or more rarely glass,[17] and examples of this kind continued to be made for the Near Eastern market in the early part of the century, but they also seem to have gained some popularity in China. How far they were simply regarded as rare novelties is uncertain, but the best of them vie in quality with those intended for the imperial household.

Interregnum

It was during the period from about 1426 to 1435 that the fifteenth-century imperial style reached its first peak, the second peak coming in the Ch'êng-hua period, thirty years later, between 1465 and 1487. In the intervening thirty years production to both government and imperial order was cut back, and it is believed that modifications were made to the kilns themselves. The products of the Interregnum are rather variable in quality and only some of the blue and white and a small number of other pieces have so far been attributed to this period (Figs. 147, 148). On the smaller pieces of blue and white, the base is recessed in two or

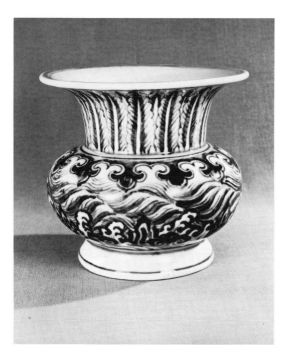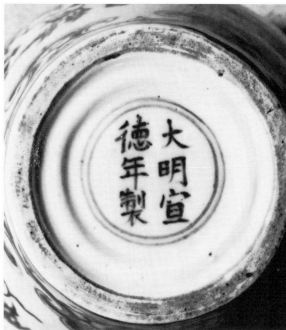

Fig. 147. Blue and white leys jar with stepped base. Diameter 16.1 cm. Hsüan-tê mark, but mid 15th century A.D. London, Percival David Foundation.

Fig. 148. Detail of underside of a stepped base vase.

three stages, and they are therefore referred to as the 'stepped base' group.[18] It was a manner of construction which must have started at the very end of Hsüan-tê, or soon after, and it continued into the beginning of the Ch'êng-hua period, from which one piece is known to date.[19] Larger pieces belonging to the series are distinguished by the low, vestigial foot-ring and glazed base, in conjunction with certain other features. These include an unusual glaze structure, and peculiarities in the cobalt reaction in the glaze evidenced among other things by reddish brown patches, where the colour is much concentrated. Most of the Interregnum pieces are heavily constructed, some are unusual shapes, and the decoration is more varied than in the earlier part of the century.

Ch'êng-hua and Hung-chih

When the production of the last thirty-five years of the century is examined, it is seen as a whole to be quite different from that of the earlier part of the century. Not only are the porcelain bodies much thinner and lighter in weight as well as more translucent, but the glaze has lost the orange peel effect and is very thick and glassy. The potters had by now refined the body materials, perfected the glaze and improved their firing technique. In terms of technical qualities, the Ch'êng-hua

202

and early Hung-chih periods were not to be equalled for another two hundred years, with only rare exceptions.

The range of material manufactured from now on was greater than it had been, but the blue and white still remained the predominant type. The decorations were to be as much changed in the last thirty-five years as were body and glaze. The 'heaped and piled' effect, which always made Hsüan-tê blue and white so desirable in Chinese eyes,[20] was replaced by a soft greyish blue applied very evenly, and because of the slight opacity of the glaze, the outlines often appear a little blurred. Dragons and phoenix continue to be popular, presumably for imperial use, but one singularly fine series of designs of lily and other flower scrolls appears on bowls always described as 'palace bowls' (Fig. 149).[21] Most of these are decorated only on the outside, but some designs appear on the inside as well. To these one can add a certain number of pieces with figures in landscape and a design of three men strolling through landscape towards a cloud-wrapped pavilion in the mountains, a design apparently unheard of in the first half of the century (Fig. 150).

Fig. 149. Blue and white palace bowl. Diameter 15.5 cm. Ch'êng-hua mark and period. London, Percival David Foundation.

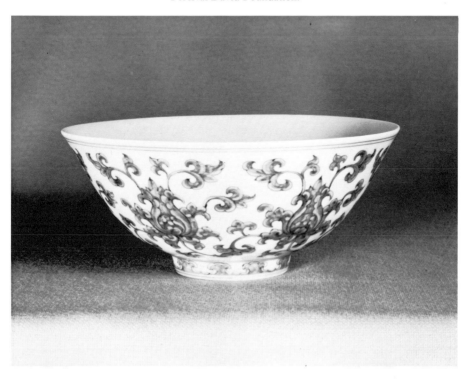

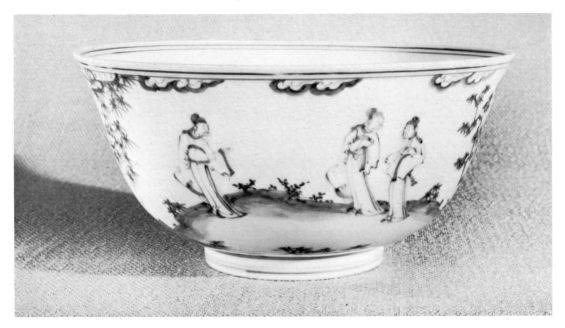

Fig. 150. Blue and white bowl. Diameter 20.5 cm. Late 15th century A.D. London, Percival David Foundation.

Polychrome Decoration

It was during the fifteenth century that overglaze enamelling began to be practised on porcelain from Jao-chou. As already recounted this technique appeared first in the stoneware of Tz'ŭ-chou type in the north, and it remained a northern treatment until about the middle of the fifteenth century, when the earliest examples, decorated only in red and green, are recorded (Fig. 151). Such enamelled porcelain, however, did not occur in any quantity until the last part of the century, when in the Ch'êng-hua period it became popular in a number of variant forms. Two well-known ones are *tou-ts'ai*, 'dove-tailed' colours,[22] and *wu-ts'ai*, literally 'five colours' but usually regarded simply as polychrome.

Of these two *tou-ts'ai* was especially admired on the courtly level. It was a nice combination of underglaze blue painting and overglaze enamelling of a very superior kind. The main outlines and some of the details were painted in blue directly on to the body in the normal way, and the piece was then glazed and fired to the high temperature required to fuse both porcelain and glaze. After being taken from the kiln, the coloured lead glazes were applied to the surface of the fired glaze in the appropriate places so they exactly filled the underlying outlines in blue (Fig. 152). The piece was then fired a second time to a temperature between 850°C and 900°C. This, as with the Tz'ŭ-chou type, was sufficient to fuse the lead glazes to the porcelain glaze, without upsetting the latter. It was a technique which required great accuracy on the part of the underglaze painter, since mistakes in the outline could not be corrected.

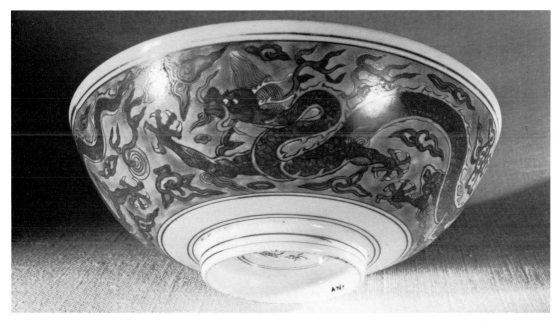

Fig. 151. Red and green enamelled bowl. Diameter 22.5 cm. Mid 15th century A.D. London, Percival David Foundation.

It was much easier, to use the *wu-ts'ai* treatment. This kind of polychrome first occurs without any cobalt blue under the glaze. It started simply, using only red and green, as on the mid-fifteenth-century dragon bowl (Fig. 151). In the Ch'êng-hua period yellow, turquoise, aubergine purple, and black were added, and the outlining of the decoration was always executed in either red or black over the

Fig. 152. *Tou-ts'ai* polychrome jar. Diameter 13 cm. Ch'êng-hua mark and period. London, Percival David Foundation.

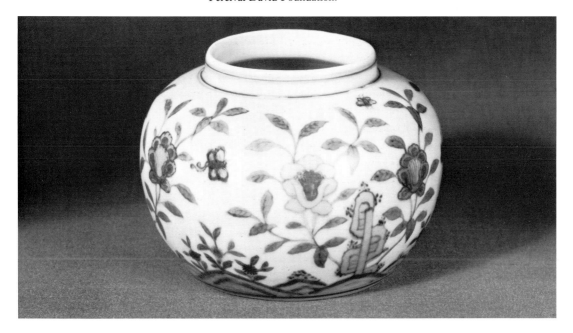

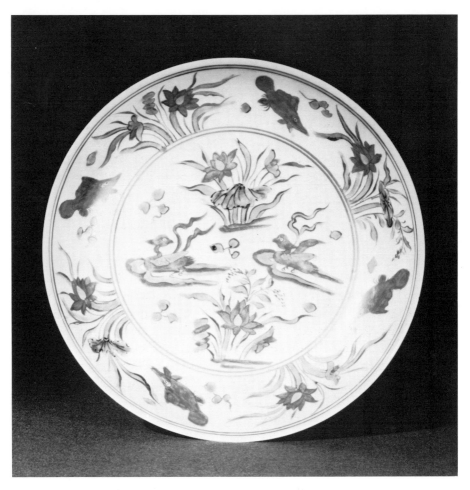

Above: Fig. 153. Polychrome enamelled dish. Diameter 21.7 cm. Ch'êng-hua mark and period. London, Percival David Foundation.

Below: Fig. 154. Green and yellow enamel on biscuit; leys jar. Diameter 14.7 cm. Chêng-tê mark and period. London, Percival David Foundation.

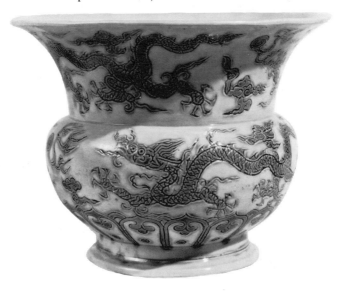

glaze. As these two colours for the outlines were painted on to a fired glaze, it was perfectly possible, if a mistake was made in the outline, to wipe off the colour and redraw the line, since the colour could not be absorbed by the fired glaze in the way that cobalt could be absorbed by an unfired body. This proved an extremely popular technique and a decorative style developed that was very different from the *tou-ts'ai* and from that of earlier periods. Fish, water weed and ducks were favoured, and figure scenes quickly became common (Fig. 153). Some very odd-looking dragons, sometimes with wings, and usually with flower sprays or jewelled strings bursting from their gaping jaws, are seen, writhing in a spirited manner round bowls and jars, or organized as circular medallions.

Enamel on Biscuit

A variant form of decoration using lead fluxed glazes was introduced towards the end of the century. It was to prove attractive and was to persist in a number of variations into modern times. This was to paint the coloured glazes, or enamels, directly on to the fired body, omitting the usual colourless porcelain glaze, a technique known as enamel on biscuit. In a sense it is a short cut, since it saves on the porcelain glaze, but it still involves two firings. The introduction of this variant treatment resulted in a quite different character in decoration from that of the overglaze type. It was infinitely more striking, with large masses of brilliant colour making a great visual impact. There are two styles to be distinguished in this group of polychrome wares. One is that known as Ming *san-ts'ai*, Ming 'three-colour' ware, in which the dominant background is yellow, with a decoration incised into the body and coloured green (Fig. 154); later other colours were to be added.

The other style, commonly recognized by the name *fa-hua*, which is untranslatable, is nearer to cloisonné enamelling than to anything else.[23] The decoration is generally outlined in thin threads of trailed slip, often has incised details, and the coloured glazes are painted on to the fired body within the slip outlines, in the same way as the enamel pastes are put into the cells, or cloisons, of the metal based cloisonné. The palette used for the *fa-hua* is much more varied than that for the *san-ts'ai* and the backgrounds are very rarely yellow, a deep cobalt blue or a copper turquoise being preferred. Moreover the pieces on which this style of decoration is found are generally rather large, with *kuan* jars, large *mei-p'ing* and garden seats in the shape of drums among the commonest forms (Fig. 155). One point of interest about the type is that the quality of the porcelain body itself was less fine than that of the other wares. This was possibly because it was going to be completely shrouded in colour anyway, and if white was needed at all it was likely to be for details which would barely show any defects in the body against the 'colours that dazzle the eye'.[24] The decorations were near in character to those usually found on such large objects. The central area or band was rather

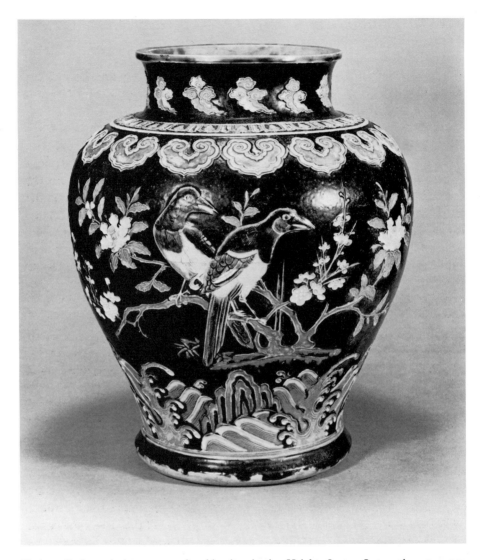

Fig. 155. *Fa-hua* polychrome enamel on biscuit; wine jar. Height 28.2 cm. Late 15th century A.D. Osaka, Ataka Collection.

freely decorated with birds, such as peacocks, with shrubs, or with figures in landscape, while above and below were more formal bands of various kinds. The petal panel motif, or a wave pattern, was common round the bottom, while above would often be large lappets alternating with strings of jewels round the shoulder, and small stylized puffs of cloud round the neck. In a few cases the potters complicated everything for themselves by making a double shell and piercing the outer one so that the main elements stood out against an openwork ground, through which it was possible to see the glazed inner shell.

Miscellaneous Polychrome Types

A number of variant combinations of underglaze and overglaze decorations, which cannot easily be categorized, are found especially in the later fifteenth century and into the first half of the sixteenth century.

One of these is an unusual little group of bowls and dishes, which were made only from some time in the Ch'êng-hua period until about the end of the Chêng-tê period. Using a porcelain of the highest quality, the potters finely incised a decoration of dragons among waves with clouds above; this was done while the porcelain clay was still fairly wet and plastic. After drying the main parts, the head, neck and body with the legs of the dragons were painted with a resist. When the pieces had been glazed and fired this left the dragons in the biscuit against the glazed ground. This presents an odd appearance which can be seen on a number of unfinished pieces which have survived to our own day (Fig. 156). The dragons were then painted green, and the claws, horns and streamers, which had not been painted with the resist were also coloured, so that the bodies and heads appear as enamel on biscuit, but the rest as overglaze enamel (Fig. 157). In the David Foundation there is one unfinished piece of the Chêng-tê period, and another of the Hung-chih period, which was decorated in recent times without the claws, horns or streamers, and in the wrong colours; it is interesting to compare these two with the green enamelled originals.

Also belonging to the series of variants are some dishes with rather bold decoration of the centre with a flower spray, two large flowers and a bud, while round the walls are disposed, rather wide apart, four large fruiting sprays (Fig. 158); round the outside is a floral scroll. The design occurs as ordinary blue and white, as white reserved against a deep blue ground, in blue with a yellow enamelled ground and in coffee brown against a white ground. It is a striking design made all the more effective by the variations in the colour combinations.

The earliest examples seem to date from the last years of the Hsüan-tê period, and it is worth noting that such largeness of scale and sparing distribution of the elements in design is extremely unusual in the first half of the fifteenth century. These earliest examples are of the white reserved on blue type and a pale coffee brown on white. The pale coffee colour is achieved from an iron oxide, and evidently it was rather sparingly used in the early specimens, for those of the late fifteenth century, bearing the Hung-chih mark, are very much darker. The combination of the two different glazes must have presented a difficult problem with regard to the firing temperature, and there are instances, such as one of the Chêng-tê period, in which the brown has flooded beyond its proper areas as the result of slight over-firing.

It was not until the Ch'êng-hua period that the practice of painting the white ground of a blue and white piece, with overglaze yellow enamel began, but once

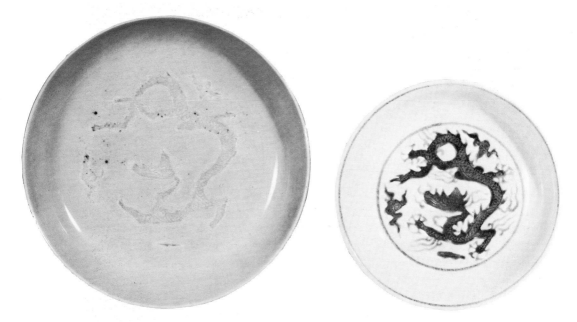

Fig. 156. Unfinished dish with biscuit dragon. Diameter 22.9 cm. Chêng-tê mark and period. London, Percival David Foundation.

Fig. 157. Completed dish with green enamel on the biscuit and over the glaze. Diameter 18.2 cm. Chêng-tê mark and period. London, Percival David Foundation.

started this became the most popular treatment and was to continue through to the Chia-ching period in the middle of the sixteenth century, when this particular design is seen for the last time.

Monochromes

The production of monochrome porcelain during the first century and a half was far surpassed in quantity by the blue and white and the polychrome enamelled wares. The monochromes, white, copper red, blue, yellow, turquoise blue and celadon, are chiefly bowls and dishes, with a few ewers, *mei-p'ing* and other vases. They are amongst the most difficult of Chinese ceramics to date and the fact that many pieces are marked is no help at all. Marks on Chinese porcelain are a special problem which is dealt with at the end of this chapter.

The white wares quite simply continue the traditions of the fourteenth century, with body and glaze gradually being refined, the body becoming thinner and more fine grained, and the glaze more translucent, glassy and more truly colourless. In the early part of Ming it is common to find what the Chinese call *an-hua*, 'secret decoration', on much of the plain white porcelain. This is decoration finely incised into the body while still wet, or it may be included as very low relief in the mould on which a dish or bowl was made. The name refers to the elusiveness of the decoration; often it is only possible to see it by holding the piece up to strong illumination. The designs used in *an-hua* are generally floral scrolls, dragons and

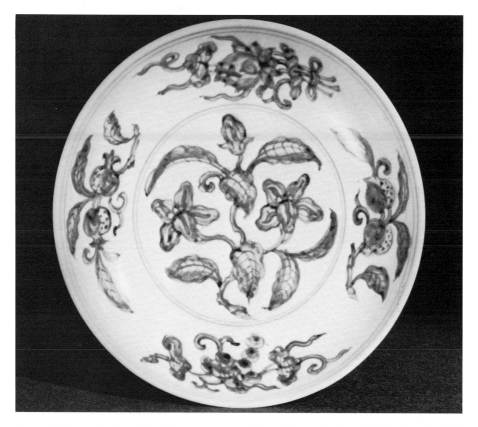

Fig. 158. Blue and yellow dish. Diameter 29.7 cm. Hung-chih mark and period. London, Percival David Foundation.

clouds, and lotus scrolls with the Eight Emblems of Buddhism. It is possible to assign quite a large number of white porcelains to the early part of the fifteenth century, but they seem to have been less popular in the later years, when colours were apparently preferred.

Copper red had, as we have seen, also been used in the earlier fourteenth century, but the colour was often brownish and muddy. The tendency to muddiness continued to the end of the fourteenth century on the bowls and dishes, but by the beginning of the fifteenth century the potters seem to have mastered the technique of reduction and there are some good examples of these shapes and some very handsome stem-cups. The control of both temperature and reduction is critical for the type and the raising of the temperature seems satisfactorily to have been achieved. As in the fourteenth century the dishes are usually decorated with dragons and clouds in low relief round the sides, but the designs are more elusive than formerly. Unlike fourteenth-century examples the base is always glazed. During the fifteenth century the glaze itself nearly always displays the familiar 'orange peel' effect, and the rims almost without exception are perfectly white (Fig. 159). The reason for the white rim is that the base glaze applied over the copper charged glaze tends to run down slightly from the sharp

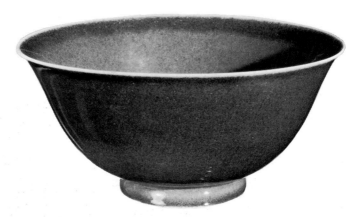

Fig. 159. Copper red glazed bowl. Diameter 20.7 cm. Early 15th century A.D. London, Percival David Foundation.

edge of the rim so that the copper beneath volatilizes through it in that area. The depth and brilliance of the red in the fifteenth-century examples is remarkably consistent, but after the end of the century it fails and for a time red, using copper, was abandoned as a monochrome.

Plain blue pieces are extremely rare in the fifteenth century, and when they are found there is usually *an-hua* relief dragon decoration round the inside of the walls under a colourless glaze, the blue being confined to the outside. Evidently the decorative use of blue for painting was preferred.

Yellow porcelains seem not to have occurred much before the Ch'êng-hua period. As an antimoniate colour, it was of course most easily employed on porcelain as an overglaze enamel, which means that it may have been applied over earlier plain white pieces. This is the reason why many of the yellow pieces are regarded with suspicion. Those specimens which seem most convincingly to be of fifteenth-century date and may be assigned to Ch'êng-hua and Hung-chih are usually slightly brownish and iridescent, a characteristic which is largely eliminated in the following century.

Turquoise glazed porcelain is rarely datable to the fifteenth century, but becomes more common in the sixteenth. Such pieces as survive from the early part of the Ming dynasty could probably be counted on the fingers of one hand. Like the yellow, the turquoise, which derives from copper, has to be fired on as an enamel, but unlike the yellow, which is fluxed with lead, the turquoise has to be fluxed in a glaze largely free of lead. It thus falls into the category of alkaline glazes, which may have a different and much wider firing range. The use of turquoise as an overglaze colour was apparently mastered in the second half of the fifteenth century, but its use on a large scale as a monochrome, evidently presented difficulties. In the Tz'ǔ-chou examples it is noticeable that the glaze is always crazed and that it may often peel off. It was this problem of glaze fit which had to be overcome. It seems likely that in applying it to the porcelain biscuit it was necessary to discover the right temperature for the glaze mix to fuse properly

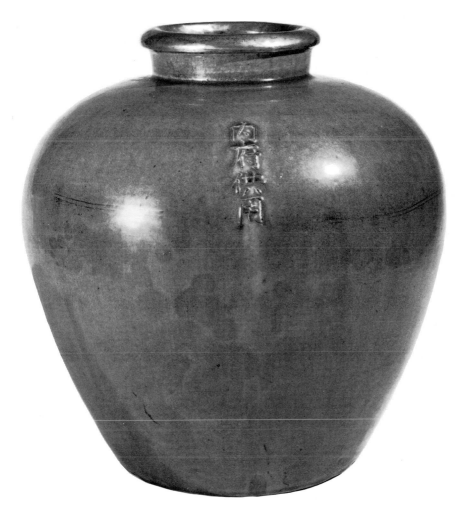

Fig. 160. Turquoise glazed wine jar. Height 33.3 cm. 15th century A.D. London, Percival David Foundation.

with the body. In fact the tendency to craze was never completely overcome even on the highest quality pieces which can be assigned to the fifteenth century (Fig. 160). There is a small number of dishes on which the colour has been applied, usually only on the outside, with a Hsüan-tê mark, but it seems more likely that these pieces should be attributed to the Ch'êng-hua and Hung-chih periods by which time the colour was being used quite commonly on the polychrome wares.

The grey green celadons of Lung-ch'üan continued in production on the fall of the Yüan, and a study of the material of late fourteenth and early fifteenth-century date reveals that in both shape and decoration they remain very close in style to the contemporary blue and white. In very many instances the decorations are identical, the only modifications being accounted for by the difference in execution between the brush and the knife. There are examples of this kind to be seen in the large dishes, the ewers, and the *yü-hu-ch'un p'ing,* the pear-shaped vase

213

with spreading lip. By the Hsüan-tê period, however, the quality was deteriorating and very few pieces of any distinction can be dated after the end of the period. The forms had become coarse, the structure being depressingly heavy, and the glaze uneven in both translucency and colour. By the end of the fifteenth century Lung-ch'üan had ceased to be a serious competitor with the Jao-chou kilns upon which, from the early fourteenth century, production had been increasingly concentrated.

Reign Marks

The question of reign marks is a vexed one which can only be raised when we come to the Ming dynasty, for it was in this dynastic period that it first became the practice to supply a mark to porcelain. It seems to have been introduced as common practice during the Hsüan-tê period between 1426 and 1435 and not before. Any marks pointing to an earlier period than this are suspect.

Either four or six characters are used.[25] If there are four characters they will be those either of the dynasty or of the reign period. If the first two characters name the dynasty only, then the last character will be either *chih* or *ts'ao*, the first implying 'made to imperial order', and the second simply meaning manufactured, and it may occur on a piece made anywhere. Once marks, which are usually written in underglaze blue or finely incised on the base of an object, had been established in regular use they were perpetuated, so that those which were first employed were likely to continue in use. Thus Hsüan-tê and Ch'êng-hua marks, which are among the earliest, and certainly, from the point of view of the ceramics, the two most popular with both Chinese and foreign collectors, are also those most open to suspicion. When a cyclical date is included, normally making the total up to eight characters, the situation is rather better, with the likelihood of the specimen being authentic considerably increased. Any assessment of authenticity must always be based on the materials, form, decoration and its style, and peculiarities associated with the particular type of ceramic ware, and not in the first instance on the mark, which should be considered last in any attempt to evaluate a specimen. The Interregnum, for instance, is a period during which the Hsüan-tê mark continued in unabated use, and the second half of the sixteenth century is well known for the use of both Hsüan-tê and Ch'êng-hua marks.

It should be emphasized in connection with marks that the use of an earlier mark was not, initially at least, done with an intent to deceive. It was done mainly to give a piece a *cachet*, and in admiration of the products of the period of the mark chosen. Finally, it should be pointed out that the style of writing is not necessarily a criterion for authenticity, nor is it even a guide to the century in which a piece was made. Some eighteenth-century copies of fifteenth-century marks are particularly deceptive.

CHAPTER NINE

Popular Taste and New Markets

By the beginning of the sixteenth century the Ming dynasty had already passed its zenith and was entering a long decline, with the administrative machinery of government starting to creak under the complex system of taxation, which had evolved piecemeal in the earlier years. Corruption was also becoming increasingly apparent in high places, while the emperor, brought up under the influence of the eunuchs, was not only unwilling, but also unable to exercise his authority as a ruler, as the autocratic Hung-wu and Yung-lo had done in the early years of the dynasty. It was the great number of eunuchs allied to their administrative power which was to be a major factor in the final collapse of the Ming dynasty in 1643. The eunuchs had gradually insinuated themselves into the higher rungs of the government hierarchy, from which the first emperors had barred them, and by now the emperor had little real authority. Attempts at the reform of the tax system, begun after the death of Chêng-tê in 1521, although not doomed to total failure, were less successful than they would have been had the emperor held greater power and shouldered his responsibilities as a ruler. The result was that the agrarian situation deteriorated even more than it had done in the previous century, because it was the peasant who paid in the end, since officials at all levels habitually passed down the demands for taxes, and the wealthy were easily able through long experience to shift the responsibility for payment to others less well equipped to withstand the pressures. By the middle of the seventeenth century, the government, wholly inept and riddled with corruption, gave way completely before the rebel Li Tzŭ-ch'êng, and then he in his turn fell before the determined pressure of the Manchus, who in the course of the previous fifty years had adjusted to Chinese systems of administration as they were found in the north-eastern frontier regions.[1]

It was in the year 1514, when cracks in the administration had begun to appear, that the Portuguese first arrived on the coast of China. They were not particularly welcomed, for they were unmannerly adventurers, but they wedged themselves into the ports and from that time on played an important part in the carrying trade to Indonesia and India.[2] It is often said that the Portuguese ousted the Arabs from this trade, but this is not entirely true, for even before the end of the fourteenth century, and much more after 1433, when Chêng Ho made his final expedition, Chinese merchants had financed and worked their own system into Indonesia, and many had travelled to, and settled down in the trading cities of Indonesia and Malaysia.[3] The Portuguese made much of their opportunities until the arrival of the Dutch, who were soon followed by the British. After the founding of the Dutch and British East India Companies the Portuguese found themselves being edged out of the international trade that developed between the Far East and Europe.

In the sixteenth century, however, another competitor for the trade was Japan. Much of the history of the sixteenth century along the south-east coast of China is tied up with Japan. Pirates from Japan were a constant and irritating menace, frequently assailing the provinces of Fukien, Chekiang and Kiangsu, often laying waste and looting large areas. But alongside this violent contact there was, in both the sixteenth and the seventeenth centuries, a more peaceful and frankly commercial meeting between the two countries, mainly on the private merchant level at the ports, with a lively trade in a number of commodities, which included not only porcelain, but swords, lacquer, and sulphur.[4]

The great quantity of porcelain required by the foreign merchants during the second half of the sixteenth century and throughout the seventeenth, did much to ease the precarious economic situation of the potters of Jao-chou, especially at Ching-tê Chên, when orders made by the government were cut back half-way through their execution for lack of money.[5] The emperor Wan-li, whose irresponsible attitude was notorious, wasted the already depleted finances of the state in the pursuit of luxury, and in death was surrounded with all the paraphernalia of a life of extravagance.

The activities of the potteries, many of them privately operated, continued unabated until after the collapse of Ming, but in the period from about 1650 to 1680, much of the production was curtailed, and Ching-tê Chên in particular suffered severely between 1673 and 1680 at the time of Wu San-kuei's rebellion, being overrun and burned at one stage in the prolonged campaign of suppression.

The Ceramic Industry

The ceramic industry, well established and very comprehensively organized, especially at Ching-tê Chên, was capable of producing virtually anything that a merchant might demand by the beginning of the sixteenth century. The Chinese potter had proved himself adaptable to changing fashions and markets, and was versatile in decorative invention. From the sixteenth century onward a great flexibility in the creation of form and in decorative techniques and styles was to be required of him as the markets grew wider. Master of his techniques, he was indeed able to submit to demands without difficulty. Only when he was required to copy an inscription in Arabic or Latin does he seem to have found himself somewhat at a loss.

The materials which the potter needed continued on the whole to be easily available, and although resources of Chinastone (*pai-tun-tzŭ*) temporarily ran short, new sources were soon found. The colouring pigments for the most part presented no problem, for although cobalt continued to be imported, and was now named *hui-ch'ing* or *hui-hui-ch'ing*, 'Muhammadan blue',[6] resources of native cobalt, which was called *shih-ch'ing*, 'stone blue', had been found in Yünnan, and had begun to be used before the middle of the fifteenth century, often being mixed with the imported pigment. This practice was to continue, and it is usually found that pure imported blue is relatively rare on its own, although the native blue was often used alone. Contrary to popular belief it is not possible to distinguish between the two types of blue as seen on a fired porcelain without scientific tests; efficient preparation of the pigment and proper firing can produce the same brilliant blue.

During the period with which this chapter is concerned, Ching-tê Chên and the minor kilns in Jao-chou prefecture were responsible for the great bulk of the ceramic output, with certain so-called provincial kilns producing a number of easily distinguishable and rather different types in more limited quantities. The best known of these are Tê-hua in Fukien, and kilns just to the north of the modern port of Swatow in northern Kuang-tung, which made a colourful ware known by the name of the port. The stonewares made during the sixteenth century and probably into the present age, came mainly from kilns in the south reasonably near the coast. Much of this type of material was in the form of large storage jars, decorated, sometimes lavishly, with incised or relief moulded dragons, and are hence often called dragon jars. Large numbers of these have been found in Indonesia and Malaysia.[7] They are usually a greyish brown stoneware, brown or green glazed, and vary in size from about ten inches in height to as much as three or four feet. A few, like the Tradescant jar, are polychrome glazed and decorated in a superior manner with floral motifs sprigged directly to the body.[8]

Blue and White and Polychrome in the Sixteenth Century

At the beginning of the sixteenth century many of the familiar shapes and decorations continued with little immediate change. Orders continued to be

Fig. 161. Blue and white brush rest inscribed in Persian, 'Pen rest'. Length 22.5 cm. Chêng-tê mark and period. London, Percival David Foundation.

despatched from the capital to Ching-tê Chên and other kilns fulfilling government contracts. The Chêng-tê reign, 1506–21, however, is marked by the manufacture of an unusual group of blue and white wares on which appear inscriptions in Arabic and Persian.

Most of the pieces making up the group are objects intended for the scholar's study, for there are writing boxes of various kinds, ink stones, brush rests, small lamps, incense burners, and hat stands (Fig. 161). The number of bowls and dishes amounts to about half a dozen small examples, there being only two recorded really large pieces. One of these two is in the Ardebil collection in Tehran,[9] and the other, now in America, is in fact a plate formerly in the Eumorfopoulos and Sedgwick collections.[10] These two large pieces are very different in character from the rest of the group and were probably made to special order for a Near Eastern merchant.

The decoration of the group differs in almost every respect from that found on any other pieces at this time. The inscriptions, usually moral precepts or bald descriptive terms, are included in medallions that punctuate a background of scroll work defined by the name 'Muhammadan scrolls'. The outlines are painted with thin lines of a slightly darker blue than that of the wash which fills in the spaces. Occasionally a rather stylized lotus makes its appearance, as it does on the only example on which there is a Koranic inscription, a table screen of considerable size, now in the David Foundation (Fig. 162). The inscriptions, while generally quite easy to read, are clearly copied by painters unfamiliar with the Arabic script.

The explanation for the existence of the group is that the eunuchs, who at this time were chiefly Muslim by religious persuasion, had achieved positions of great power both in relation to the emperor, over whom they exerted a baleful influence, and in relation to the government, in which many now held important administrative posts at a high ranking level to which, under the early emperors,

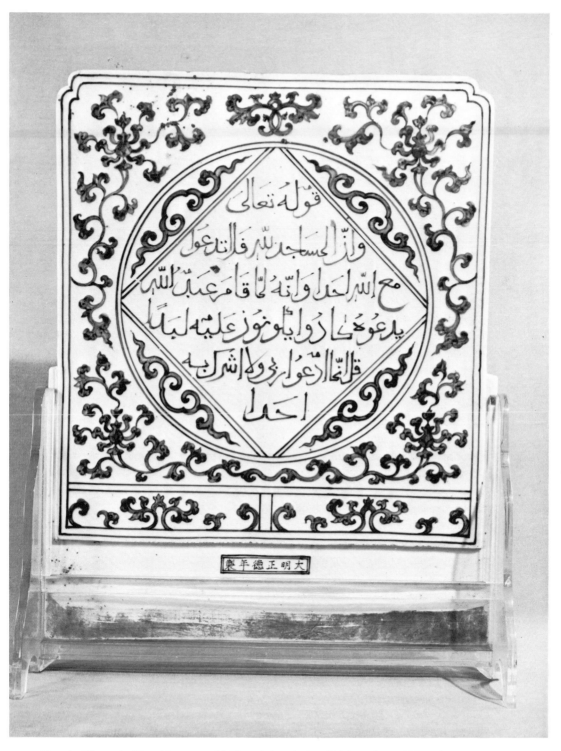

Fig. 162. Blue and white table screen with Koranic inscription. Height 45.8 cm. Chêng-tê mark and period. London, Percival David Foundation.

they had been unable to aspire. Their power was now such that it was easy for them to order whatever they wanted for the furnishing and decoration of their houses and offices.

Two points of interest with regard to the pieces in the group should be noted. One is that they are always marked with a six character mark in underglaze blue of Chêng-tê, while almost without exception all other pieces marked and made in this reign have only a four character mark. This is perhaps an indication of the extent of eunuch power. The second point to notice is that on the death of Chêng-tê the type ceases to be made. The only pieces with similar inscriptions in succeeding reign periods are of poor quality by comparison, and often have polychrome decoration. These later inscriptions are rarely decipherable, some of them being no more than absurd scribbles.

Other porcelain in blue and white and polychrome during the Chêng-tê period includes examples with dragons among lotus scrolls of a familiar kind, but the drawing is weaker than it had been, and the organization is more crowded on bowls, dishes, and the globular jars with wide flaring neck known as leys jars (*cha-tou*; Fig. 163). Much less fine are the many small jars, ovoid in elevation, and round, rectangular or hexagonal in plan. It is on these small jars that a marked departure is seen from the traditional canons of decoration, for they are often painted with herons in lotus ponds, children at play, and other themes more popular in their appeal than the rather formal lotus and other floral scrolls (Fig. 164). Diaper patterns of various kinds are also introduced more often, especially on the overglaze enamelled wares.

It is a significant feature of the sixteenth century, to be continued even into the late seventeenth century, that there is a steady movement away from the specially drawn designs intended for execution in various media so characteristic of the fifteenth century, towards designs of wider more popular appeal. The change becomes very noticeable in the Chia-ching period from about 1522 onward, with children, scholars, animals, birds and flowers in natural surroundings such as gardens, on terraces, or in open landscapes (Fig. 165). While there are still examples of the more formal designs that reflect the high style of the fifteenth century, they are much less common and less well executed (Fig. 166). Interest in the earlier designs flagged and new sources of inspiration were being sought. The new sources seem chiefly to have been the illustrated books, which were beginning to enjoy wide circulation. Books of poems and anecdotes, each with a facing illustration, editions of novels with illustrated supplements, and dramas with a running head of illustration, provided the painter of porcelain with a profusion of lively themes (Fig. 167). A few examples of bird and flower drawings have been identified, and in future perhaps many more will be found. Into this repertory were also introduced Shou Lao, the god of longevity, and the Eight Immortals, together with many symbolic elements associated with immortality.

The handling of these themes was very free with a finely drawn outline and a

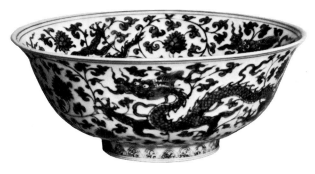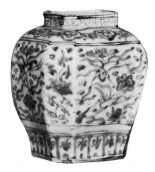

Fig. 163. Blue and white bowl. Diameter 23.3 cm. Chêng-tê mark and period. Croydon, Riesco collection.

Fig. 164. Blue and white jar with herons and lotus. Height 11.8 cm. Chêng-tê period. Formerly Mrs Alfred Clark.

wash filling. The outlines were usually executed in a dark blue, and the wash filling was in two or more shades of lighter blue, a treatment that often gave great liveliness to these popular designs,

In the blue and white and in the overglaze enamelled polychrome the new approach is amply illustrated on a wide range of shapes, which were augmented in the Chia-ching period by handsome ewers and gourd-shaped vases, the latter shape having been allowed to drop out of the repertory in the second half of the fourteenth century (Fig. 168). There remained a tendency to break up the surface

Fig. 165. Blue and white wine jar with children in landscape. Diameter 26.7 cm. Chia-ching mark and period. Washington, Freer Gallery of Art.

Fig. 166. Blue and white bowl imitating fifteenth-century style. Diameter 14.2 cm. Hsüan-tê mark but 16th century A.D. London, Percival David Foundation.

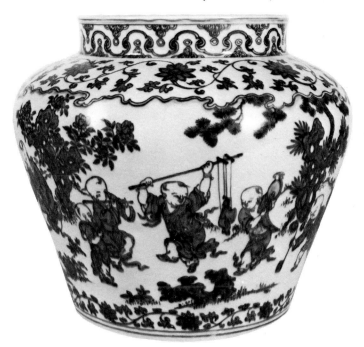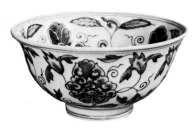

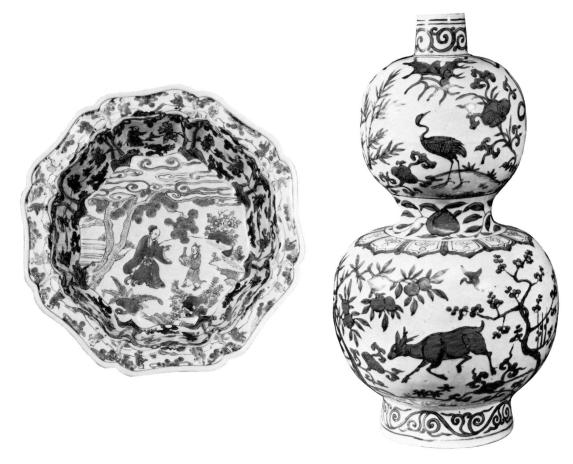

Fig. 167. Polychrome basin with figures in landscape. Diameter 30.5 cm. Wan-li period, late 16th century A.D. Osaka, Ataka collection.

Fig. 168. Gourd vase painted in blue. Height 44.5 cm. Chia-ching mark and period. London, British Museum.

of the large upright forms into a series of formal and informal bands, a treatment well-suited to the gourd vases with their waisted middle zone.

In the overglaze enamelled group a variant sub-group appears about the middle of the century. This is composed of pieces on which the predominant colour is red in combination with lesser amounts of green and yellow, with limited additions of turquoise and black; sometimes there is underglaze blue as well. In some cases the red is applied as a flat ground colour, with panels left white in reserve and then delicately painted with bird and flower scenes. After the second firing, the red ground was decorated in gold with floral scrolls, the gold being lightly burnished on using a suitable adhesive. Some ewers made in the form of dancing girls are also decorated in this way (Fig. 169). In many cases bowls were wholly covered on the outside with either red or green and similarly gilt. The type is known by its Japanese name, *kinrande*, 'gold brocaded', and it seems to have been made purely for the Japanese market.[11] A unique example of the type is a high-footed ewer

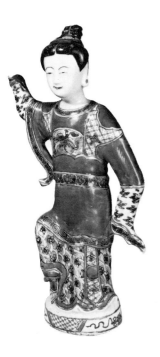
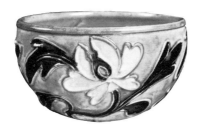
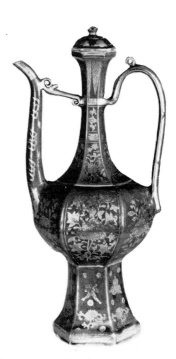

Left: Fig. 169. *Kinrande* ewer in form of a dancing girl. Height 31.8 cm. 16th century A.D. London, Percival David Foundation.

Centre: Fig. 170. *Fa-hua* enamel on biscuit bowl with lotus decoration. Diameter 17.8 cm. 16th century A.D. Mr Pierre de Menasce.

Right: Fig. 171. Gold, *kinrande*, decorated aubergine glazed ewer. Height 33 cm. Mid 16th century A.D. Baur collection.

based on a contemporary Chinese metal form, on which the gold has been applied to a plain aubergine purple ground (Fig. 171).

During the sixteenth century the palette of the *san-ts'ai* type of enamel on biscuit was enlarged, and aubergine purple, turquoise blue, and black or sepia made their appearance, the black or sepia generally only being used for outlines, which began to be preferred to incising. One reason for this may have been that the stability of the colour helps to prevent the other colours running into each other. It does not always do this, but the running is certainly less frequent. Some of the designs became smaller in scale, and slightly more fussy.[12] Despite the availability of additional colours, and the possible variation in the colour combinations, the original green and yellow type continued to be used well into the Wan-li period. As a decorative treatment it has been revived at intervals ever since that time, occurring in the K'ang-hsi, Ch'ien-lung, and other later periods into the nineteenth century.

The type of enamel on biscuit referred to as *fa-hua* completely changed in character in the course of the century. The objects became much smaller, while the scale of the decoration was enormously enlarged, so that the surface was no longer organized in bands as on the late fifteenth-century examples. The small vases and rotund bowls had boldly outlined lotus or chrysanthemum designs, which were painted in a restricted range of colours, often only two or three being used, with aubergine purple or turquoise blue tending to predominate as the ground colour (Fig. 170).

Monochrome in the Sixteenth Century

The monochrome glazes used in the previous century all continued in use, except for the copper red, which deteriorated so obviously in the Chêng-tê period that it had to be abandoned. The potters seem to have lost the perfect control of reduction necessary to achieve a good even red over the whole surface. Thus during the rest of the Ming dynasty, if a red monochrome was wanted, the copper was replaced by an overglaze iron red. It is a rather bright, slightly orange colour, lacking the sumptuous depths of the copper glaze, which when it was reintroduced in the late seventeenth century was to be rather different in appearance.

About the middle of the century a copper green enamel began to be used for monochrome effect, thus joining the red and the earlier yellow in the overglaze monochrome range. Plain cobalt blue became rather more common during the century, and just occasionally small bowls are given the *kinrande* treatment. White bowls and vases also occur, but the dating of white wares in the Ming dynasty is a subject bristling with difficulties, and it is hard to distinguish any clear line of development in the sixteenth century. Colour seems to have been preferred, or else many plain white pieces have subsequently been given a coloured enamel coating, which leaves us with a false impression of the period.

1573- 1619

Decorative Style under Wan-li and his Successors

There is a marked continuity of the sixteenth-century decorative style into the second half of the Wan-li period in the seventeenth century, and even beyond that reign. This means that in the absence of dated or convincingly marked pieces it is difficult to state with certainty whether a specimen should be dated to Chia-ching, Lung-ch'ing or Wan-li and his immediate successors. Often the best one can do is to assign it to the first or second half of the sixteenth century, or broadly to late Ming. The Lung-ch'ing period from 1567 to 1572 is so short that no specific decorative style can fairly be associated with it; the traditions established in the preceding Chia-ching period continued without interruption.

Opposite: Plate VII. Swatow type dish painted in overglaze enamels. Depth 39.9 cm. 16th century A.D. London, Percival David Foundation.

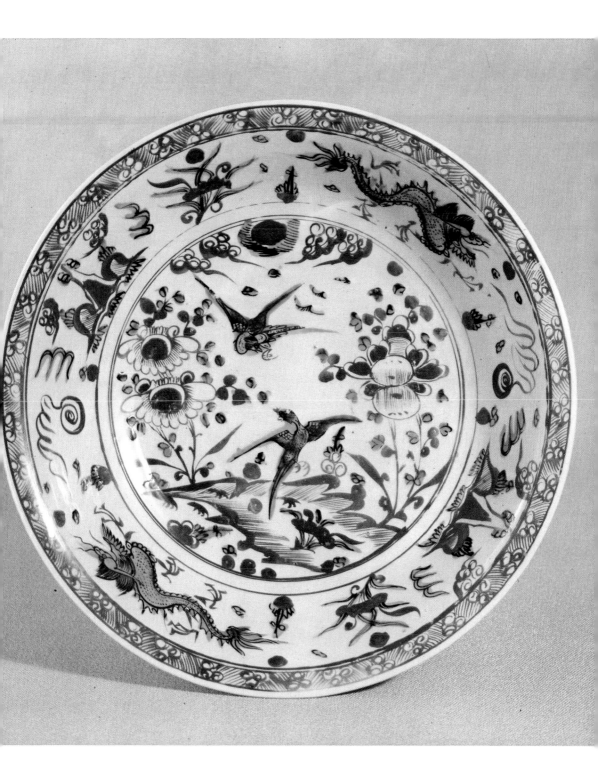

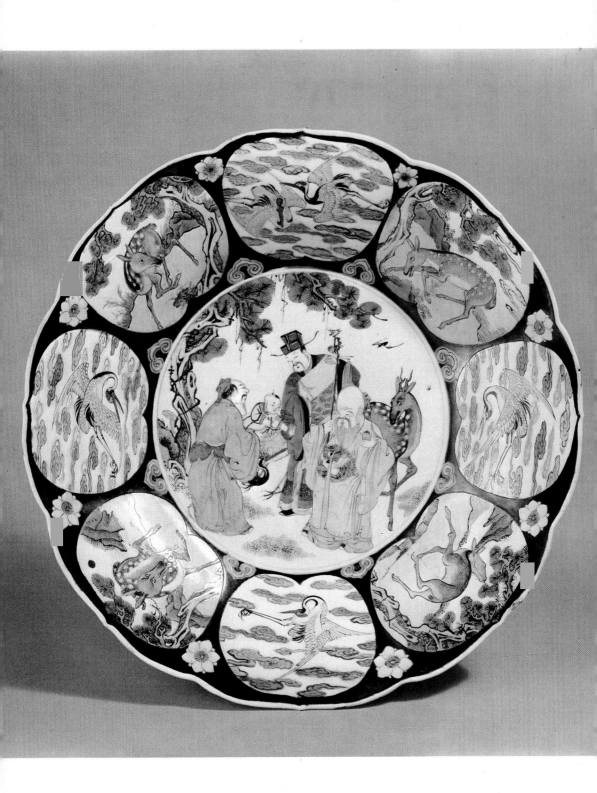

Towards the end of the sixteenth century, when Wan-li was reducing the country's financial resources to even lower levels than had his recent ancestors, and the government was rapidly breaking down in the face of agrarian troubles, certain significant changes in the ceramic industry began to occur. There were two reasons for the changes. One was that although the palace still sent orders for hundreds of thousands of pieces, patterns of specific kinds were apparently not demanded. The second reason was that orders once given tended to be at least partly countermanded before completion on account of the cost.

The results can be seen in the increasing use of free decoration in preference to the dragon and phoenix designs used for pieces intended for the personal use of the emperor and empress. The second result was that the potters, finding themselves in dire economic straits with perhaps part of an imperial order left on their hands and no further work immediately in prospect, had to look elsewhere for new customers. The way was therefore opened not only for new decorative treatments, but also to explore new markets. The vacuum was filled by the Japanese, for whom as we have seen the potters had already been working, the Portuguese, and then in the early seventeenth century by the Dutch, soon followed by the British.

A number of distinctive styles and treatments can be distinguished apart from the central tradition, which continued from the sixteenth century. Two of the new styles had their origin in native tradition, and a third, which was subject to overwhelmingly strong Japanese influence, was exploited for the Japanese market.

The two treatments to emerge from the native tradition, which qualify as artistic styles in their own right from about the end of the sixteenth century, are quite distinctive. One developed in the Wan-li period and persisted virtually unchanged until about 1683. It is found almost exclusively in the blue and white. The other attained its apogee between about 1630 and 1670, and, as it was of much greater importance in the development of style, it will be discussed under its stylistic name of Transitional.

Kraak Porselein

The first style, which is curiously static, has been associated with the name Kraak ware, a type commonly exported to South-East Asia, Indonesia and countries to the west, and it was carried throughout the seventeenth century to Europe by the various East India Companies. The name Kraak owes its origin to the Dutch form of the name for a Portuguese carrack, a type of galleon, in which the porcelain was

Opposite: Plate VIII. *Famille verte* dish with *famille noire* rim. Depth 34.7 cm. Second half of the 17th century A.D. London, Percival David Foundation.

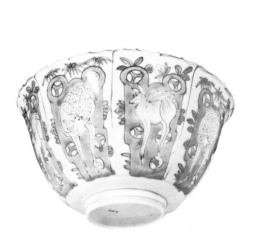

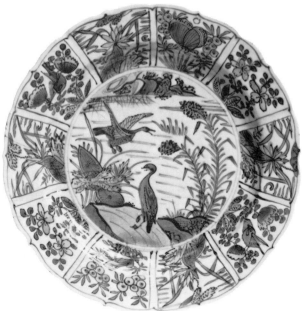

Fig. 172. Blue and white bowl with panelled decoration. Diameter 15 cm. Late 16th century A.D. London, Percival David Foundation.

Fig. 173. Kraak porcelain plate. Diameter 20.3 cm. 17th century A.D. London, Victoria and Albert Museum.

transported from China to Indonesia. The Dutch, having captured a ship of this kind deeply laden with porcelain in 1603, thereafter referred to the wares as *Kraak porselein*, a name which has come down in the literature to the present day. It is a convenient name for a type which is distinctive, but curiously difficult to describe with any precision.

The body material is of reasonably good quality, and it is generally found that the vessels are fairly thin and light in relation to their size. Bowls, dishes, plates, vases, and ewers share the same characteristics of construction, with a rather thin base and foot-ring. The base often has what are known as chatter marks, which are irregular radiating lines from the centre to the foot-ring. This is the result of the craftsman holding his foot cutting tool at the wrong angle when cutting the base and foot-ring, or it may be due to the wheel on which this operation is carried out being slightly off-balance and imperfectly centred. The marks are a common feature of Wan-li and later material of the kind that was widely exported (Fig. 172).

The glaze usually has a high gloss, is reasonably thick over the main part of the body, but may be rather thin on the base, and it is not unusual to find a little grit adhering to the foot-ring. One feature peculiar to much of the porcelain produced in the seventeenth century is the fault known as 'tender edges', or, as the Japanese more graphically described it, 'moth-eaten' edges. This is the tendency of the glaze to break off in patches along any sharp edge in a rather irregular

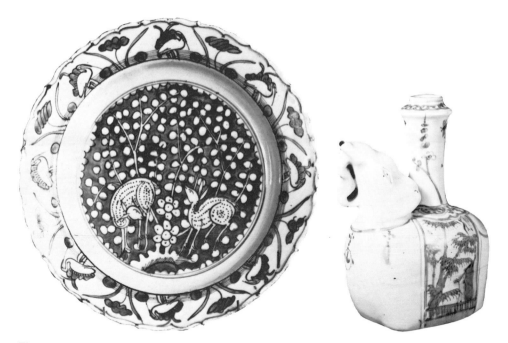

Fig. 174. Plate with white decoration on a blue ground. Diameter 20.3 cm. 17th century A.D. London, Victoria and Albert Museum.

Fig. 175. Blue and white *kendi* ware bottle. Height 15.7 cm. *c.* 1600. London, Percival David Foundation.

manner; it is particularly common on the rims of bowls, dishes and plates. The cause is complex, but is mainly due to the physical properties of the raw materials and the varying surface tensions of the different ingredients of body and glaze. The fault can be overcome only by adjustments in the raw materials and their proportions one to another.

The cobalt blue is often thin and watery looking, and sometimes even a pale almost silvery grey. In the really good pieces, however, the blue is very clear and bright. The pigment is evenly applied in washes in various tones within rather dark outlines.

The decoration of bowls and dishes, and of some plates and vases is characterized by the division of the surface into panels (Fig. 173). On bowls, dishes and plates they radiate from a central circular field, which may be framed by a complicated series of diaper patterns. The central field is usually freely painted, with birds or animals, especially deer (Fig. 174), in landscape, figures in pavilions looking out over river and landscape scenes, or with a flower-filled wicker basket. The radiating panels are sometimes separated from each other by much narrower panels filled with ribbons with bows on them, or small diaper patterns. The main panels are filled in a great variety of ways, the most popular motifs being flower sprays, emblems of the Eight Immortals, deer with rocks and flowers, and lotus scroll patterns reserved in white on a blue ground; the variety of motifs both naturalistic and abstract is enormous.

227

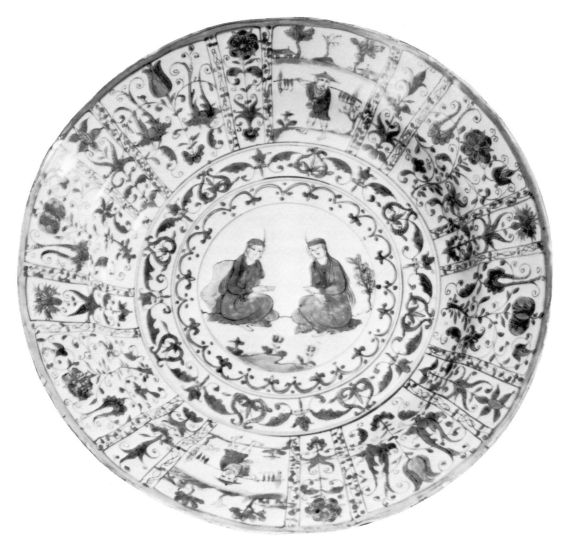

Fig. 176. Blue and white dish with mixed decoration. Diameter 45.7 cm. *c.* 1640. London, Percival David Foundation.

Plates, as flat wares, often lent themselves to a slightly different treatment, though still with the central field freely painted, sometimes with the decoration reserved in white against a blue ground. The shallow well was frequently left undecorated, while the flat rim was painted in a variety of ways, one popular theme being herons in a lily pond, a design originating early in the sixteenth century, and often seen round the rim of the large bowls exported to the Near East.

Vases and ewers were commonly treated in the same manner, in as much as the

228

surface was broken up into panels, but on account of its odd shape the *kendi,* a peculiar form of water bottle made for the Indonesian market, was usually treated with greater freedom. As many of these pieces were made as squatting animals or toads, they lent themselves to more imaginative treatment (Fig. 175).

By about the middle of the seventeenth century the decorations were beginning to incorporate motifs and pictorial themes alien to the Chinese vocabulary, such as the tulip and other floral elements derived from European sources, or landscape and figure scenes, some of which can be traced back to Islamic sources (Fig. 176). However the basic schemes remained unchanged throughout the period from Wan-li until the end of the third quarter of the seventeenth century. By about the middle of the seventeenth century it is not always easy to distinguish between some of the vases of this class and those associated with the Transitional style, for the latter borrowed scrolling patterns and panel diapers; nevertheless the Transitional style porcelain is easily distinguished from the Kraak ware in its most important characteristics.

Transitional Style Porcelain

The Transitional style porcelain differs from the Kraak wares not only in being thicker and heavier, but in generally being better quality. Moreover the use of overglaze enamelling, with or without blue, but having green as a predominant colour, gives it a greater variety. The examples with green as the predominant colour are in effect the forerunners of the *famille verte* of the K'ang-hsi period from about 1662 onward, a period into which the Transitional style wares continued.[13] The porcelain at its best is of a quality comparable to that termed 'imperial', the body being well prepared, the shapes well made and the painting of a high standard. The glaze is exceptionally good, rarely suffering the fault of tender edges so common in other seventeenth-century material and particularly common in the Kraak wares (Fig. 177).

Fig. 177. Transitional style jar. Diameter 19.1 cm. Mid 17th century A.D. London, Percival David Foundation.

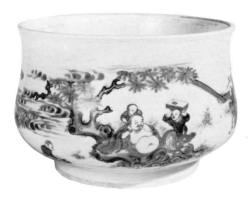

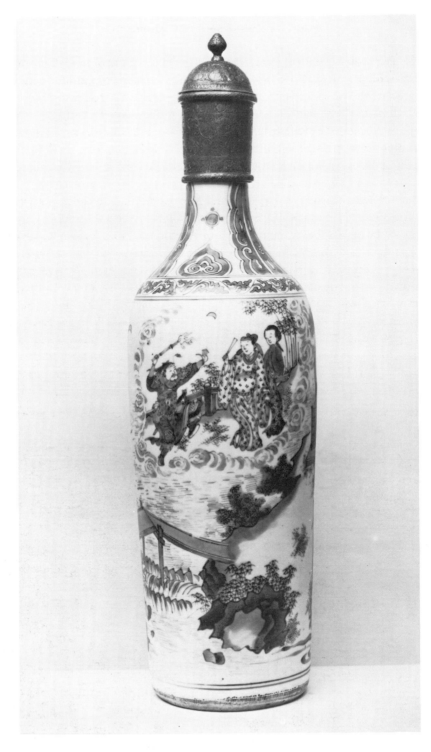

Fig. 178. Transitional style vase with romantic scene. Height 47.7 cm. 17th century A.D. London, Victoria and Albert Museum.

The shapes include a very great number of vases, many of large size. In this repertory of vases are shapes not previously encountered in Chinese ceramics. There are some sturdily constructed ovoid ones on flat unglazed bases; indeed an unglazed base is commonly found in the type. Other vases are tall and waisted, spreading to a flared mouth rim, and some are straight, cylindrical, occasionally with a thickened mid-section. To these should be added numerous tall perfectly cylindrical vases with a narrow sloping shoulder and small neck, usually quite short, with a slightly flared mouth.

The decoration, especially on the smaller vases and jars, is large in scale and runs freely over the surface, the old practice of dividing vertical forms into a series of horizontal bands being almost totally abandoned (Fig. 178). Occasionally grouped vegetal elements form a narrow repeating band, or there may be a finely incised scrolling border above and sometimes below the main decoration; it is usually not easily seen unless sought. The subjects of decoration are as varied as the shapes on which they appear: flowers, landscapes with or without figures, scenes of romance, illustrations from legend and history all find a place. The broad free treatment and often superlatively good execution make a refreshing change from the more formal designs found on material intended for the palace. Inscriptions, which can be long and poetical, are sometimes found dated, so that it

Fig. 179. Transitional style polychrome box with domed cover. Diameter 30.3 cm. 17th century A.D. Amsterdam, Rijksmuseum.

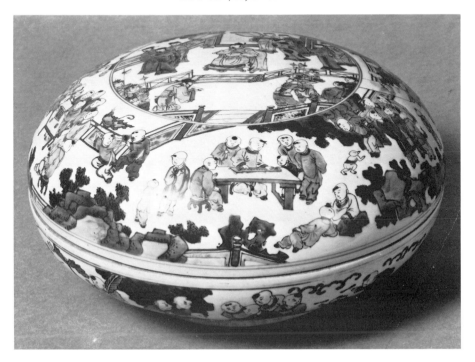

is possible in many instances to relate undated examples quite closely into a chronological succession running well into the K'ang-hsi period. ⟨1642-1722⟩

On the rectangular vases, which for the most part date from the later stages, landscape scenes are particularly favoured. In the polychrome examples, the colour is generally bright and clean, imparting a gaiety not always seen in the less well executed polychromes of the Wan-li period and those of late Ming; possibly the slightly increased use of yellow contributes to this general impression.

In addition to the innumerable vases there are round boxes with domed covers (Fig. 179), bowls of various sizes, brush pots, and incense burners, many of them decorated in a similar fashion, but on a smaller scale. Some of the incense burners, which are deep, heavy, cylindrical jars, have a bold decoration of two confronted dragons with a panel between them enclosing a suitable dedicatory inscription, usually dated. Some of these incense burners are of less fine quality and may suffer from glaze faults similar to those on the Kraak wares. They qualify for the name Transitional mainly on the basis of the wildness of treatment accorded to the dragons, which is quite unlike the more formal, almost heraldic handling of the beast on other wares.

Tê-hua Ware

The kilns in the province of Fukien associated with the name of Tê-hua originally came into operation in the Sung period, but little is known of the early history, although some white wares found in the Philippines and Indonesia, dating from the fourteenth century have been traced back to the district.[14] It was not until the sixteenth century that the kilns began to achieve fame for the products that are now recognized by their French name of *blanc de chine*. The reputation of the kilns is now mainly dependent upon the figures of Buddhist deities, of which Kuan Yin, goddess of mercy, Bodhidharma, the reputed founder of Zen Buddhism, Maitreya, the Buddha of the age to come, and the Buddha himself are the best known. In addition there are incense burners and bowls, but these are less numerous. Recent study has enlarged knowledge of the material, especially in the later periods, but even the late Ming and other seventeenth-century material up to the K'ang-hsi period from 1662, is still not well understood.[15]

The porcelain is pure white, and when fired has a very glassy fracture. The glaze, which is colourless and transparent, is exceptionally smooth and brilliant. The marriage of glaze to body is remarkable, the two merging more perfectly into each other than is usually the case, even in the best porcelain from Ching-tê Chên. When fired the colour of the material varies from a warm, sometimes pinkish, ivory tone to a pale skimmed-milk white, depending on local oxidation or reduction. A few pieces may display both extremes of colour, which is clearly an accidental effect.

The figures, although hollow, are thick and heavy. They appear to have been

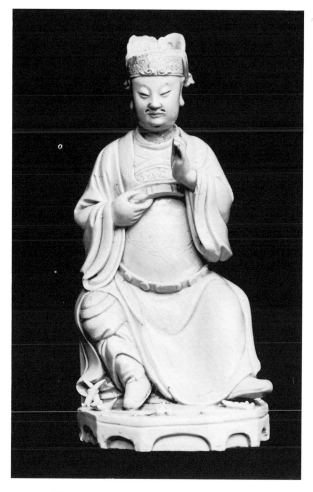

Fig. 180. Tê-hua figure of Kuan-ti, god of war. Height 25.7 cm. Dated to 1610. London, British Museum.

roughly moulded and then carefully worked by hand, the heads being made separately and then luted in, often with small holes left in the ears and mouth so as to permit the escape of gases in the firing. Artistically the figures are rightly regarded as sculptural works of the first order, combining a well expressed sense of mass with controlled handling of detail, as in the rhythmic treatment of the robes with which most are adorned. The majestic figure of Kuan-ti, the god of war, dated to 1610 and in the British Museum, is a fine example of an early stage in the evolution of these famous figures (Fig. 180).

The problems to be faced in attempting to date Tê-hua porcelains to the earlier part of the seventeenth century are formidable. With only the figure of 1610 and the rather poor quality vase of 1639 in the David Foundation, there is little solid evidence on which to depend. A greater body of dated material is essential to the understanding of the earlier history of the ware.

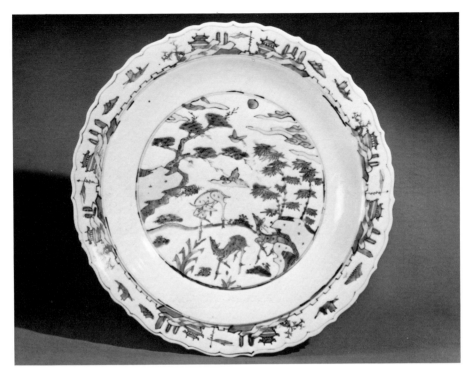

Fig. 181. Swatow ware blue and white plate. Diameter 41.3 cm. 16th century A.D. Mr Max Robertson.

Swatow Ware

The porcelain included under this somewhat artificial name comprehends a greater variety of wares than used at one time to be believed. Made at kilns north of Swatow in the extreme north of Kuang-tung, they seem to have been developed mainly for export to South-East Asia, Indonesia and Japan.[16] They make their appearance first, as far as is known, in the sixteenth century and continue into the seventeenth century, but it is not known exactly how early the kilns began to operate, nor is it known precisely when production ceased.

The clay body is a porcelain of rather uneven quality, and the glaze varied a little depending on this. The standard felspathic glaze was normally used.

Among the products are polychrome enamelled, blue and white (Fig. 181), and slip painted wares, the last on either a light blue or light brown ground, with a transparent glaze over it.

The output was chiefly of large dishes and plates, with a smaller number of bowls of various sizes, and *kendi,* the last made especially for Indonesia, where the

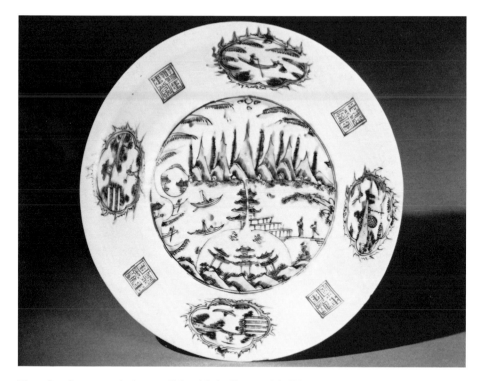

Fig. 182. Swatow polychrome dish with 'split pagoda'. Diameter 40.2 cm. 16th century A.D. London, Percival David Foundation.

majority have been found, but some pieces of all kinds have been found in India and even further afield. On almost all the wares, and it is especially characteristic of the large dishes and plates, the foot-ring and glaze splashed base is spattered with grit off the floor of the saggar, indicating carelessness in placing the wares and setting the kiln.

The polychrome wares which are the best known are boldly decorated in overglaze red, green, and turquoise blue, with a limited use of black reserved for some of the finer detail and outlining. The drawing has a spontaneity not found in the central tradition as represented by Ching-tê Chên and other Jao-chou kilns, and the designs are sometimes very strange. An example of the strangeness is the design known as the 'split pagoda', the explanation of which still eludes research. Carried out in black and turquoise in the central field of large dishes, it is dominated by what resembles a three storey pagoda split in two vertically by a funnel-like strip reserved in white, almost like a volcanic eruption. Below is a waterway with boats, a bridge and pavilions, and a few miniscule figures (Fig. 182). Round the sides, outside the central field, are red overglaze enamel cartouches with debased seal characters, which have not so far yielded anything comprehensible.

Apart from such oddities, there is a great variety of designs, which include animals, birds, flower sprays, Portuguese galleons, Chinese junks and sampans, sea monsters, fish, and representations of both the European and the Chinese mariners' compass (Plate VII, opposite page 224).

In the blue and white many of the designs are more closely related to the central tradition than is the case with the polychrome. There are landscape scenes with deer not unlike some of those produced at Ching-tê Chên, and with similar borders to those of mid sixteenth-century date. Others, probably later in date, bear a strong resemblance to some of the Kraak porcelain, but often have a more extravagant use of diapers, which may form a ground in which are reserved shaped panels painted with greater freedom with landscapes.

A much smaller group is made up of large dishes with a light blue or brown ground. These are painted in white slip, and slips coloured dark blue or dark brown. They differ from the other wares, mainly on account of the technique used, and are more sparingly decorated with rather simple flower sprays and inexpertly composed inscriptions in rectangular cartouches; these are mostly indecipherable. In the central field of some of the large dishes weird-looking dragons often replace the flower sprays.

The Japanese Market

Kinrande had been established in the middle of the sixteenth century as an export ware for Japan, and it may have continued into the beginning of the seventeenth century, but this is uncertain. The seventeenth century, however, saw other types of ware gain popularity with the Japanese, and these fall broadly into two categories. First there is the Tenkei and *kosometsuke*, which are polychrome wares and blue and white, both groups to be assigned to the late Ming. The second category is an unusual kind of blue and white known as Shonzui, which is generally dated to about the middle of the seventeenth century, thus bridging the Ming and early Ch'ing dynasties.

Tenkei and the Kosometsuke

Tenkei is the Japanese pronunciation of the Chinese name T'ien-ch'i, the reign name of the emperor who reigned from 1621 to 1627. To the Japanese the name in connection with porcelain implies polychrome porcelain of the late Ming period and the blue and white, the latter more generally recognized by the name *kosometsuke*, 'old blue and white'.

The earliest of this polychrome and blue and white was probably not made with the Japanese specifically in mind, but very soon the Chinese potters were working with Japanese designs and made shapes to please Japanese taste. This applies

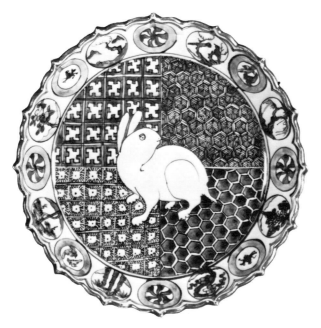

Fig. 183. *Kosometsuke* plate with brocading designs. Diameter 23 cm. 17th century A.D. Baur collection.

mainly to the *kosometsuke*, which in both shape and decoration scarcely resemble anything the Chinese had ever made (Fig. 183). Jars, vases, small bowls in rather fancy shapes, and unusual small boxes were made in large quantities. The bowls and plates were made in sets of five specially to suit the Japanese requirement.

The decoration, often naïve in its simplicity and spontaneous and free, is far removed from the studied effects of the central tradition. Poems are frequently inscribed and a few are dated. Landscape scenes were among the most popular decorations, and these seem usually to have been inspired by Chinese painting or book illustration. An identifiable example of this adaptation from book illustration is seen in an example (Fig. 184) with the hen and chicks by a plant of coxscomb, adapted from the woodcut included in *Chi-ya ts'an hua-p'u: Ts'ao-pên hua-shih-p'u*, a volume of poems with facing illustrations published in 1621.

The Japanese-inspired designs are often directly dependent upon illustration or are strongly influenced by the contemporary textiles of Japan, which are so distinctive, with diaper designs cutting across each other and with inset panels of totally different decorations, often naturalistic and contrasting sharply with the geometric diapers.[17] These designs are more common among the blue and white than the polychrome, in which diapers are used as no more than frames for the central decoration, or are omitted altogether. There is a rustic charm about much of this late Ming porcelain not found to the same extent even in the Swatow.

The body material is somewhat variable, the best being equal to that of the

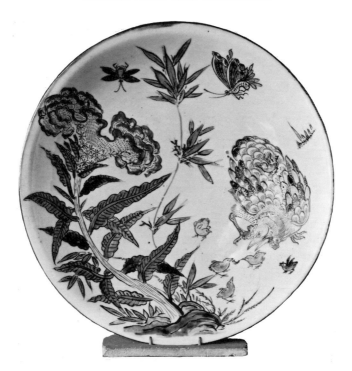

Fig. 184. Polychrome dish with hen and chicks. Diameter 21.2 cm. 17th century A.D. London, Victoria and Albert Museum.

better examples of Kraak ware, and frequently displaying the same characteristics of chatter marks on the base and moth-eaten edges. Some of the bodies are heavier and rather coarser, with a glaze that is thick and of a faint bluish skimmed-milk colour. It is likely that some of the material was made at Ching-tê Chên, but other outlying kilns were also making it. Unfortunately the types included under the terms *kosometsuke* and Tenkei are among the easiest to imitate, and the Japanese have done this themselves very successfully in the past; there are also many modern copies of remarkable excellence.

Shonzui

The porcelains known by this name, are all blue and white of a kind distinct from the *kosometsuke,* not only in style, but also in being inscribed on the base with an eight character inscription, which is usually read in Japanese, *Gorodaiyu Wu Shonzui tsukeru,* and translated, 'Made by Gorodaiyu Wu Shonzui'. There are a number of theories as to the origin of the inscription, the name, and the place of manufacture.[18] It seems likely that the inscription should be read in Japanese, and may represent what the Japanese themselves wanted written on the porcelains, since a translation from the Chinese reading makes poor sense, involving as it does the translation of the first four characters, which can be read as a name in Japanese.

As the Shonzui wares are of the finest quality porcelain, the painting of an exceptionally high standard, and the shapes so unusual, it would be reasonable to accept that all were made to special order, and probably for the tea ceremony. This at least seems to be the concensus of opinion on the extremely complicated problem posed by the inscription combined with that of the shapes. The covered jars and bowls are often carefully pushed in a little on one side so as to upset the perfect symmetry natural to an object thrown on the wheel. The painting, in a very good blue, which is varied in tone to suit the designs, is very accomplished whatever the subject, be it landscapes with figures, birds, animals and flowers, or diaper and scrolling patterns (Fig. 185). All these may appear together on a single piece. The influence of Japanese textile design is even stronger on the Shonzui porcelain than it is on the *kosometsuke*.

Like the *kosometsuke* it has been much imitated and faked. It is, however, held that the genuine pieces can be distinguished at least from the earlier imitations, by the presence of the originals of a little man on a donkey. Sometimes he appears as a minute figure in landscape, and at other times only in a small medallion making up one of a series enclosing other motifs on the same surface, but he always appears. Whether this will remain a valid criterion on which to judge the type is another matter. The problems relating to this attractive ware need careful investigation, but the situation is complicated by the conflicting traditions in the literature that has accumulated in Japan. There is nothing tangible to be gained at the moment from the Chinese sources. They have so far been combed with diligence but little success.

Fig. 185. Shonzui jar and cover. Diameter 17.4 cm. Second quarter of the 17th century A.D. Tokyo, Idemitsu Foundation.

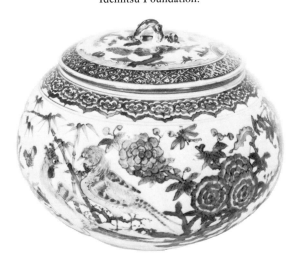

CHAPTER TEN

Technical Virtuosity

When in 1644 the Manchus from the north-east in Manchuria took over the Chinese empire and ruled as the Ch'ing dynasty, the last great era in the history of Chinese ceramics began. The zenith of this last period was reached in the eighteenth century, after which a long slow decline in both production and quality began. By the nineteenth century the industrial revolution in Europe was beginning to have an impact in China. Europe was rapidly catching up in the field of ceramics, in which the Chinese had held a substantial lead since early times, having discovered porcelain nearly a thousand years earlier. Now that lead was to be reduced to very little as the cost of shipping rose against European efficiency and production costs.

Reorganization at Ching-tê Chên

The ceramic industry underwent changes in organization following the destruction of a large part of Ching-tê Chên in 1675, at the time of the Wu San-kuei rebellion. Even apart from the destruction there had been a good deal of unrest over labour conditions, so that when in 1680 the enlightened young emperor K'ang-hsi ordered a commission to enquire into the state of the industry at Jao-chou, he was doing what should have been done about a century earlier under Wan-li, when the labour force had not infrequently refused to pay taxes. On the basis of the report submitted to the throne in 1682, a superintendent of the kilns was personally appointed by the emperor and for the first time an industrial kiln complex was properly organized to supply the palace, alongside the many other kilns operating in the region. At the same time the old system by which a proportion of the work force had been forced labour was changed and from now on the men were paid craftsmen and labourers.

The change in organization meant that two distinct levels of production were gradually to emerge. The imperial kilns, administered by a superintendent directly appointed by the emperor through the Board of Public Works, made porcelain exclusively for the palace, while others were engaged on production for both the domestic and foreign markets. At first there was an all round effort to improve standards, and the distinction between palace wares and general production for the other markets was not clearly defined. The distinction only becomes fully apparent at the beginning of the eighteenth century, by which time the imperial kilns had had time and opportunity to recruit the finest craftsmen to work as a team under a superintendent wholly conversant with the industry, and who must have had considerable knowledge of the practical problems, and possibly a strong interest in the chemistry and firing of ceramics. Quite a lot is known of the scale and the organization of the kilns at Ching-tê Chên, and the specialization that was a necessary part of this, from the two famous letters of the Jesuit Père d'Entrecolles, who, while he misunderstood some of what went on, was yet able to convey a fairly clear picture of the system of work and the processes used in the early years of the eighteenth century.[1]

The emperor K'ang-hsi's personal interest, his open mind, and his willingness to learn from the Jesuits at the court at this time, must have had much to do with the rapid development, and the new experimental period which was initiated under the first of the three great superintendents, Ts'ang Ying-hsüan. It would, however, be a mistake to overestimate the influence of K'ang-hsi as a patron of the arts; his interest lay more in efficiency than in art as such.

It was during the last few years of the emperor K'ang-hsi's reign that Europe made her one contribution to the technical repertory of Chinese ceramics; the introduction of the rose pink overglaze enamel derived from colloidol gold, which gave rise to the name *famille rose*.[2]

In the short reign of Yung-chêng (1723-35), during the first three years of which Ts'ang Ying-hsüan continued as superintendent, there was increasing stress on technical perfection, and this was maintained both by Nien Hsi-yao and his even more famous successor T'ang Ying, the latter continuing his work until his death in 1753 under the emperor Ch'ien-lung. Under Ch'ien-lung a certain contradiction became apparent, for while there was still curiosity about what was new, and what could further be developed, there was also an almost compulsive emphasis on technique and its perfection, often at the expense of form, and sometimes of good taste as well. Experiment was thus largely abandoned, and any stimulus from foreign sources tended to fade away, until after Ch'ien-lung production at almost every level became mere repetition.

The wares continued to be as technically varied as during the Ming dynasty, but blue and white gradually declined in popularity, especially from about the middle of the eighteenth century as interest grew in the overglaze enamels of the *famille rose* group. The other overglaze enamels of the *famille verte*, and the *tou-*

ts'ai, which was briefly revived under Yung-chêng, constituted the bulk of the
polychrome wares, but it was in the monochrome glazing that the most interesting
developments took place.

Famille verte and its Variants

The class of ceramics to which the name *famille verte* is given has two parts. One
consists of ordinary overglaze decorated pieces, and the other of enamel on biscuit
pieces, the distinctions between them not always being very clear. It is generally
found that the enamel on biscuit type lends itself to slightly denser treatment and
the use of white areas is drastically reduced.

The name *famille verte* was coined by Jacquemart in the nineteenth century

Fig. 186. *Famille verte* dish with Immortals. Diameter 41.9 cm. 17th century A.D. London, Victoria
and Albert Museum.

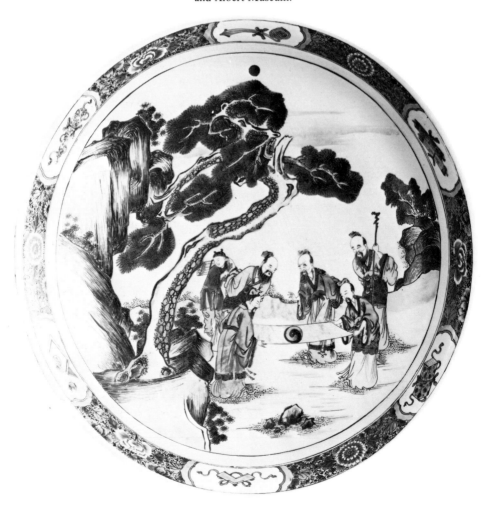

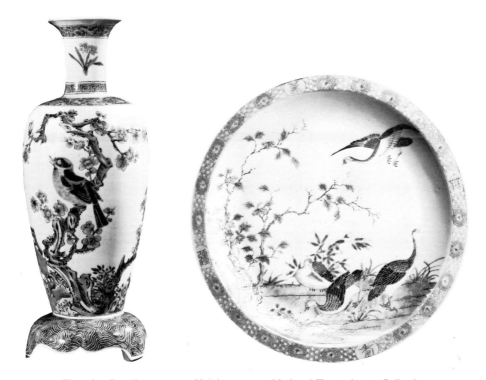

Fig. 187. *Famille verte* vase. Height 30.2 cm. National Trust, Ascott Collection.

Fig. 188. *Famille verte* 'Birthday Plate'. Diameter 25.1 cm. Early 18th century A.D. Kansas, W. R. Nelson Gallery of Art.

and has remained convenient for the porcelain decorated in translucent enamels, among which green is dominant.[3] Towards the end of the seventeenth century the use of underglaze blue in combination with the overglaze colours diminished. It was finally abandoned in favour of an overglaze blue, and it is to this type that the name truly applies. To the *famille verte* there may be limited additions of gold for some details, but gold does not normally occur on the enamel on biscuit type.

The decorations are enormously varied, as are the shapes (Figs. 186, 187). Birds, flowers, landscape scenes with or without figures, scenes of romance, often with tall elegant young ladies, auspicious emblems, and flower baskets are a large part of the repertory. Diaper patterns of many kinds are used either as borders or fillers.

The overglaze enamel group is usually more freely decorated, and when diaper designs are employed they are used with greater restraint than on the enamel on biscuit pieces, being restricted to borders. The most refined pieces can be dated to the second decade of the eighteenth century, and are at their best in a famous series of plates known as 'birthday plates', because they are believed to have been made for the emperor K'ang-hsi's sixtieth birthday in 1713. They are of the finest quality porcelain, extremely white, thin, and very translucent; they appear faultless. The flattened rim, which is quite narrow, is decorated with a diaper pattern in iron red broken in four places by cartouches bearing the characters

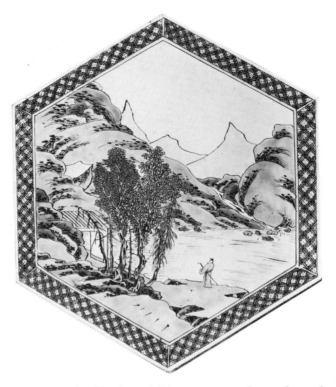

Fig. 189. *Famille verte* enamel on biscuit stand. Diameter 25.4 cm. Late 17th or early 18th century A.D. London, Victoria and Albert Museum.

wan-shou wu-chiang, 'Long life without limit', the imperial birthday greeting. In the centre, painted with the utmost delicacy, are either birds on fruiting branches, or beautiful women with flowers and lanterns, or, in a very few cases, birds of various kinds in landscape (Fig. 188). All are marked on the base in underglaze blue with a six-character mark of K'ang-hsi. Closely related to these and of the same quality, but smaller and with the Ch'êng-hua mark, is another series of plates with a variety of figure scenes in the centre and a butterfly and flower border in light red with touches of gold (Fig. 190).

The enamel on biscuit group varies in its shapes, including as it does such things as teapot stands (Fig. 189), incense burners, ornamental panels for setting in furniture, and small models and figures, some of the last being large and handsome (Fig. 191). The decoration is also different, and includes many more diapers, often over considerable areas. There is also an increase in the use of aubergine purple and yellow, while the green may be in a variety of tones, with black used almost exclusively for outlines. The use of white is extremely limited.

Under the general heading of *famille verte* the variants *famille noire* and *famille jaune* may be admitted. They use the same palette but the emphasis is either on the black or the yellow rather than the green, and in both cases these tend to be

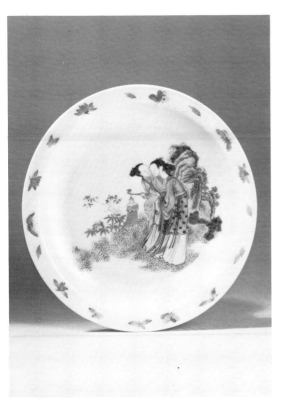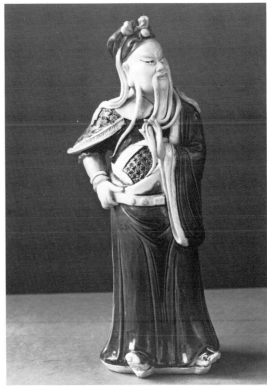

Fig. 190. *Famille verte* overglaze enamel. Diameter 17.2 cm. Late 17th century A.D. London, Percival David Foundation.

Fig. 191. *Famille verte* enamel on biscuit figure. Height 25.4 cm. *c.* 1700. London, Victoria and Albert Museum.

background colours. The black is peculiar because it is applied to the biscuit, and then a translucent green enamel is added over the rather dull surface; a treatment which in fact results in an extremely dense black (Plate VIII, opposite page 225). Many pieces of this kind, especially the really large ones, are believed to have been made in the nineteenth century.

The *famille verte* has survived intermittently, having reached its apogee early in the eighteenth century, and it is still found today in bowls, dishes, and vases. But it is of obviously less fine quality than in the period before it was displaced in imperial favour, and in that of the wealthier patrons, by the newer and in some respects more exciting *famille rose*.

Famille rose and Ku Yüeh Hsüan

It was in about 1720, right at the end of the reign of K'ang-hsi, that the opaque rose-coloured enamel was introduced into the Chinese decorative repertory, and it was one in which the new emperor Yung-chêng was to take a personal interest.

245

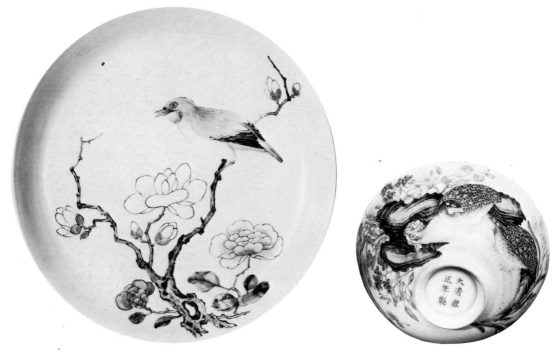

Fig. 192. *Famille rose* dish with bird. Diameter 20.3 cm. 18th century A.D. London, Percival David Foundation.

Fig. 193. *Famille rose* bowl with quails. Diameter 12 cm. Yung-chêng mark and period, 1723–36. Mount Trust Collection.

Through the Jesuit fathers at the court he sought additional help from Europe, so that the craftsmen could perfect their handling of the new ingredient.

The origins of the *famille rose,* so named by Jacquemart in the nineteenth century, are likely to be found in the European enamelling tradition of Limoges, and the use of enamelling on metal.[4] The rose colour, derived from gold, is made opaque by additions of tin oxide to the frit, and is fired on to the glaze surface of a ceramic vessel in the same way as any other overglaze colour. The difficulty which the Chinese encountered, when they first began using the tin oxide opacified enamels, probably lay in controlling the firing. It seems that opacified enamels were first tried on a copper base, like European ones, and that they were only subsequently attempted on a porcelain glaze. It was apparently not much before about 1730, approximately ten years later, that the firing of this type of enamel was satisfactorily mastered. From about that date the best that China could produce not only equalled, but even surpassed anything similar made in Europe.

Rose enamels were used at first rather sparingly, and a study of eighteenth-century porcelain reveals that on early pieces the colour was often muddy and sometimes a weak lilac, although the other colours might be quite good. Once the firing was mastered, the Chinese much extended the use and varied the tone. In the imperial kilns it became common and designs were specially drawn by court

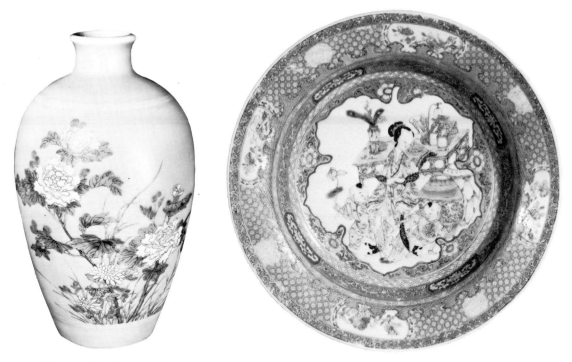

Fig. 194. *Famille rose* painted vase with blue glaze. Height 19 cm. Mid 18th century A.D. Mount Trust Collection.

Fig. 195. *Famille rose* ruby back dish with diaper borders. Diameter 21 cm. Mid 18th century A.D. London, Percival David Foundation.

artists to fit the shapes of different vessels intended for imperial use (Figs. 192, 193). The style of decoration differed from that of *famille verte* in the much more meticulous treatment of detail, while the stability of the enamel pastes permitted delicate shading of tones and a wide variety of colour combinations. Minute details could be picked out in different colours without fear of these running, so that birds and flowers, for instance, could be painted with a marvellous attention to detail rivalling that of the European miniaturist.

Bird and flower subjects and figural themes were the most popular, and occur on most of the current shapes such as bowls, dishes and vases (Fig. 194). Diaper patterns taken over from textile designs are painted with incredible accuracy (Fig. 195).[5] On dishes the decorations normally appeared only on the inside, the outside being either left plain white or sprayed with a total covering of a soft, dark rose, giving rise to the name 'ruby back'. The use of the dark rose on the back may have been intended to cut down the translucency of the very thin, often 'egg-shell' porcelain on which the *famille rose* colours so commonly occur.

Most of the finest *famille rose* can be dated to the late years of the Yung-chêng and through most of the Ch'ien-lung period, but there were still good pieces being made in Tao-kuang in the middle of the nineteenth century; on many of these there is a K'ang-hsi mark. Among other nineteenth-century pieces, often with the

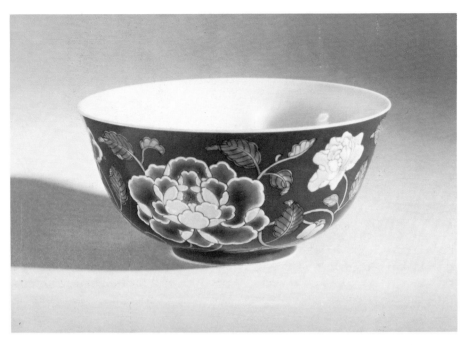

Above: Fig. 196. Bowl painted in opaque enamels of *famille rose* palette, with Yung-chêng mark. Diameter 11.1 cm. Late 19th century A.D. London, Percival David Foundation.

Below: Fig. 197. Teapot painted in Ku Yüeh Hsüan style. Diameter 11.4 cm. Ch'ien-lung mark, mid 18th century A.D. London, Percival David Foundation.

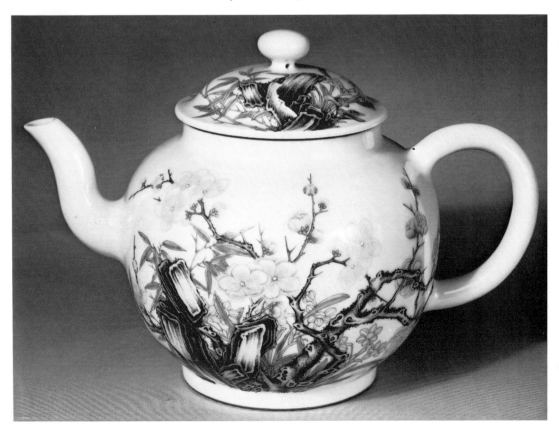

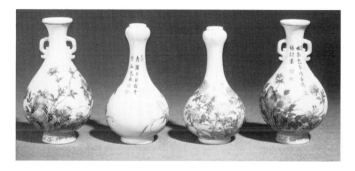

Fig. 198. Two pairs of Ku Yüeh Hsüan type vases. Maximum height 4.3 cm. Mid 18th century A.D. London, Percival David Foundation.

K'ang-hsi mark, are some bowls and depressed globular jars with opaque colour ground, against which are painted elaborate floral scrolls on an unusually large scale (Fig. 196). Neither technically nor stylistically can these have appeared as early as the K'ang-hsi period, and it seems likely that the earliest date to which they can be assigned with any confidence is the very end of the eighteenth century.[6]

If it is accepted that the *famille rose* cannot have reached a satisfactory stage until about 1730, it follows that the most refined and delicately painted porcelains of the Ch'ing dynasty known as Ku Yüeh Hsüan, in which the rose enamel is combined with both opaque and translucent enamels, cannot have been produced before this date. Some pieces, all of the finest quality porcelain, bear the Yung-chêng mark in blue enamel on the base, four characters being used in a double rectangle, but most belong to the Ch'ien-lung period, and it is said that the best comes to an end in 1753 on the death of T'ang Ying, the last of the three great superintendents of the imperial kilns.

The pieces making up this group are all small, rarely being more than twenty centimetres in any dimension (Fig. 197). Bowls, saucers, small wine cups, wine pots, and very small garlic-headed vases are the most usual shapes (Fig. 198). All are painted with the utmost delicacy with birds, flowers and birds in landscape

Fig. 199. Glass cups painted in Ku Yüeh Hsüan style in *famille rose* enamels. Height 4.3 cm. 18th century A.D. London, Percival David Foundation.

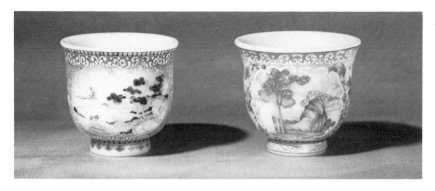

249

settings. Black often plays an important role in the decoration, and is always used for the writing of a poetic couplet on some suitable part of the surface. All the pieces have a four-character mark in blue enamel, but the blue does not always mature properly so that it may be greyish.

The name Ku Yüeh Hsüan given to this select group presents a problem over which much ink has been spilt, but generally it is looked on now as a style name,[7] and as such has also been used in connection with a group of small milky glass vessels, brush pots, small vases (Fig. 199), snuff bottles and wines cups, which have been decorated in a similar manner, but without the poetic inscriptions.[8] The marks on these are engraved and then filled in with enamel. It is worth noting that pieces actually marked with the characters Ku Yüeh Hsüan, instead of the reign mark, are regarded with some suspicion as being late nineteenth or even twentieth-century imitations.

Monochrome Glazes

In the late seventeenth century following the appointment of Tsang Ying-hsüan, the most notable achievement of the potteries of Ching-tê Chên was in the realm of monochrome glazing. There must have been deliberate experiments aimed at producing new glaze colours and transmutations, as well as attempts to revive old glaze effects.

One of the best of the revivals, for instance, was the reintroduction of the Kuan-type glaze. The colour and crackle is remarkably deceptive in really good pieces (Fig. 200). We know from a number of sources, both Chinese and European, that Kuan was very popular under Tsang Ying-hsüan and that the kilns made many examples of the type under his supervision.[9] In most cases the shapes are subtly different, but one can be deceived, especially if the foot-ring adheres closely to the Sung pattern with its neat square cutting. The fact that the body is usually stained a dark purplish brown sometimes makes attribution difficult, and occasionally the glaze has characteristics that make it hard to distinguish the copy from the original.

Less deceptive were the attempts to imitate Ting, partly because the artistic atmosphere of the period made it almost impossible for the potters to recapture the sensitive treatment in both design and decoration of the original, even apart from the skill in carving. Moreover the body material was quite different, either being too purely white porcelain, or too obviously off-white, to make up for the lack of ivory tone in the transparent glaze.

The most striking achievement in the use of traditional glaze colours was in the reintroduction of copper red, and the development from this of the 'peach bloom' and other transmutations using copper in a reducing atmosphere. It is not known precisely when attempts were first made to revive the difficult technique of firing

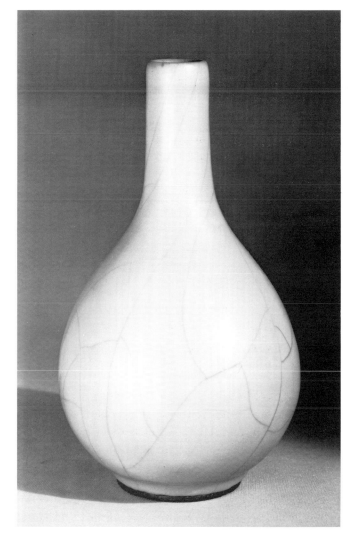

Fig. 200. Kuan-type vase. Height 21.5 cm. Early 18th century A.D. London, Percival David Foundation.

copper in this way, but by the end of the seventeenth century it was securely established, and some very fine examples are found.

The new copper red came to be known as Lang-yao, or in Europe as *sang de boeuf,* the first believed to be the name of a potter, and the second a term found first in E. Grandidier's *La Ceramique Chinoise.*[10] The method used to produce the new type differed from that of the fifteenth century. The body was different, being much thicker and heavier, and it was biscuit fired before the glazes were applied. First a copper charged glaze was applied and then a base glaze was added

251

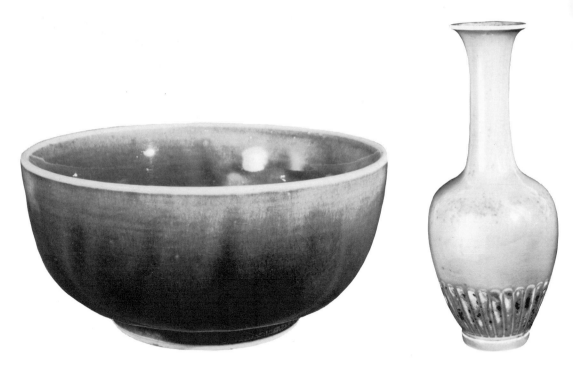

Fig. 201. Copper red glazed bowl. Diameter 24.2 cm. *c.* 1700. London, Percival David Foundation.

Fig. 202. Peach bloom vase with green speckles on the lower part. Height 21.2 cm. K'ang-hsi mark and period, early 18th century A.D. London, Percival David Foundation.

over this in the usual way (Fig. 201). After this the ware was fired a second time at a very much higher temperature than that used for the biscuit firing, which was probably the temperature required to fuse the porcelain body. It is likely that the temperature for the glost firing was taken up to between 1,350°C and 1,400°C.[11] Such a much higher temperature accounts for the persistent appearance of a fine crackle on all these later pieces in comparison with those of the fifteenth century, which, with very rare exceptions, are free of this feature.

It was not until the early eighteenth century that the glaze transmutation known as 'peach bloom' appeared, and since it was even more difficult, and correspondingly expensive to produce, it seems to have been largely reserved for small pieces of exceptional quality intended for the scholar' s desk, such shapes as water pots, brush washers and small jars and vases being among these pieces (Fig. 202). They were not fired to such a high temperature but the critical problem was the control of the firing cycle, even in a kiln so constructed as to reduce the variation of atmosphere in the chamber to the absolute minimum. Minute variation in temperature and atmosphere from one part of the kiln to another would be sufficient to ruin a firing. At its best the peach bloom is a soft pinkish red that darkens in some parts and pales in others, and displays green, often a bright moss green, either in patches or in small speckled areas. The green can be produced at will by slightly increasing the copper in predetermined areas, so that

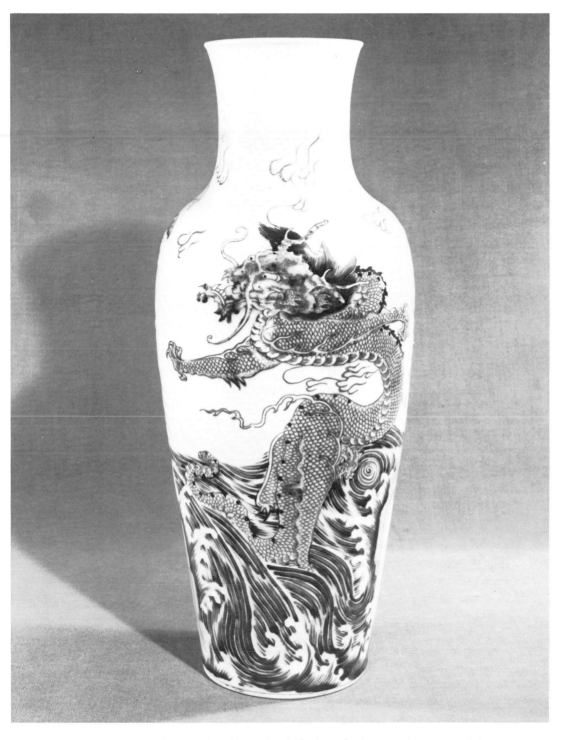

Fig. 203. Vase decorated in underglaze blue and red, the latter having turned green round the dragons' jaws. Height 42 cm. K'ang-hsi mark and period, *c.* 1700. London, Percival David Foundation.

253

in the firing the base glaze covering of the copper will be penetrated by the overloading of mineral oxide and volatilize out to oxidize on the surface. That this could be achieved deliberately can be seen in a number of underglaze copper red painted vases with dragons on them (Fig. 203). On these the faces, especially round the jaw, are consistently bright moss green, the colour appearing nowhere else on the creature.[12]

Other copper red effects include a large series of eighteenth and early nineteenth-century ones known as 'flambé' in which the red is streaked with greyish and bluish tones.[13] Like the copper red of the peach bloom series it was a transmutation induced by varying concentrations of copper and adjusting the firing cycle in critical ways, in some instances following a reduction period with one of oxidation, and then at a later point repeating this. Experimental work has been carried out in attempts to reproduce the effects, but not very successfully, probably because the really critical areas are not fully understood, and the variations in temperature in the kilns used have been too wide to ensure consistency.

Of very different character are other monochrome glazes developed in the first half of the eighteenth century under Nien Hsi-yao and T'ang Ying, especially under the supervision of the latter, who was fully trained in the techniques of pottery, and whose main interest seems to have been in the chemistry of glazes.

The use of cobalt continued, and although very often used in the usual concentration to produce a deep rich blue colour, it was also employed in very small quantities, sufficient to tint the glaze only a very pale blue (Fig. 204). It was used in this way on the finest porcelain, and is described in the contemporary texts as yüeh-pai, 'moon white', or in French, 'clair de lune'. Unfortunately the term yüeh-pai in Chinese literature is also applied to pure white and to a great number of blues including the blue of Chün ware.

Another use of cobalt was as a powdered colour blown on to the unglazed body using a bamboo tube spray. A colourless transparent glaze was added over this and a pleasing mottled effect was achieved. A further step, but away from monochrome effects, was to reserve panels in white by sticking shaped pieces of paper on the surface, so that certain areas were protected from the sprayed blue. The paper panels were then removed and sometimes these areas were painted in blue in the ordinary way before being glazed. On other occasions the piece would be glazed and the white glazed panels would then be painted in famille verte or famille rose enamels (Fig. 205).[14]

Iron oxides were also used in lower concentrations to produce pale colours, such as a very pale celadon green (Fig. 206). The use of a pure white porcelain body in place of the pale grey Lung-ch'üan type of body, however, meant that the colour was robbed of the more subtle depths so characteristic of the originals. Nevertheless the quality is unsurpassed, some extremely fine examples demonstrating a superb control of every process. In an oxidizing atmosphere the

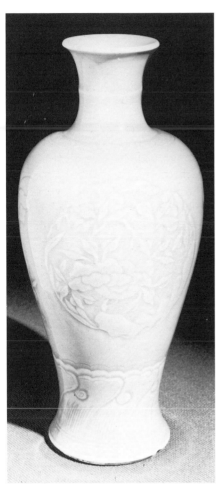
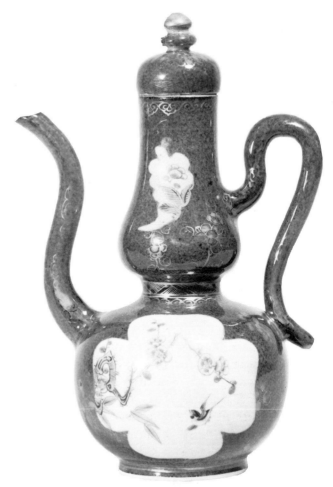

Fig. 204. Pale cobalt blue glazed vase with carved decoration. Height 20.6 cm. 18th century A.D. London, Percival David Foundation.

Fig. 205. Powder blue ewer with reserved panels painted in overglaze enamel colours, with gilt decoration on the blue ground. Height 22.2 cm. 18th century A.D. Mrs R. H. R. Palmer.

iron oxides were used to produce a range of lustrous browns, a pale type of which has been aptly named 'café au lait'. The oxidized iron brown was also used like the powder blue on vessels with panels reserved in white and decorated in either underglaze blue or overglaze enamels.

More exciting effects were achieved by trying what were fundamentally variations in the reducing cycles, such as those used on twelfth and thirteenth-century black wares. The most striking was the production of a glaze known as iron rust, which is a streaked reddish brown with a metallic sheen, achieved by sharp reduction from a high temperature in cooling.

The use of double glazing, using two totally different glazes, was successfully tried in the first half of the eighteenth century. Two of the most remarkable effects were gained by using lead silicate enamels. One of these was the tea-dust glaze

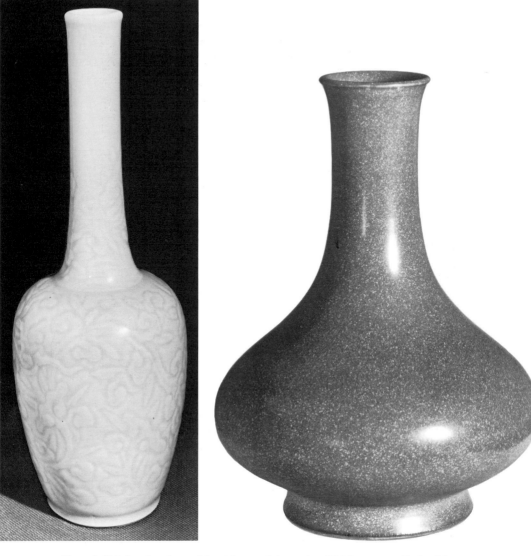

Fig. 206. Celadon glazed porcelain with carved decoration. Height 23.5 cm. Early 18th century A.D. London, Percival David Foundation.

Fig. 207. Tea-dust glazed vase. Height 21 cm. 18th century A.D. Geneva, Baur collection.

produced by blowing a very fine spray of green lead silicate glaze on to a yellowish brown iron oxide glaze (Fig. 207). The other was the attractive robin's egg glaze. A light pale turquoise opaque spray was blown on to a deep blue ground, also opaque, to produce a fine speckled effect. Most of the pieces with these two glazes are small, but there are a few large ones.

During the Yung-chêng period the use of opaque monochrome glazes increased and the colours include the rose pink from gold, opacified with tin

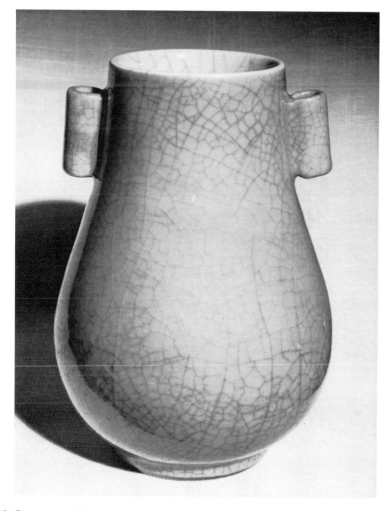

Fig. 208. Green enamel glaze over a crackled grey, Kuan-type glazed vase. Height 21 cm. Late 17th century A.D. London, Percival David Foundation.

oxide. A rather acid yellow of great brilliance made its appearance at this time, together with an opaque pale turquoise blue. It seems likely that the yellow and turquoise were both opacified with tin oxide, but the bright pale green, which came in slightly later was compounded and opacified using a mortally dangerous arsenical oxide; not surprisingly this enjoyed only very brief favour.

Transparent green lead silicate glazes continued in use and are found not only over a plain white porcelain, but also over a crackled grey Kuan-type glaze (Fig. 208). The effect of the greyish glaze underneath is to impart a darker softer tone to the green. The combination remained popular into the present century, but good early pieces are fairly rare.

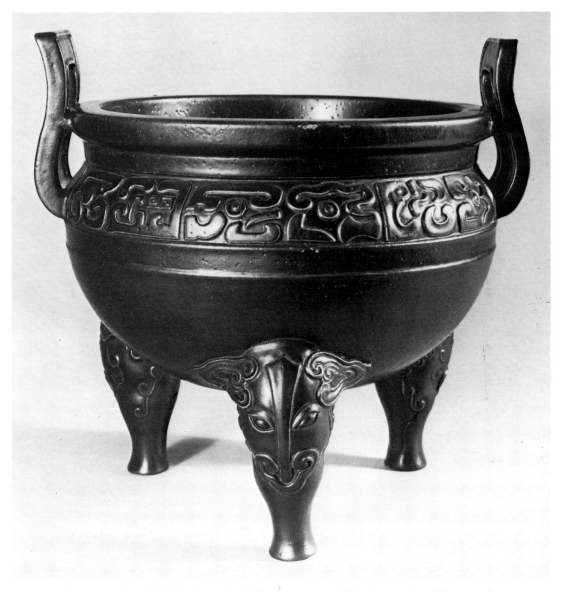

Fig. 209. Greenish black glaze imitating bronze on an archaistic bronze shape. Diameter 26.7 cm. Ch'ien-lung mark and period. London, Percival David Foundation.

Green was also used in combination with black to cover vessels imitating ancient bronzes, and some good examples can be dated to the Ch'ien-lung period when antiquarianism again became popular (Fig. 209). Some examples are clearly inspired by the illustrated catalogues of collections, but others were simply archaizing inventions, frequently of incredible ugliness.

A pure dense black, developed from a nicely balanced mixture of iron, cobalt and manganese oxides, and known as mirror black, was a further achievement which had its origin in the seventeenth century. The early examples tended to be slightly iridescent, but in the eighteenth century this fault disappeared, and the glaze took on a smooth glassy character of great brilliance. Many examples of this kind were decorated in gold with fine diapers, decorative panels and roundels, dragons, and birds and flowers.

White Wares

The white wares of the late seventeenth and eighteenth centuries fall into three groups; first those of the Ching-tê Chên high quality porcelain, second the so-called 'soft-paste', and third the Tê-hua, which had begun to achieve real fame in the sixteenth century.

There is little to be said of the Ching-tê Chên high quality ware, as this includes all the shapes found in other wares, but covered only with a perfectly colourless glaze of great brilliance. Pieces of extreme thinness, known as bodiless wares, were decorated with an incised or very low relief decoration of the *an-hua*, or 'secret decoration' type, which can only be seen properly using transmitted light. There were also pieces with pierced decoration, much of it very fine with diaper patterns into which poetic couplets are sometimes incorporated.

The so-called 'soft-paste' group requires some explanation. Chinese 'soft-paste' must not be confused with European soft-paste as the two are completely different. The Chinese material is a natural white-firing clay, probably of the pegmatite group of clay minerals. The Chinese call it *hua-shih*, 'slippery stone', and it was sometimes added to poor quality porcelain, perhaps for its plastic quality.[15] The European soft-paste is a fritware and thus artificially constituted of a glass frit combined with ball clay. The Chinese material in the fired state is rarely translucent, while the European type usually is. The Chinese seem to have begun using the material on its own about 1700 and it continued into the late nineteenth century, possibly even longer. Most pieces are small and include boxes for seal paste as well as a variety of vases, small bottles and miniatures (Fig. 212). The decoration is often finely incised and almost invisible, but there are also many moulded pieces which incorporate complex decoration in relief of dragons among waves, swastika diaper patterns, and stylized forms of the Chinese character *shou*, 'longevity', which enjoyed perennial popularity. The glaze is thin, sometimes uneven, and inclined to craze. A certain number of pieces are decorated in underglaze blue painted in a finely pencilled style quite unlike that used on the ordinary porcelain of the period.

The fine white porcelain of Tê-hua, *blanc de Chine*, reached its apogee in the period from about the middle of K'ang-hsi's reign in the seventeenth century to some time towards the end of the first quarter of the eighteenth century. Figures remained the predominant output (Fig. 210), and the names of some of the potters are recorded in the impressed seal marks that sometimes appear on the backs of

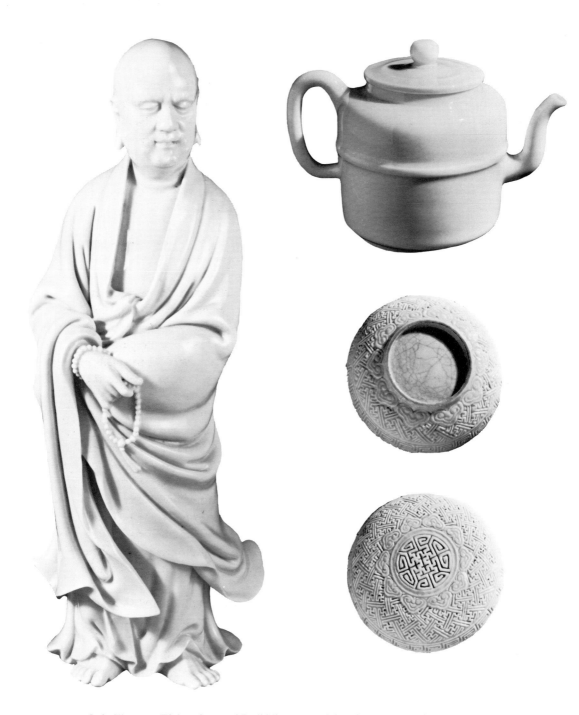

Left: Fig. 210. Tê-hua figure of Bodhidharma. Height 26 cm. Late 17th century A.D. London, Percival David Foundation.

Top right: Fig. 211. Tê-hua wine pot. Diameter 10.5 cm. 18th century A.D. London, Percival David Foundation.

Bottom right: Fig. 212. Soft-paste moulded box. Diameter 6.4 cm. Late 18th or 19th century A.D. London, Percival David Foundation.

the figures.[16] The quality of the porcelain is impressive, and so too is that of the modelling, which has a strength combined with a sensitivity not seen in the later figures of the nineteenth century, which display a clumsiness in the handling of both form and construction and a cursory treatment of detail. In addition to the many figures are small cups, some of them modelled in imitation of rhinoceros horn marriage cups and with similar relief decoration;[17] incense burners of various shapes, some of them based on archaic bronze forms; wine pots (Fig. 211); small boxes; and conical bowls and dishes.

Export Wares for Europe

The export of porcelain to Europe continued to flourish through the early Ch'ing dynasty, but began to decline in the second half of the eighteenth century, when the wild craze for things Chinese was largely over. But at the same time the multiplicity of kilns, which had sprung up partly as a result of the stimulus provided by the Chinese porcelain, had made great improvements in the quality of their wares. Nevertheless the European kilns could not keep up with the demand and there was still a need to import considerable quantities from the east. It is important to remember that even after Johann Friedrich Böttger had discovered porcelain at Dresden in 1709, and the Meissen works had been established in the following year, porcelain manufactured in Europe remained very much more expensive than the imported commodity. It was not until the nineteenth century that European porcelain really became a commercial as opposed to a luxury product. At the height of the period of import in the late seventeenth century, calculations based on the figures given in the Dutch East India Company registers in Batavia alone, indicate that at that time three million or more porcelains were being shipped annually to Europe, almost all of them made to order with shapes and decorations based on models and designs sent out by the East India Company agents.[18]

The bulk of the production was the now well-known and admired blue and white, commonly called Nanking, or Nankeen, after the port where it was transhipped on the lower Yangtse river, and to which it was sent by boat from the Po-yang lake in Kiangsi. Not all of it went this way; some was sent up the Kan river to the south and over the Mei-ling pass on a porterage stage, and then down to Canton on the river.

The *famille verte* also became very popular, and among the forms which enjoyed exceptional popularity for a time were those referred to as *garniture de cheminé*. These comprise three large lidded jars and two elegant beakers. While the blue and white always retained its popularity, it was not always the most suitable type for some shapes, and the colours of the *famille verte* palette were obviously the most appropriate for the innumerable models of birds (Fig. 213),

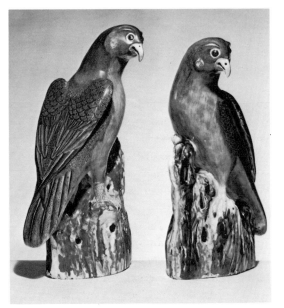

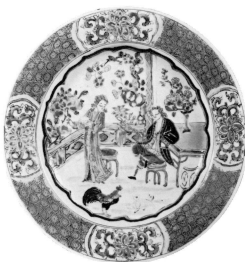

Fig. 213. Polychrome glazed figures of hawks. Height 25.4 cm. Mid 18th century A.D. Cambridge, Fitzwilliam Museum.

Fig. 214. *Famille rose* plate with European figures. Diameter 23 cm. Mount Trust Collection.

animals, Buddhist lions known as 'Dogs of Foh', and human figures, both Chinese and European. Many of the figures were made in pairs to furnish cabinets, recesses, and mantelpieces in fashionable houses.[19] After the *famille rose* was introduced many more figures were made using this group of enamels in preference to those of *famille verte*.

The *famille rose* was extensively used for the decoration of export wares and the demand for table ware, such as plates, dishes, soup tureens, coffee pots, and cream jugs for aristocratic use, grew rapidly (Fig. 214). Pattern books, drawings, and engravings, some of them identifiable, were sent out for the Chinese decorators to copy for special orders. Customers were accustomed to wait for up to about three years for delivery since so much time was involved in travelling. The manufacture of whole dinner sets of sixty or more pieces became quite normal. Many were decorated with floral designs of a usual kind, but the eighteenth century saw a growing demand for sets decorated according to European taste with cyphers and coats of arms, the borders also following European designs. There exist, in fact, a number of pattern plates, each quartered and painted with four different border patterns, and with four different styles of cyphers or armorials near the centre. Everything was numbered, so that all the customer was required to do was to give an order by numbers.[20]

The earliest armorials, in blue and white, date from the last decade of the seventeenth century, while *famille verte* was adopted in about 1710. The *famille rose* palette seems to have been introduced, rather sparingly and not always very well fired, at some time between about 1722 and 1730, but once established and properly fired, it became the most popular, with iron red and gold also holding an important place. The use of gold for armorials was of course to be expected, and it was used, often lavishly, with whatever overglaze enamels might be selected, but as a rule it was not used with the plain blue and white.[21]

The enormous range of shapes and decorations of the porcelain exported to Europe from the seventeenth to the end of the nineteenth century is a subject for special study in its own right and one which still has seriously to be undertaken. It is worth bearing in mind that the production of high quality European porcelain would have been impossible in only a hundred years following the discovery of its secret had not the European chemists and potters found inspiration in the Chinese material. The long centuries of experience of the Chinese potters in the use of clay, the understanding of shape, and the techniques of production and decoration gave them an enormous advantage over their European counterparts, whose products were rough and homely.[22] The Chinese were able to show that this common material, so much scorned for aristocratic use until the eighteenth century, was, when properly used, fit in every way for kings and emperors.

I-hsing and Kuang-tung Stonewares

Different from the central tradition of Ching-tê Chên were the products of two famous provincial centres. These came from I-hsing near Shanghai in Kiangsu, and from kilns not far from Canton in the south of the province of Kuangtung, from which the second type takes its name. Both products were stonewares with a dark reddish body.

I-hsing, sometimes spelled Yi-hsing, began to make the familiar reddish stoneware as early as the sixteenth century, but little is known of the earliest products. The ware is a very fine grained stoneware, and when well handled the clay yielded a product that had a slight gloss on the unglazed surface which was much admired. The teapots, the best-known objects, were often decorated with neatly incised inscriptions or with low relief designs of various kinds. Among the unglazed wares were also miniatures and models which stand out as exceptional in the eighteenth-century output; it was fashionable among connoisseurs to collect such pieces. It is among these smaller novelty pieces that the glazed I-hsing is found. The glaze is a pale bluish grey and is usually found to run thin enough along sharp edges to show a hint of the brown of the underlying body. Both the glazed and the unglazed I-hsing are difficult to date because of the lack of archaeological evidence. Nor is it always easy to distinguish glazed examples from the better and smaller pieces of Kuang-tung ware.

The Kuang-tung stoneware, like the I-hsing, has a history that is really only known at all in the eighteenth and nineteenth centuries. Most of the Kuang-tung, which is still made today, and imitated in many local potteries, is large and heavy. The body is generally coarser than I-hsing and is always glazed. In such details as the finishing of the foot and base, there is often a lack of the neatness found in the I-hsing wares. Some shapes are handsome and well proportioned, including *mei-p'ing* vases and the so-called ginger jar shapes, but it is flower pots and pot stands that are best known, and are still made in quantity. The glaze is thick, opaque, and a dark bluish tone suffused and streaked with pale grey, or more rarely purple (Fig. 215). In some ways the ware is reminiscent of the later Chün, and it is sometimes assumed that Kuang-tung represents a provincial attempt to imitate the famous Chün. The body colour, however, makes it easy to determine its origin, for even the late Chün of the north had a dense grey body and not a reddish brown one.

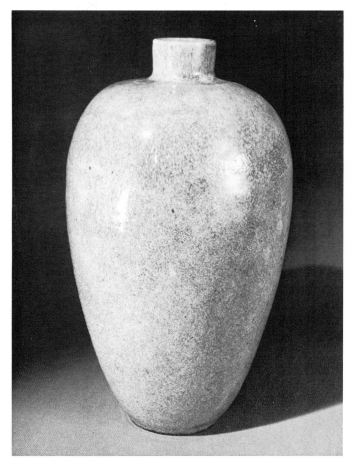

Fig. 215. Reddish brown stoneware *mei-p'ing* with dark blue glaze flecked with grey. Height 32.9 cm. Kuang-tung ware, *c.* A.D. 180. London, Percival David Foundation.

The real interest in this last period of ceramic history lies in the changes in patronage and the fluctuations in taste that these brought. It is more a matter of art history than of technological evolution, for the basic problems had all been solved reasonably well. It was now the turn of the designers and decorators to show what could be done. While in the earlier period of the tenth to the fourteenth century it had generally been the potters who had designed the forms and conceived and executed the decoration, it was now the court artist, with no knowledge of the technology, who designed both forms and decoration, although naturally certain standard forms continued. The change meant that from early Ming times the potter began to lose his control over his own products. An additional factor was the increasing degree of industrialization, as the result of the very techniques that the potter himself had developed.

Thus the Chinese potter eventually became in a sense a victim of his own skill and ability to create. The consequences of his own ingenuity could not have been foreseen, but from early Ming his opportunities to work as an individual, or even as a member of quite a small group, steadily diminished, as first imperial interest grew, and then as the foreign markets in the sixteenth century made new demands.

It was only for a short period in the seventeenth century, when the Transitional style wares were produced, apparently by private potteries, that the master potters and ceramic designers in Jao-chou enjoyed a brief period of freedom to experiment and initiate a new approach to decoration. In this short respite in which to work freely, they laid the foundations for the decorative achievements of the early K'ang-hsi period, which is famous for the broad treatment of surface.

The reorganization of the kilns at Ching-tê Chên and in Jao-chou generally, at the end of the seventeenth century, pushed the process of industrialization a stage farther. The potters, while still experts in their chosen field, became much more the servants of the state and of commerce in a newly capitalized industry, which frequently worked for the foreigner. The potters had lost the opportunity to be individually creative in the face of the demand for efficiency and quantity production.

That in these circumstances the Chinese potter was still able to produce great masterpieces is a tribute to his pride in craftsmanship and to his self-discipline. In the later years of the eighteenth century and through the nineteenth century he was barely able to maintain his standards, partly because of the deterioration of the domestic situation, and partly because of the growing impact of contacts with Europe and America, where, as the result of the industrial revolution, production at all levels was beginning to price his work out of the market. Nevertheless in his finest work he could still far surpass anything made in Europe, even into the present century.

Conclusion

The great achievements in the earliest centuries of China's ceramic history lay not so much in the skill learned in handling the clay materials found in the natural surroundings, as in the development of kilns which were capable of reaching relatively high temperatures, and the control of these temperatures together with the atmospheres suitable for particular effects. This is not to say that the potters did not attain mastery in throwing simple well-proportioned forms on the wheel; this indeed they did at a very early stage. Even in neolithic times they allied this skill to a delight in constructing complex forms from a variety of small parts, and this delight remained with them all through the centuries. Yet, surprisingly, in the early centuries the shapes showed that there was a lack of variety. The cause may have been the absence of immediate stimulus from outside, but may also have been due to the weighty influence of the bronze tradition, which had for so long been dominant.

The situation was remedied in the late sixth century and through T'ang, when, after the basic techniques were mastered, the Chinese were open and ready to accept influences from the Near East, India, and Central Asia. The variety of form was immensely enriched in this age, and development was rapid. As before, simple wheel-made forms, often majestic, are seen alongside constructions, and both are partly dependent on the natural development of the craft and partly on inspiration from abroad, even in the decoration.

In the Sung period the stoneware tradition, which had become firmly established in the previous centuries, suddenly blossomed. The tactile sense, always strong, and the increasingly refined appreciation of form, ensured a strict control of decoration, which for the first time began to be studied seriously in relation to stoneware. Thus decoration was so perfectly subordinated to shape that it became a part of the visual poetry of the age. It is particularly evident in

266

Ting, in which the subtle variation of line and tone of glaze is a stimulus to the imagination. In some instances the elusiveness of this kind is even more apparent in the *ch'ing-pai,* the ware which led on into the later porcelain tradition.

In the fourteenth century the impact of blue and white on a national personality so sensitively attuned to texture, form, and restraint in decoration, was almost horrific, so that for a time it was regarded as unendurably vulgar and totally unacceptable to educated taste. Painted decoration, however, for which there was already a precedent in Tz'ŭ-chou, could not long be rejected. Thus by the end of the fourteenth century it gave a new direction to Chinese ceramics, and was ultimately to result in some instances, particularly in the later stages, in a much less refined appreciation of shape, so that lavish decoration occasionally covered a multitude of sins against the canons of good taste.

The enormous numbers of craftsmen employed, as time went by and the industry developed a more complex structure to meet the greater demands, led to a less personal approach on the part of the potter to his materials. In spite of the organizational changes, especially those of the late seventeenth century, the Chinese personality managed to survive, and not even the disasters of the nineteenth century could wholly destroy it. Thus the Chinese potter, a master of his chosen material, continued to adapt himself to changing conditions and to be prolific in the production of vessels displaying pleasing visual effects. He was nevertheless forced to abandon personal aspirations in expressing delight in the ceramic medium, and was gradually compelled to submit to the discipline of a factory worker. He had to learn to execute the wishes of, and give expression to the taste of others who knew nothing of the problems which he had slowly and painfully resolved down the centuries. The final achievement was one of extreme technical accomplishment, and any failures there were, were due rather to the directions to which the potter had to submit than to the character and capability of the potter himself.

Notes

INTRODUCTION
The Potter and his Materials

1. The excavation of the Western Han tomb at Ma-wang-tui near Chang-sha, shows this to be the case. See *Ch'ang-sha Ma-wang-tui i-hao Han mu fa-chu chien-pao*, Peking, 1972, especially Pls 8, 14, 18–23.
2. Stoneware bodies can be fired to lower temperatures, but the full strength of the body is not attained and it behaves like earthenware in as much as it is porous and capable of being lead glazed.
3. Lead glazed biscuit might be a convenient way out of the difficulty, but 'enamel on biscuit' is an expression in such common use that it seems appropriate to retain it in the present context.
4. The best general reader's introduction to the constitution and character of glazes is, Rhodes, D., *Clay and Glazes for the Potter*, London, 1958. For the more technically minded, Green, D., *Understanding Pottery Glazes*, London, 1963, is a useful guide.
5. For more detail on aspects of reduction firing see Rhodes, D., op. cit. p. 178 *et seq.*

CHAPTER ONE
Pre-Han Unglazed Earthenware

1. Andersson, J. G., 'An Early Chinese Culture', *Geological Survey of China*, Peking, 1923, and the same author's *Children of the Yellow Earth*, London, 1934, and papers published in the *Bulletin of the Museum of Far Eastern Antiquities*, Stockholm, Vols 15 and 19.
2. Academia Sinica, Institute of History and Philology, 'Ch'êng-tzǔ-yai. The Black Pottery Culture Site at Lung Shan Chên in Li-ch'êng Hsien, Shantung Province', Peking, 1934 (Chinese text, translated by K. Starr as *Yale University Publications in Anthropology*, No. 52, 1956).
3. An Chih-min,'*Chung-kuo ku-tai li-shih tao'*, *K'ao-ku hsüeh-pao*, 10, 1955, pp. 27–51, in Chinese. See also Watson, W., *Cultural Frontiers of Ancient East Asia*, Edinburgh, 1971, pp. 9–37. It should be mentioned here that the material from both Hsin-tien and Li-fan is omitted from this account because it adds nothing to our knowledge of the early technological development; it is also rather late in date and overlaps with the Bronze Age. For the description of these potteries see Chêng Tê-k'un, *Archaeology in China*, Vol. 1, *Prehistoric China*, Cambridge, 1959.
4. Known to archaeologists as a paddle.
5. The report in one Chinese account that a temperature of 1,400°C was used must be discounted. Earthenware bodies would slump and melt long before this temperature could be reached, as would many of the stoneware bodies.

6. Examples of some of the different styles may be seen in the exhibition catalogue *The Genius of China*, London, 1973, Nos 15–22 and 33–41.

7. Watson, W., *China before the Han Dynasty*, London, 1961, pp. 37–54.

8. A fairly complete classification is included in the archaeological report on Ch'êng-tzǔ-yai. See note 2 above.

9. Imbibing method, see glossary.

10. The best collection of Yang-shao pottery outside China is to be seen in the Museum of Far Eastern Antiquities in Stockholm. Many of the examples have been published by J. G. Andersson and others in *Bulletin of the Museum of Far Eastern Antiquities* (hereinafter referred to as *BMFEA*), from 1929 onward, and by Palmgren, N., *Kansu Neolithic Urns*, Peking, 1934.

11. Little of this material has been published outside China, but an interesting selection from recent finds may be seen in *Historical Relics Unearthed in New China*, Peking, 1972.

12. For a general account of Shang culture, Creel, H. G., *The Birth of China*, London, 1935, still remains a classic although out of date in some respects. A more recent account is Watson, W., *China before the Han Dynasty*, London, 1961.

13. Hochstadter, W., 'Pottery and Stoneware of Shang, Chou and Han', *BMFEA* 24, 1952, pp. 81–108.

14. Ibid., Pl. 18, figs 71 and 72.

15. Sundius, N., 'Some aspects of the technical development in the manufacture of Chinese pottery wares of the pre-Ming age', *BMFEA* 33, 1961, pp. 103–24.

16. See below Chapter 5, p. 117.

17. *Wên-wu* 1956, No. 12, pp. 53–4, in Chinese. From the description and the rather poor photographs of the excavation it has been possible to propose a workable reconstruction. I am grateful to Henry Hodges for his help and for the trouble he has taken to make the reconstruction drawings. It is worth noting that the kiln is basically of the same down-draught, wood-fired type as the old kilns at the Sèvres factory. At Sèvres, however, the draught enters from the sides, is taken over a bag-wall and then down through the centre, thus reversing the Chinese direction of draught, but still going out through the sides, a much more complex arrangement.

18. Since this section was written a Chinese report published in *K'ao-ku* 1974, No. 1, pp. 16–17, indicates that the primitive form of 'horse-shoe shaped' kiln has now been found in southern Shensi and dates from about the fourth century B.C.

CHAPTER TWO

Glazed Wares from Shang to Han

1. Watson, W., *China before the Han Dynasty*, Chang, K. C. *The Archaeology of Ancient China*, Yale, 1963, and the Chinese language reports in *K'ao-ku hsüeh-pao, K'ao-ku* and *Wên-wu*.

2. Creel, H. G., op. cit.

3. Much has been written about this early period of empire, but for the best account of the society of China at this time see Loewe, M., *Everyday Life in Early Imperial China*, London, 1968.

4. *Wên-wu* 1972, No. 10, p. 20 *et seq.*, and Pl. 3. Report in Chinese.

5. The Chinese report states that these pieces were all made by hand and makes no reference to the use of the wheel, even for finishing, despite the obvious evidence of this in the inked squeezes of the bases of a number of the pots on which potters' marks have been incised. See *K'ao-ku hsüeh-pao* 1959, No. 4, p. 70 *et seq.*

6. The Chinese report uses a term which has been translated by Chêng Tê-k'un in *Archaeology in China*, Vol. 3, *Chou China*, Cambridge, 1961, as 'soaked', but this is impossible in practical terms. In the context it is clear that dipped is meant.

7. The material is represented by several pieces in the Ingram collection in the Ashmolean Museum, Oxford. They were first assigned to this early period by Orvar Karlbeck; see his article 'Early Yüeh Wares', *Oriental Art* 2, 1949, pp. 3–7. More recent work confirms his attributions.

8. Hochstadter, W., 'Pottery and Stonewares of Shang, Chou and Han', *BMFEA* 24, 1952, pp. 81–108, especially pp. 101–2.

9. The wide currency of textile design should be noted. It is also found in early bronze mirror decoration and on the painted lacquers. For examples on mirrors see

Karlgren, B., 'Huai and Han', *BMFEA* 13, 1941, Pls 22–39, and for painted lacquer examples see Willetts, W., *Foundations of Chinese Art*, London, 1965, figs 105–9, and for comparison with textiles the same, margin figs 19–25, 95, 97, 100 and 116. Other examples of textiles from Central Asian finds are illustrated in Stein, A. M., *Innermost Asia*, Vol. 3, Pls XL–XLIII. Such textiles were exported and have been found as far west as Palmyra in Syria; they were illustrated by Pfister, R., *Textiles de Palmyre*, Paris, 1934–40, Vol. 3, *Nouveaux Textiles de Palmyre*, Pls XI–XII.

10. In ancient practice the temperature rarely exceeded about 1,050°C.

11. I only know of one example on which green and brown have been used, and this is a piece in the Tenri Ethnographical Museum, near Nara, Japan. It is illustrated in *Sekai tōji zenshū*, Vol. 8, Colour Pl. 13.

CHAPTER THREE
Technical Consolidation: The Period of the Northern and Southern Dynasties

1. Balazs, E., *Chinese Civilization and Bureaucracy*, New Haven and London, 1964, pp. 206–7.

2. See examples in Mahler, J. G., *The Westerners among the Figurines of the T'ang Dynasty*, Rome, 1959.

3. The type is admirably illustrated by Sickman, L., and Soper, A. C., *The Art and Architecture of China*, Harmondsworth, 1956, Pls 30b and 34–5.

4. The best-known series of impressed bricks is that in the Royal Ontario Museum, Toronto. See White, W. C., *Tomb Tile Pictures of Ancient China*, Toronto, 1939. The more prestigious panels in stone are illustrated by Chavannes, E., *Mission Archéologique dans la Chine Septentrionale*, Paris, 1909, Vol. 1, Hsiao-t'ang Shan, Pls XXIII–XXX, and Wu Liang-tzǔ, Pls XXXVIII–LXXXV.

5. Two good examples are illustrated from the Têng-hsien series in *Chūgoku Bijutsu*, Vol. 1 (*Sekai Bijutsu Taikan* Vol. 8), Tokyo, 1965, p. 122. The complete series is

published with Chinese text in *Têng-hsien tsai-sê hua-hsiang chuan-mu*, Peking, 1958.

6. See Pelliot, P., *Les Grottes de Touen-Houang*, Paris 1920, Sirén, O., *Chinese sculpture*, London, 1925, Vols. 2 and 3, and Mizuno S. and Nagahiro T., *Ryūmon sekketsu no kenkyū* (A Study of the Buddhist Cave Temples at Lung-mên), Tokyo, 1941.

7. All the figures and trees illustrated in *Chūgoku Bijutsu*, Vol. 1, p. 123. A similar treatment of figures may be seen in the famous painting 'Admonitions of the Imperial Preceptress' attributed to Ku K'ai-chih in the British Museum, partly illustrated by Sickman and Soper, op.cit. Pl. 48. Trees displaying similar features also occur and are illustrated in the same volume from a stone sarcophagus, see Pls 52 and 53. See also Soper, A. C., 'A new Chinese tomb discovery; the earliest representation of a famous literary theme', *Artibus Asiae*, Vol. 24, 1961, pp. 79 *et seq.*, and *Wên-wu* 1960, Nos 8–9, pp. 19–24 and 37–42 (in Chinese).

8. The Chinese term 'green glazed ware' is of course self-explanatory and was introduced only in 1947. The term 'proto-Yüeh' was proposed by W. Watson in 1971 in a paper in *Transactions of the Oriental Ceramic Society (TOCS)*, 38, 1969–71, p. 23, in order to make clear the distinction between pre-T'ang material from northern Chekiang and that which can be dated to T'ang and later; the distinction is a valid one and brings our terminology into line with accepted Chinese practice.

9. For examples of roulettes see Sanders, H. H., *The world of Japanese Ceramics*, p. 77, fig. 30.

10. An example is that in Ayers, J., *Chinese and Korean Pottery and Porcelain (The Seligman Collection of Oriental Art*, Vol. 2), Pl. 6, No. D102.

CHAPTER FOUR
New Inspiration in T'ang

1. An important source for the study of the period is Bingham, W., *The Founding of the T'ang Dynasty*, Baltimore, 1941.

2. Balazs, E., op.cit., Ch. 5, 'Fairs in China',

pp. 55–65.

3. The introduction of polychrome lead glazing is discussed by Watson, W., 'On T'ang soft glazed pottery', *Pottery and Metalwork in T'ang China: their chronology and external relations* (Percival David Foundation Colloquies on Art and Archaeology in Asia, No. 1), London, 1970.

4. Charleston, R., 'Glass "cakes" as raw material and articles of commerce', *Journal of Glass Studies* 5, 1963, pp. 54–68.

5. Such opacity, producing whiteness, is not very common. It is likely to be due to massive quantities of some form of calcium, since tin oxides were not used in China until the eighteenth century. Careful chemical analysis would be helpful here.

6. Fêng Hsien-ming, '*Honan Kung-hsien ku-yao chih t'iao-ch'a pao-kao*', *Wên-wu* 1959, No. 3, pp. 21 *et seq.* In Chinese.

7. Medley, M., *Metalwork and Chinese Ceramics* (Percival David Foundation Monograph Series, No. 2), London, 1972.

8. Sanders, H. H., *The World of Japanese Ceramics*, Tokyo, 1967, pp. 144–5; the author uses the Japanese term *neriage* in his description of the technique. The illustrations in fig. 81 show very clearly how marbled wares are produced. The name 'agate ware' is also associated with the type. See glossary.

9. *Wên-wu* 1960, No. 3, pp. 67 *et seq.* In Chinese.

10. Whitehouse, D., 'Chinese stoneware from Siraf; the earliest finds', *South Asian Archaeology*, London, 1973, pp. 241–55.

11. For Hao-pi-chi see *Wên-wu* 1964, No. 8, pp. 1 *et seq.*

12. *Shensi T'ung-ch'üan Yao-chou yao* (Excavation of the Yao-chou kiln sites at T'ung-ch'üan, Shensi), Peking, 1965. In Chinese with summary in English.

13. See below, Chapter Five, Popular Wares, Tz'ŭ-chou etc.

14. *China's Beauty of 2000 Years.* Exhibition of ceramics, Tokyo, 1965, item No. 12 in colour.

15. The Philippine finds are among the most recent and least generally known. See Locsin, L. and C., *Oriental Ceramics Found in the Philippines*, Tokyo, 1968.

16. Ayers, J., *Chinese and Korean Pottery and Porcelain (The Seligman Collection of Oriental Art*, Vol. 2) London, 1964, p. 7.

17. Sarre, F., *Die Ausgrabungen von Samarra* II, *Die Keramik von Samarra*, Berlin, 1925, Pls XXIII–XXV, and two Wa-ch'a p'ing types on Pl. XXIX. The site is the subject of much controversy, since the palace area continued to be a habitation site long after the Abbāsid court removed to Baghdad in A.D. 883, but the Chinese white ware certainly belongs to the ninth or early tenth century. The two Wa-ch'a-p'ing pieces are likely to be ninth-century on the basis of the Chinese reports.

18. Sundius, N., 'Some aspects of the technical development in the manufacture of Chinese pottery in the pre-Ming age', *BMFEA* 33, 1961, pp. 103–24. See also the scientific section of Palmgren, N., *Sung Sherds*, Stockholm, 1963, pp. 377 *et seq.*, by Sundius, N., and Steger, W., 'The Constitution and Manufacture of Chinese Ceramics from Sung and Earlier Times.'

CHAPTER FIVE

North China from the Tenth to the Fourteenth Century

1. Discovered by Fujio Koyama and reported in a paraphrased translation, 'The Ting-yao kiln sites: Koyama's significant discoveries', by J. M. Plumer in *Archives of the Chinese Art Society of America* 3, 1948–9, pp. 61–6.

2. Reports in Chinese in *Wên-wu* 1953, No. 9, 1959, No. 7, and in *K'ao-ku* 1965, No. 8, the last available in abstract translation in *Oriental Ceramic Society Chinese Translations*, No. 4, 1968.

3. The Chinese reports state that the kilns were put out of action at the end of the Northern Sung period, but this is not borne out by the evidence of the material itself, some of which is dated to the twelfth and thirteenth centuries, as for instance the mould illustrated here, and others recorded in other collections. See Wirgin, J., *Sung Ceramic Designs*, Stockholm, 1970, pp. 124 *et seq.*

4. I am indebted to Sister Johanna Becker for this information. She is an experienced potter, and although she has not done this

herself, she has seen it done by a Japanese potter. The carving could not be done after the operation of placing over the mould because the continuity of line would be broken.

5. Firing tests carried out in Sweden are reported in Palmgren, N., *Sung Sherds*, pp. 461 *et seq.*

6. See for instance the painting reproduced on Pls 208–10 in Sirèn, O., *Chinese Painting*, London, 1956, Vol. 3.

7. A great number of designs in the form of line drawings is included in the Chinese report *Shensi T'ung-ch'üan Yao-chou yao*.

8. The report on Lin-ju Hsien, in Chinese, appears in *Wên-wu* 1964, No. 8, pp. 15 *et seq.*

9. *Wên-wu* 1964, No. 8, pp. 15–26. On the design and construction of the kiln found at Wu-sung Shan, mentioned in the report, the author's interpretation of the second chamber should be disregarded. An abbreviated translation of the report is available in *Oriental Ceramic Society Chinese Translations*, No. 3, 1968.

10. Hetherington, A. L., *Chinese Ceramic Glazes*, Cambridge, 1937, pp. 66–72.

11. A list of 31 pieces was published by Gompertz in *Chinese Celadon Wares*, London, 1958, but a new list might be smaller, and certainly at least one of the pieces he records should now be eliminated; some specimens have changed ownership.

12. The most comprehensive study of Liao history and culture is Wittfogel, K. A., and Fêng, C. S., *History of Chinese Society: Liao 907–1125*, New York, 1949.

13. A useful article is Wirgin, J., 'Some notes on Liao ceramics', *BMFEA*, 32, 1960, pp. 25–46.

Oriental Ceramic Society Chinese Translations, No. 2, 1968.

3. I am grateful to Henry Hodges for the suggestion that shrinkage in drying was likely to be the cause which led to this unusual practice.

4. *Chi-chou yao*, Peking, 1951 (in Chinese).

5. The Chinese report states that the leaves were placed on a small area painted yellow in order to produce the yellowish colour of the leaf after firing. This, however, was not the case. J. Wirgin in his 'Some ceramic wares from Chi-chou', *BMFEA*, 34, 1962, unfortunately follows the report at the top of p. 57, and accepts this method of decoration.

6. *Wên-wu* 1961, No. 11, Pl. 5, fig. 6, and pp. 48–52.

7. Some of the kilns were discovered by James Marshall Plumer in 1933, and his posthumously published book *Temmoku*, Tokyo, 1972, should be consulted for illustrations of the various forms and the glaze transmutations, the latter being in colour.

8. The earliest text in which the term *ch'ing-pai* occurs is *T'ao-i chih-lüeh* by Wang Ta-yüan, published in 1349–50, an important geographical text, which is so far untranslated. See also, David, Sir P., 'Ying-ch'ing, a plea for a better term', *Oriental Art*, (new series) 1, 1955, pp. 52–3.

9. Evidence for fritting the glaze materials is clear from Chiang Ch'i's 'Appendix on the Ceramic Industry', of which a new translation is urgently needed. The translation, with gaps, included in Bushell, S. W., *Oriental Ceramic Art*, New York 1899, pp. 178–83, is inaccurate and dangerously misleading.

10. Wirgin, J., *Sung Ceramic Designs* for a range of the decorations.

CHAPTER SIX

South China from the Tenth to the Fourteenth Century

1. A long, extremely technical study in Chinese on this subject was published in *Kao-ku hsüeh-pao*, 1973, No 1, pp. 131–56.

2. See *Wên-wu* 1963, No. 1, pp. 27–35, of which there is an abstract translation in

CHAPTER SEVEN

The Last Great Innovation

1. See *Ibn Battuta: Travels in Asia and Africa*, translated by H. A. R. Gibb (Hakluyt Society), Cambridge, 1958–71, in three volumes; also Ferrand, G., *Relations de Voyages*, Paris, 1913–14, in two volumes, and of course *Marco Polo*, Vol. 2, in

Yule's translation.

2. Wang Ta-yüan, *T'ao-i chih-lüeh*, 1349–50.

3. This is the implication of a passage in Chiang Ch'i's 'Appendix on the Ceramic Industry' of 1322.

4. ibid.

5. A term introduced in the author's *Yüan Porcelain and Stoneware*, London, 1974, Ch. 2.

6. Locsin, L. and C., *Oriental Ceramics discovered in the Philippines*, Tokyo, 1968, and Addis, J. M., 'Chinese porcelains found in the Philippines', *TOCS* 37, 1967–9, pp. 17–36.

7. Ayers, J., 'Buddhist porcelain figures of the Yüan Dynasty', *Year Book of the Victoria and Albert Museum*, London, 1969.

8. Medley, M., *Yüan Porcelain and Stoneware*, Ch. 3.

9. According to Sir Harry Garner, the mines were located at Khemsar, about twenty miles from Kashan, where until recently it could be found as an outcrop of the brilliant puce form, erythrite. See his *Oriental Blue and White*, Preface to the Third Edition, 1970, pp. xviii–xix. It should also be noted that according to R. J. Gettens and G. L. Stout, smalt has been identified as an artists' pigment with certainty from the Ming dynasty. It has also been found as a pigment at Kara Khoto in Central Asia on a wall painting of the eleventh to the thirteenth centuries; see *Painting Materials*, New York, 1942, p. 159. I am grateful to Henry Hodges for bringing this latter reference to my notice.

10. The Chinese names for cobalt up to the beginning of the sixteenth century were *su-ma-ni, su-ma-li, su-po-ni, su-ni-po*, and *sa-po-ni*. It has been mistakenly supposed that these names should be equated with Sumatra, where the material is believed to have been transhipped on its way from the Near East. In *Yüan Porcelain and Stoneware*, p. 34, I suggested that these names constituted a linguistic and dialect problem and not a geographical one. It has now emerged that 'Abu'l-Qasim of Kashan in Persia, in his treatise on ceramics, written in A.D. 1301, refers to cobalt as *sulimānī*, which provides a much better approximation to the Chinese names transmitted through the various coastal

dialects than Su-mên-ta-li, the Chinese name for Palembang in fact and not Sumatra. On the identification of place names on the sea routes see Wheatley, P., *The Golden Khersonese*, Oxford, 1961

11. For a detailed discussion of early blue and white see *Yüan Porcelain and Stoneware*, Ch. 3.

12. Medley, M., 'Chinese Ceramics and Islamic Design', *Percival David Foundation Colloquies on Art and Archaeology in Asia*, No. 3, 1972, pp. 1–10.

13. Pope, J. A., *Fourteenth century Blue and White*, Washington, 1952 and 1970, pp. 30–48, Pls A–C.

14. Ayers, J., 'Some characteristic wares of the Yüan Dynasty', *TOCS* 19, 1954, Pl. 45, fig. 46.

15. Saito K, '*Gendai no sometsuke*', *Kobijutsu* 18, 1957, in Japanese with English summary. The author has identified several dramatic scenes.

16. For lacquer examples see Lovell, H. C., 'Sung and Yüan monochrome lacquers in the Freer Gallery', *Ars Orientalis* 9, 1973, pp. 121–30. For good silver examples see *The Genius of China;* An exhibition of archaeological finds in the People's Republic of China, London, 1973–4, catalogue entries 372 and 374; also Medley, M., 'A Fourteenth-century blue and white box', *Oriental Art* 19, 1973, pp. 433–7.

17. Locsin, L. and C., op. cit., Pls 82, 142 and 143, and Addis, J. M., op. cit., pp. 17–36, Pls 39 and 40.

18. The problem of dating is difficult, but some of the arguments in favour of a late date in the fourteenth century will be found in *Yüan Porcelain and Stoneware*, Ch. 3.

CHAPTER EIGHT
Imperial Patronage

1. 'Tribute' was often a euphemism for trade, and in certain compounds actually means 'to open up the trade'.

2. *Ming shih-lu, Ming T'ai-tsu shih-lu*, Ch. 95, f. 3a

3. The equivalent of a cattie is about one and one third of a pound, but whether the early Ming cattie was the precise equivalent of

this is uncertain.

4. *Ming T'ai-tsu shih-lu,* Ch. 105, f. 3b.

5. op. cit., Ch. 156, f. 2b–3a.

6. A study of the changes is found in Medley, M., 'The Yüan-Ming transformation in the blue and red decorated porcelains of China', *Ars Orientalis* 9, 1973, pp. 89–101.

7. Some of the workshops are named in *Ta Ming hui-tien,* Wan-li edn., Ch. 201, f. 25a *et seq.*

8. *Ta Ming hui-tien,* Ch. 194, f. 3b–4a.

9. *Ming Hsüan-tsung shih-lu,* Ch. 9, f. 4a and Ch. 34, f. 4a; the story here falls into two parts and is fuller than in other sources.

10. See note 6 above.

11. One of these two is in the Palace Museum in Taiwan. See *Ku-kung tsang-tz'ü: Ming yu-li-hung tz'ü* (Porcelain of the National Palace Museum, Underglaze Red Ware of the Ming Dynasty), Hong Kong, 1963, Pl. 6.

12. This was found to be the case following the examination by X-ray emission spectroscopy in 1962 of a large sample of blue and white pieces. The report was published in *Archaeometry* 10, 1967, pp. 101–3.

13. *Ming Jên-ts'ung shih-lu,* Ch. 9, f. 4a and Ch. 11, f. 4b–5a.

14. *Ta Ming hui-tien,* Ch. 194, f. 3b–4a.

15. Two examples in textiles are illustrated in *Wên-wu* 1960, No. 1, and two cloisonné enamel examples using similar motifs, and treating them in much the same way were shown in the exhibition 'The Arts of the Ming Dynasty' organized by the Oriental Ceramic Society for the Arts Council of Great Britain, London, 1957, Nos 299 and 300.

16. *Ta Ming hui-tien,* Ch. 194, f. 3b.

17. The shape named 'precious moon vase' is one based on Syrian glass; an example is shown in the British Museum's Islamic Collection.

18. Medley, M., 'Re-grouping fifteenth-century blue and white', *TOCS,* 34, 1962–63, pp. 83–96

19. Formerly in the Sedgwick collection and illustrated in the paper quoted in the previous note, Pl. 11.

20. Chu Yen *T'ao-shuo* of 1774, translated by S. W. Bushell as *Description of Chinese Pottery and Porcelain,* London, 1910, p. 60. The sentence is repeatedly quoted in the handbooks for antiquarians.

21. It is not known how they acquired the name.

22. The term 'dove tailed' is explained in the introduction to Section 3 of the *Catalogue of Ming Polychrome Wares in the Percival David Foundation,* London, 1966, p. x.

23. The term *fa-hua* was invented by an auctioneer before the First World War, so from the Chinese point of view there is no justification for its retention, but the Japanese in writing of the type introduced two characters which are read in this way in Chinese. For convenience of identification for European and Japanese readers it thus seems sensible to keep the term with the proviso that it should only be used for the type of enamel on biscuit described here. The description of the type as 'cloisonné style' is possible in some cases, but there are so many exceptions in which the outlines are incised that the artificial, blanket term, arbitrary as it may seem, is easier.

24. This phrase describes the type in the Chinese antiquarian handbook *Po-wu yao-lan,* compiled in the late sixteenth century, and published at the end of the seventeenth, possibly with textual additions.

25. See page 277.

CHAPTER NINE

Popular Taste and New Markets

1. For a good survey of Ming history see Fairbank, J. K., and Reischauer, E. O., *East Asia: The Great Tradition,* Boston, 1960.

2. On the Portuguese in the Far East works by C. R. Boxer are recommended; of these *Fidalgos in the Far East, 1550–1770,* The Hague, 1948, *South China in the Sixteenth Century,* London, 1953, and *The Dutch Seaborne Empire, 1600–1800,* London, 1965, are recommended.

3. A valuable study of the trade is Meilink-Roelofsz, M.A.P., *Asian Trade and European influence in the Indonesian Archœpelago between about 1500 and about 1630,* The Hague, 1962.

4. Wang, Y. T., 'Official relations between China and Japan, 1368–1549', *Harvard Yenching Institute Studies,* No. 9, Cambridge, Mass., 1953.

5. *Kiang-hsi T'ung-chih.*

6. During the sixteenth century cobalt as *hui-ch'ing* was evidently imported overland via Samarkand as well as by the sea route, and it is explained in *Shui-pu fu-k'ao*, a Chinese civil service handbook compiled and issued in 1587, that *Hui-ch'ing* is another name for *su-ma-ni ch'ing*, 'which comes from Java and other places'.

7. They figure largely in the Batavia Museum collection, see Ottema, N., *Chineesche Cerameik Handboek*, Amsterdam, 1946, figs 145–58.

8. Illustrated in *The Ceramic Art of China*, London, 1971, Pl. 117, No. 165.

9. Pope, J. A., *Chinese Porcelains from the Ardebil Shrine*, Pls 75–6.

10. Hobson, R. L., *Catalogue of the George Eumorfopoulos Collection of Chinese and Corean Pottery and Porcelain*, Vol. IV, Pl. IV, D19, with other examples of the group. See also Garner, Sir H. M., *Oriental Blue and White*, Pls 43–5.

11. Much of the best of this type has been illustrated in *Sekai tōji zenshū*, Vol. 11, Pls 96–101 and in *Tōki zenshū*, Vol. 27 *(Min akae)*, Colour Pls 5–7 and Pls 34–46.

12. A good example is illustrated in *Catalogue of Ming Polychrome Wares in the Percival David Foundation*, London, 1966, No. 790.

13. The only extended study of the type is Jenyns, S., 'The Wares of the Transitional period between the Ming and the Ch'ing, 1620–1683', *Archives of the Chinese Art Society of America* 9, 1955, pp. 20–42, with a good cross section in illustration.

14. Chinese reports giving this information are in *Wên-wu* 1955, No. 4, pp. 55 *et seq.*, and 1957, No. 9, pp. 56 *et seq.*

15. Donnelly, P., *Blanc de Chine*, London, 1969, is the fruit of much research. It is not an easy study to follow, but is lavishly illustrated and contains translations of two Chinese reports not otherwise easy of access.

16. The largest and most comprehensive collection of Swatow wares is that in the Princessehof Museum at Leeuwarden in Holland, of which a catalogue *Swatow* was published in 1964.

17. Sato, K., *Kosometsuke (Tōki zenshū 15)*, Pls 28b, 31 and 48.

18. These theories are examined by Jenyns, S., 'The Chinese *Kosometsuke* and Shonzui wares', *TOCS* 34, 1962–63, pp. 13–50.

CHAPTER TEN
Technical Virtuosity

1. 'Lettres du Père d'Entrecolles, Missionaire de la Cie de Jésus.' Reprinted in full from *Lettres Edifiantes et Curieuses'* in the appendix to Bushell's translation of Chu Yen's *T'ao-shuo* of 1774. The two letters are dated 1712 and 1722.

2. The name *famille rose* was coined by Jacquemart, A., and Le Blant, E., *Histoire artistique, industrielle et commercielle de la Porcelaine*, Paris, 1862, pp. 77 *et seq.*

3. Jacquemart again was responsible for the introduction of this name, *op. cit.*, pp. 67–8.

4. Garner, Sir H. M., 'The origins of *famille rose*', *TOCS* 37, 1967–9, pp. 1–16.

5. d'Entrecolles, 'Lettres . . .'

6. Garner, op.cit., pp. 13–14. A few pieces with the Yung-chêng mark may have had the enamel background added at a later date, like on the small cup, No. 889 in the Percival David Foundation. On this the delicacy of the floral decoration is sharply at variance with the heavy yellow ground.

7. Jenyns, S., *Later Chinese Porcelain*, Appendix 1, pp. 87–95, and Hardy, S. Y., 'Ku Yüeh Hsüan – a new hypothesis', *Oriental Art* 2, 1949–50, pp. 116–25.

8. The largest collection of both porcelain and glass examples outside the Palace Museum in Taiwan is in the Percival David Foundation in London.

9. Louis le Compte, *Memoirs and Remarks on the Empire of China*, translated by Benjamin Tooke in 1698, published in 1737.

10. Paris, 1894.

11. Experiments carried out in recent years indicate this temperature range for the later material. Verbal communication from Fance Franck.

12. See No. C644 in the Percival David Foundation, *Underglaze Blue and Copper Red Decorated Porcelain*, London, 1963.

13. Examples in the Salting Collection at the Victoria and Albert Museum.

14. Examples in the Salting Collection.

15. Honey, W. B., *Guide to Later Chinese Porcelain*, p. 15, refers to other names such as 'steatitic' and 'soapstone' porcelain among the misnomers for this white ware.

16. Donnelly, P., *Blanc de Chine*, Appendix 4, pp. 355–60.

17. The Chelsea potteries seem to have been particularly attracted by these cups and made many imitations of them.

18. Volker, T., *Porcelain and the Dutch East India Company,* Leiden, 1954, pp. 21–4.

19. Well-known collections included that of Queen Mary at Hampton Court Palace, and that of the Swedish royal family in the Kina Slott at Drottningholm outside Stockholm. The latter survives in some-thing very close to its original condition.

20. Victoria and Albert Museum ceramics department.

21. Howard, D. S., *Chinese Armorial Porcelain,* London, 1974, a recent monumental study.

22. Up to the seventeenth century wood, pewter, or silver, according to social status and income, was used for table ware, only jugs and large mugs were of humble clay.

Reign Marks

Ming Dynasty

Hung-wu
1368–1398

Yung-lo
1403–1424

Yung-lo
1403–1424

Hsüan-tê
1426–1435

Ch'êng-hua
1465–1487

Hung-chih
1488–1505

Chêng-tê
1506–1521

Chia-ching
1522–1566

Lung-ch'ing
1567–1572

Wan-li
1573–1619

T'ien-ch'i
1621–1627

Ch'ung-chêng
1628–1643

治年製　大清順 Shun-chih 1644–1661

熙年製　大清康 K'ang-hsi 1662–1722

正年製　大清雍 Yung-chêng 1723–1735

隆年製　大清乾 Ch'ien-lung 1736–1795

年製　嘉慶 Chia-ch'ing 1796–1820

光年製　大清道 Tao-kuang 1821–1850

豐年製　大清咸 Hsien-fêng 1851–1861

治年製　大清同 T'ung-chih 1862–1874

緒年製　大清光 Kuang-hsü 1875–1908

統年製　大清宣 Hsüan-t'ung 1909–1912

年製　洪憲 Hung-hsien 1916 (Yüan shih-k'ai)

278

Glossary

Alkaline glaze A glaze constituted virtually without lead, but with varying quantities of the most important fluxes, potassium, sodium, and calcium. The firing temperature is adjusted according to the variations in quantities and the physical characteristics of the raw materials.

Antimony oxide A poisonous oxide producing yellows in lead glazes.

Bag wall A lightly constructed wall inside the firing chamber, built to force the flame up towards the roof before being reflected down among the wares.

Biscuit The name given to a once fired ceramic body on which there is no glaze. A biscuit firing usually varies in temperature between about 950°C and 1,100°C, but it may be higher if vitrification is required.

Chia A three or four legged archaic bronze vessel with a handle at the side; current in the Shang period.

Chüeh A three legged bronze vessel of the Shang period, with an open spout and a side handle at right angles to the line of the spout. On the rim at the base of the spout are two small capped columns

Crackle A deliberately induced type of crazing. Sometimes finely ground iron oxide is rubbed in, and fused in an additional firing with another thin layer of glaze over the top.

Crazing A very fine network of cracks in the glaze, not to be confused with crackle. Crazing may be due to a wrong balance in the glaze mixture, or it may be the result of age

and the effects of burial.

Deflocculation The separation of the aggregate particles into the individual particles, as in a slip in which the proportion of particles in suspension is increased through the reduction in particle size.

Dolomite A common rock compound of calcium and magnesium carbonates, which can be included in both bodies and glazes.

Earthenware A non-vitrified, porous ceramic ware, variable in colour and texture, fired at temperatures between about 850°C and 1,100°C, and not exceeding 1,150°C; it may be glazed or unglazed.

Engobe Another name for slip, now largely obsolete.

Feldspar, or felspar A basic ingredient in many clay bodies as well as glazes. It is an igneous rock material occurring in a number of forms, all containing alumina and silica, together with varying proportions of fluxing elements. The most common feldspars in Chinese ceramics are Potassium Feldspar or Orthoclase ($K_2O.Al_2O_3.6SiO_2$), and Calcium Feldspar or Anorthite ($CaO. Al_2O_3 2SiO_2$).

Flocculation The clustering or coagulation of suspended particles.

Flux Any material that encourages fusion and lowers the melting point of substances.

Frit The product of fritting. See next entry.

Fritting Two or more materials heated together to the point of fusion and then quenched in water and ground. An important process employed to render lead harmless for use in glaze, but widely used in the preparation of glazes.

Fritware A ceramic ware made by combining a ground glass frit with a small percentage of plastic ball clay; popular in Near Eastern ceramics on account of its whiteness.

Glaze fit The stability of a glaze on the fired body. A glaze that fits well displays no crackle or blistering, and it does not peel or flake off easily. A glaze that does any of these things, and so fails properly to adhere, is wrongly constituted for the type of body on which it is used.

Glost A potter's adjectival word for glaze; hence a glost firing, that in which the glaze is fired on to the body.

Green fired A ceramic body that is allowed to dry naturally in air and is glazed and fired in a single process.

Hu A wine vase in the broadest sense. Usually of wide bellied shape narrowing slightly towards the neck and lip.

Imbibing method One way in which reducing conditions can be produced to alter the appearance of a ceramic ware. When the critical maturing temperature is reached earth, damp straw, and other vegetation are shovelled on to the top of the kiln or bonfire, and water is dribbled over it. This causes a rapid drop in temperature as the damp penetrates the kiln roof, or the casing of the bonfire, and the oxygen is sucked out.

Kaolin A white relatively aplastic clay, largely free of ferrous impurities, which fires white. It occurs in many parts of China and is an essential ingredient in porcelain. When used alone, virtually an impossibility, it fuses into an homogenous mass at about 1,750°C.

Leather-hard A clay body which is firm but not dry. The clay is no longer plastic and can be handled easily without becoming deformed, yet is still soft enough to permit clean carving and incising.

Lei A tall wine vessel with short neck and wide shoulders from which the body narrows towards the base; circular or rectangular in cross section. A bronze form.

Li An archaic bronze vessel round at the mouth and globular in the body, with three hollow legs.

Lute To lute is to put two clay bodies together using slip to seal the join. Spouts and handles, as well as some decorative elements are attached to vessels in this way.

Marbled ware, or **Agate ware** Strictly this is covering a ceramic ware with coloured slips and then shaking or combing them on the surface. In Chinese wares the whole body may be composed of different coloured clays and it is not always easy to determine which process has been used. The use of different coloured clays in construction is usually termed Agate Ware.

P'an A wide, shallow, circular bowl raised on a wide, spreading foot.

Porcelain A ceramic ware constituted of two ingredients, kaolin and Chinastone, or petuntse *(pai-tun-tzŭ)*, a felspathic material from decomposed granite. It fires at temperatures from about 1,280°C upward, and is generally covered with a felspathic glaze. When fired it is very hard, normally white, vitrified and translucent.

Porcellanous An adjective used to describe ceramic wares made from kaolinic clays. It may be translucent and vitrified, but the ingredients producing these features are derived from other materials than the felspathic Chinastone, such as dolomite. The firing temperatures are in the upper stoneware range and into the porcelain range.

P'ou A large sub-spherical vessel with a straight plain mouth rim, on a slightly splayed high foot.

Resist The use of a wax or grease on an unglazed surface will prevent the glaze adhering when applied to the pot. In firing the wax or grease is burnt off leaving a patch of unglazed biscuit.

Rilling Lines Lines scoring the surface horizontally round a pot. They are due to small hard particles in the clay being caught by the potter's hands and then being dragged along the surface in the process of throwing on the wheel.

Roulette An instrument shaped in wood and similar to a small cotton reel, on which a decoration is carved. It is mounted on a spindle to a handle so that it can be rotated easily, and is used for impressing wet clay with a repeating decoration.

Saggar A fireclay box made to contain fine quality ceramic ware in the kiln and protect it from sudden falls of ash and direct flame. A saggar helps to ensure even temperature; it also makes the wares easy to stack on top of each other in the firing chamber.

Setting A setting is the name given to a kiln stacked ready for firing, and may also be used as an alternative, rather loose name for the firing.

Sintering Heating to the point at which some cementation of the clay particles occurs as the result of softening the constituents of the body.

Slip Clay reduced to a liquid, often creamy in consistency, by the addition of water.

Slump A term used to describe a pottery body which has been heated to the point of collapse which precedes liquefaction.

Sprigging Decoration by applying small clay elements directly to the body, usually from moulds.

Sprig moulding Specifically using small moulds for clay used in applied decoration.

Stoneware A ceramic ware of variable colour and texture, firing at temperatures from about 1,200°C to about 1,280°C. Usually glazed in its finished form.

Tabby weave The simplest form of weaving by which the threads are one over and one under in both directions.

Temper An organic or inorganic material, usually the latter, added to plastic clay to improve its handling and firing qualities.

Ting A round vessel of bronze on three columnar legs. One of the most persistent bronze forms.

Tou A wide bowl on a high spreading foot, common in the middle and later periods of the Bronze Age.

Tui A roughly spherical vessel made in two identical halves, each with three projections which serve as feet. A Middle Chou period bronze vessel in origin.

Vitrification The formation of glassy material in a ceramic body.

Water smoking The removal of mechanically held water during the early stage of firing. In the firing cycle it is the period during which the kiln and wares are slowly and evenly warmed up, and it is indicated by steam being given off instead of smoke.

Bibliography

NOTE. Every effort has been made to confine the bibliography to English-language literature, but to ensure a fair balance and adequate illustrative material one French and two Japanese titles have been included.

Historical and Geographical Background

BALAZS, E., *Chinese Civilization and Bureaucracy*, New Haven and London, 1964.

CHANG, T. T., *Sino-Portuguese Trade from 1514 to 1644*, Leyden, 1944.

CREEL, H. G., *The Birth of China*, London, 1935.

FAIRBANK, J. K., and REISCHAUER, E. O., *East Asia: The Great Tradition*, Boston, 1958 and 1960.

GERNET, J., *Daily Life in China, on the Eve of the Mongol Invasion*, London, 1972.

GOODRICH, L. C., *A Short History of the Chinese People*, London, 1969 (Revised Edition).

LOEWE, M., *Everyday Life in Early Imperial China*, London and New York, 1968.

LOEWE, M., *Imperial China*, London, 1966.

TREGEAR, T. R., *A Geography of China*, London, 1965.

WANG YI-T'UNG, 'Official relations between China and Japan, 1368–1549,' *Harvard Institute Studies* No. IX, Cambridge, Mass., 1953.

WHEATLEY, P., *The Golden Khersonese*, Kuala Lumpur, 1961.

Ceramics

ADDIS, J. M., *Chinese ceramics from datable tombs*, London and New York, 1978.

ADDIS, J. M., *Chinese porcelain from the Addis Collection*, London, 1979.

AYERS, J., *The Seligman Collection of Oriental Art* Vol. 2, *Chinese and Korean Pottery and Porcelain*, London, 1964.

BOSTON, MUSEUM OF FINE ARTS, *The Charles B. Hoyt Collection*, Boston, 1964, 1972, 2 vols.

BRANKSTON, A. J., *Early Ming Wares from Ching-te-chen*, Peking, 1938. Reprinted 1970.

BUSHELL, S. W., *Chinese Art* (Victoria and Albert Museum), London, 1909 (2nd edition).

BUSHELL, S. W., *Oriental Ceramic Art*, New York, 1899.

CHÊNG TÊ-K'UN, *Archaeology in China*, Cambridge, 1960–63 with Supplement, Cambridge, 1966.

CHU YEN, *Description of Chinese Pottery and Porcelain, being a translation of the T'ao-shuo . . . by S. W. Bushell*, Oxford, 1910.

DAVID, S., *Ch'ing Enamelled Ware in the Percival David Foundation of Chinese Art*, London, 1973.

DONNELLY, P. J., *Blanc de Chine*, London, 1969.

GARNER, SIR H. M., *Oriental Blue and White*, London, 1970, 3rd edition.

GODDEN, G. A., *Oriental export market porcelain*, London, etc., 1979.

GOLDSCHMIDT, D. L., *Les Potteries et Porcelaines Chinoises*, Paris, 1957.

GOLDSCHMIDT, D. L., *Ming porcelain*, London, 1978.

GOLDSCHMIDT, D. L., *Les poteries et porcelaines chinoises*, Paris, 1978.

GOMPERTZ, G. ST. G. M., *Chinese Celadon Wares*, London, 1958.

GRAY, B., *Early Chinese Pottery and Porcelain*, London, 1953.

GYLLENSVÄRD, B., *Chinese Ceramics in the Carl Kempe Collection*, Stockholm, 1964.

HAMER, F., *A potter's dictionary of materials and techniques*, London and New York, 1975.

HENTZE, C.,*Chinese Tomb Figures*, London, 1928.

HOBSON, R. L., *A Catalogue of Chinese Pottery and Porcelain in the Collection of Sir Percival David, Bart.*, London, 1934.

HOBSON, R. L., *Catalogue of the George Eumorfopoulos Collection of Chinese and Corean Pottery and Porcelain*, London, 1925–8, 6 vols.

HOBSON, R. L., *Catalogue of the Leonard Gow Collection of Chinese Porcelain*, London, 1931.

HOBSON, R. L., *Chinese Pottery and Porcelain*, London, 1915, 2 vols.

HOBSON, R. L., *Handbook of the Pottery and Porcelain in the Far East in the Department of Oriental Antiquities*, (British Museum), London, 1948.

HOBSON, R. L., and others, *Chinese Ceramics in Private Collections*, London, 1931.

HOBSON, R. L., *The Later Ceramic Wares of China*, London, 1925.

HOBSON, R. L., and HETHERINGTON, A. L., *The Art of the Chinese Potter*, London, 1923.

HONEY, W. B., *The Ceramic Art of China and Other Countries of the Far East*, London, 1945.

HONEY, W. B., *Guide to Later Chinese Porcelain in the Victoria and Albert Museum*, London, 1927.

HOWARD, D. S., *Chinese Armorial Porcelain*, London, 1974.

HOWARD, D. S., and AYERS, J., *China for the West*, London and New York, 1978.

JENYNS, R. S., *Later Chinese Porcelain*, London, 1965.

JENYNS, R. S., *Ming Pottery and Porcelain*, London, 1953.

LAUFER, B., *The Beginnings of Porcelain in China*, Chicago, 1917.

LE CORBEILLER, C., *China trade porcelain*, New York, 1974.

LETH, A., *Catalogue of Selected Objects of Chinese Art in the Museum of Decorative Art, Copenhagen*, Copenhagen, 1959.

LOEHR, M., *Relics of Ancient China from the Collection of Dr. Paul Singer*, New York, 1965.

MEDLEY, M., 'Ching-tê Chên and the Problem of the Imperial Kilns', *Bulletin of the School of Oriental and African Studies*, 29, 1966, pp. 326–38.

MEDLEY, M., *A Handbook of Chinese Art*, London, 1964, (paperback reprint 1973).

MEDLEY, M., *Metalwork and Chinese Ceramics* (Percival David Foundation of Chinese Art, Monograph Series No. 2), London, 1972.

MEDLEY, M., *Ming and Ch'ing Monochrome in the Percival David Foundation of Chinese Art*, London, 1973.

MEDLEY, M., *Ming Polychrome Wares in the Percival David Foundation of Chinese Art*, London, 1966.

MEDLEY, M., *Porcelains decorated in Underglaze Blue and Copper Red in the Percival David Foundation of Chinese Art*, London, 1963. Reprinted as *Underglaze Blue and Copper Red Decorated Porcelains*, 1976.

MEDLEY, M., *Ting and allied wares in the Percival David Foundation of Chinese Art*, London, 1980.

PALMGREN, N., *Kansu Mortuary Urns* (Geological Survey, Series D), Peking, 1934.

PALMGREN, N., *Sung Sherds*, Stockholm, 1963.

POPE, J. A., *Chinese Porcelains from the Ardebil Shrine*, Washington, 1956.

POPE, J. A., *Fourteenth Century Blue and White in the Topkapu Serayi Muzesi, Istanbul*, Washington, 1952 and 1970.

SAITO K., '*Gen-tai no sometsuke*' (Blue and White in the Yüan Dynasty), *Kobijutsu* 18, 1967, pp. 25–41. (Japanese text with English Summary.)

SANDERS, H. H., *The World of Japanese Ceramics*, Tokyo, 1973.

Sekai Tōji Zenshū (Catalogue of World Ceramics), Vols 8–12, Tokyo, 1956 (Japanese text, with English summaries and lists of illustrations), and New Edition, Vols. 10–15, 1976–80 (English summaries and lists of plates).

TAICHUNG: NATIONAL PALACEN MUSEUM, *Kukung tsang-tz'ŭ* (Porcelain in the Palace Museum Collection), Hong Kong, 1962–9, 33 vols. (Chinese and English text.)

TREGEAR, M., *Catalogue of Chinese Greenware* (Ashmolean Museum, Oxford), Oxford, 1976.

VALENSTEIN, S. G., *Ming Porcelains: A Retrospective*, New York, 1970.

VALENSTEIN, S. G., *A Handbook of Chinese Ceramics*, New York, 1975.

VOLKER, T., *Porcelain and the Dutch East India*

283

Company, Leiden, 1954.

WATSON, W., *China Before the Han Dynasty,* London, 1961.

WATSON, W., *The Cultural Frontiers of Ancient East Asia,* Edinburgh, 1971.

WATSON, W., *Handbook to the Collections of Early Chinese Antiquities, British Museum,* London, 1963.

WASHINGTON: SMITHSONIAN INSTITUTION, *Catalogue of the Hippesley Collection of Chinese Ceramics,* Washington, 1902.

WILLETTS, W., *Foundations of Chinese Art,* London, 1965.

WIRGIN, J., *Sung Ceramic Designs,* Stockholm, 1970.

WU, G. D., *Prehistoric Pottery in China,* London, 1938.

Exhibitions

Cleveland: Chinese Art under the Mongols, 1968.

Copenhagen: Kinas Kunst i svensk og dansk eje, 1950.

London, Royal Academy: International Exhibition of Chinese Art, 1935–6.

London, Royal Academy: The Genius of China, 1973–4.

London, Oriental Ceramic Society:
Pre-T'ang Wares, 1953.
The Arts of the T'ang Dynasty, 1955.
The Arts of the Ming Dynasty, 1957.
The Arts of the Sung Dynasty, 1960.
The Arts of the Ch'ing Dynasty, 1964.
The Ceramic Art of China, Jubilee Exhibition, 1971.

Los Angeles, County Museum: Chinese Ceramics from the Prehistoric Period through Ch'ien-lung, 1952. The Arts of the T'ang Dynasty, 1957.

New York: The Arts of the Han Dynasty, 1961.

Philadelphia: Ming Blue and White Porcelain, 1949.

Seoul: Special Exhibition of Cultural Relics found off Sinan Coast, National Museum of Korea, 1977.

Stockholm: Ming Blue and White from Swedish Collections, 1964.

Stockholm: Sung-Ming: Treasures from the Holger Lauritzen Collection, 1965.

Tokyo: Chinese Ceramics: One Hundred Selected Masterpieces, 1960.

Tokyo: Far Eastern Ceramics, 1970.

Washington: Chinese Art Treasures. Exhibited in the United States by the Government of the Republic of China, 1961–2.

Index

285